What's Wrong With My Houseplant?

What's Wrong With My Houseplant?

SAVE YOUR INDOOR PLANTS WITH 100% ORGANIC SOLUTIONS

David Deardorff and Kathryn Wadsworth

TIMBER PRESS
Portland, Oregon

Published in 2016 by Timber Press, Inc.

The Haseltine Building
133 S.W. Second Avenue, Suite 450
Portland, Oregon 97204-3527
timberpress.com

The information in this book, including as it relates to toxic plants, is accurate and complete to the best of our knowledge. All recommendations are made without guarantee on the part of the authors or Timber Press. The authors and publisher disclaim any liability in connection with the use of this information. In particular, individuals vary in the physiological reactions to remedies and plants that are touched or consumed.

Printed in China

Jacket design by Kristi Pfeffer

Library of Congress Cataloging-in-Publication Data

Deardorff, David C., author.
 What's wrong with my houseplant? : save your indoor plants with 100% organic solutions/David Deardoff, Kathryn Wadsworth.—First edition.
     pages cm
 Includes bibliographical references and index.
 ISBN 978-1-60469-633-2 (hardcover)—ISBN 978-1-60469-590-8 (pbk.) 1. House plants. 2. Organic gardening. I. Wadsworth, Kathryn B., author. II. Title.
 SB419.D417 2016
 635.9'65—dc23
                                    2015013389

A catalog record of this book is also available from the British Library.

For all our brothers and sisters:
Judy, Meg Elaine, Jeanne, Daniel,
Randy, Rick, John, Sarah, and
Lauren, with love and gratitude

Contents

Prepare for Success

Houseplants are a relatively recent phenomenon. For most of human history we did not have glass windows, and the insides of our homes were too dark for plants. When glass was first manufactured, only the very wealthy could afford it, but 150 years ago inexpensive pane glass became available for the first time, allowing ordinary homes to have large glass windows. That was during the Victorian era, the Age of Exploration, when botanical wonders from all over the world were brought back to England and Europe. Exotic palm trees and ferns from tropical climes were all the rage in Victorian parlors. During the 1960s, interest in growing houseplants peaked again, and making macramé plant hangers for hanging baskets became a national fad. Today, houseplants are once again popular and affordable, a result of newer production technologies, like tissue culture, combined with low-cost labor in Asia, and efficient distribution systems.

It's hard to resist gorgeous orchids in full bloom, now available at moderate prices in supermarkets, big box stores, and garden centers. Not so long ago these plants were rare and costly, enjoyed only by a privileged few.

Split-leaf philodendron makes a perfect houseplant. Besides loving the low light and warm nighttime temperatures of most homes, it is one of the plants known to rid indoor air of pollutants.

Why grow plants indoors? Houseplants satisfy the atavistic need many of us have for contact with green growing things, a need that is apparently encoded in our genes. Flowers beautify our personal spaces, brightening the home and lightening the heart. Flowering houseplants, like orchids and African violets, can decrease stress, a therapeutic value that has only recently been recognized and studied. Simply arranging a collection of houseplants can be a creative outlet. Some people like to grow a variety of bromeliads on a large, artistic branch or piece of driftwood which they call a bromeliad tree. Even the act of caring for our plant companions is therapeutic.

More impressive still, indoor plants improve air quality. Chemicals that have an adverse effect on human health commonly outgas from plywood, carpets, upholstery, and cleaning products. Research at the University of Georgia and elsewhere shows that certain houseplants reduce our exposure to these chemicals and filter pollutants from the air, providing clean air for us to breathe. A two-year study undertaken by NASA and the Associated Landscape Contractors of America identified several different houseplants that were able to remove the organic chemicals benzene, trichloroethylene, and formaldehyde from indoor air. All the philodendrons and many other plants in this book (see sidebar) are valued members of the household for their proven ability to remove chemicals from indoor air.

Tropical broadleaf evergreens adapted to low light and warm nights generally make the best houseplants. They are pre-adapted to grow well in our warm, dark homes because they evolved in similar habitats, such as the floor of tropical rainforests. As permanent members of the household these plants succeed with minimum fuss.

Cacti and succulents that come from the tropical deserts of the world also make good houseplants. Their native habitat has full sun and warm nights, and many require bright light indoors.

Culinary herbs commonly grown on kitchen windowsills make acceptable houseplants. These temperate zone plants come from the Mediterranean, which makes them generally more temperamental than tropicals. Few temperate plants are able to tolerate warm night-time temperatures.

And finally, plants that function as "living bouquets," such as spring bulbs, florist azaleas, and Persian violets, can reside in our homes only temporarily. When their flowers fade, the plants go back outside or are discarded.

What is not a houseplant? Perennial plants from temperate zones that require cool night-time temperatures are physiologically incapable of growing well inside our homes. Warm temperatures at night kill them. Perfect examples of this category include miniature roses and dwarf apple trees.

To flourish, houseplants need the right amount of light, the right temperature, the correct amount of water and humidity, and appropriate potting media and fertilizer. Like all other plants, they respond to the changing seasons of the year. The number of hours of daylight changes with the seasons, along with the temperature and humidity; these environmental cues signal the plant to respond with active vegetative growth and flowering, or dormancy and rest. Adapting your care to an individual plant's needs and to seasonal changes will assure success.

LIGHT

Plants eat light! They harvest solar energy and convert it to chemical energy. They turn sunlight into sugar and they "burn" the sugar in order to grow, flower, and thrive. In the complete absence of light all plants die sooner or later. The amount of time they can live without light depends on how much sugar, starch, or complex carbohydrates they have manufactured and stored in their tissues. If they cannot manufacture food they have to metabolize stored food until the stores run out. Without light, plants starve to death.

All houseplants originally came to us from native habitats where they had evolved and adapted to local environmental conditions for millions of years. Houseplants whose native habitat is the shady floor of a rainforest, for example, thrive under low light conditions. But keep in mind that even in shady natural habitats, plants are not really in permanent shade. They still receive a significant amount of ambient light from the sky (aka skylight: blue light that radiates from the sky). Conversely, plants whose native habitat is the brilliant sun of a desert require the maximum amount of light your home can provide.

The intensity and duration of light, and a plant's distance from the light source are the most important environmental parameters to consider as you prepare for success with any houseplant. Houses designed for humans are dark compared to houses built for plants—such as a greenhouse filled with bright light. When we bring a companion plant into our homes we need to be very cognizant of the intensity of light that particular plant needs and how long it needs it. In the plant portraits section of this book each plant's light requirement, whether high, medium, or low, is listed.

As you place your plants in the right light, bear in mind that they need to be acclimated to their new home. Acclimatize a recently acquired plant to full sun slowly over a period of a couple of weeks. Give it two hours a day for four days, then four hours a day for four days, then six hours for four days, and so forth. By the time your plant tolerates eight hours a day of full intense sun it will be acclimated well enough to tolerate full sun all day without burning.

Light attributes in your home. The first thing you'll need to do is figure out which window faces which direction. In the morning, when you're having your coffee, which window gives you the best view of the sunrise? That window faces east. As you face that east window, know that south is on your right and north is on your left. West is behind you.

The second thing you'll need to figure out is how far away from the window your plant is going to live. If the leaves of your plant are 2 feet away from the window then your plant is only getting one-fourth of the light it would receive if it were right next to the window. This phenomenon is called the inverse square law, and you can use this simple mathematical formula to help your plants get the light they need. Who knew there'd be math when all you want to do is grow a plant? But really, it's simple. All you need is a tape measure and a calculator (or a piece of paper and pencil if you're old school).

According to this law, the intensity of light decreases as the square of the distance from the source of the light. So, if the plant is 2 feet away,

then 2 squared (2×2) = 4, and your plant is only getting one-fourth of the light available. Four feet away = one-sixteenth the light (4×4 = 16), and so forth. As you can see, the further your plant is from a light source, the less energy it receives. The same rule applies to artificial light, by the way.

High light. Full sun all day, south-facing window. The brilliant, intense sunlight of a cloudless summer day at noon as it pours through a south window is the brightest possible light for a houseplant. Imagine a houseplant sitting in its pot on the sill of a south window. The plant has received direct sunlight all morning and will receive it all afternoon as well. The intensity and duration of light is at its maximum. The number of hours of light in a south window changes

These houseplants get full sun all day in a south-facing window. They're also in the laundry room, where they get plenty of humidity.

from summer, when the days are long, to winter, when the days are short, but it is always intense, direct, full sunlight. A barrel cactus or agave thrives under these conditions, while an African violet would die. In fact, the majority of good houseplants will not do well in the intense unfiltered light of a south window but those that require high light will do very well indeed.

High light. Bright indirect light, south-facing window. Imagine drawing a sheer, lacy, or gauzy white curtain over a south window. The curtain hangs between the plant and the window; your plant is now receiving very bright, but filtered light. Though the plant is no longer exposed to direct sun, it's still in a high light situation. You can further modify the light intensity by your choice of curtains. The more "see through" the curtain the brighter the light, and the heavier the curtain the less light.

Medium light. Full sun half a day, east- and west-facing windows. In contrast to the light of a south window, it is impossible for an east or west window to receive a full day of sunshine. They receive only a half-day of intense, direct sunshine; the rest of the day they receive only skylight. East or west windows give plants a medium light regime.

An east window will be high light intensity in the morning when the sun is rising and the air is cool. East windows will be low light intensity all afternoon. Most houseplants will perform quite well in an east window with cool morning light.

A west window will be high light intensity all afternoon when the sun is setting and the air temperature is hot. West windows will be low light intensity all morning long. Heat lovers like many cacti and succulents will actually do fine in a west window because they prefer those hot afternoons.

Medium light. Dappled light. Venetian blinds on a south, east, or west window that gets full, direct, intense sunlight simulate the kind of dappled light a plant receives from an overhanging tree. A plant on the sill of a window with Venetian blinds receives alternating bands of intense hot sun and cool shade that move across the leaves as the sun moves across the sky. You control how much light the plant gets by opening or closing the blinds to make the bars of light and shade narrow or wide. Thus, the plant gets half direct, intense sun and half cooling shade, both of which move across the plant's surface.

Medium light. Filtered light. Drawing a sheer or gauzy curtain over a south-, east-, or west-facing window creates filtered light.

Low light. Shade all day, north-facing windows. Windows that face north never receive any direct sunshine. The only light they receive is the ambient blue light that radiates from the sky. North windows are a low light regime, especially in winter when the sun is low in the sky and the days are short. The majority of houseplants will not do well in a north window; cast-iron plant and a few others do okay in a north window. If a north window is all you have to work with, you might consider growing houseplants in artificial light rather than natural daylight.

Low light. Ambient light all day from skylights in the ceiling. Many homes have skylights in the ceilings of various rooms in the house. They bring the ambient blue light of the sky into your home all day long. Plants that prefer low light levels will do especially well in the light provided by these skylights. However, skylights also allow a patch of direct, intense sunshine to move across your room from morning to night. If your plant is in a location that will be spotlighted by a patch of brilliant, intense

(top left) This graceful parlor palm thrives in the medium light of an east-facing window.

(top right) A position to the side of a north-facing window will never give this palm the light it prefers. All palms featured in this book require medium to high light as houseplants.

(left) This palm's owner keeps a careful eye on the sun that enters through the skylight above, so that the plant's leaves do not burn.

sunlight, you might need to move it out of that patch for a couple hours each day. The path that patch of sunshine takes across your room changes with the seasons. Observe the patch's path so that your plant does not get sunburn.

Artificial light. With artificial light you can forget about your windows and skylights and grow houseplants anywhere. Well, almost anywhere, and not all houseplants.

A very large array of light fixtures suitable for houseplants is available today. They range from simple desk lamps with containers for houseplants at the base to complex systems of multi-stacked shelves with lighting above each shelf. With these light systems in place, any dark corner can be brightened up with houseplants.

No matter what system you use, choose a light source that gives off the proper wavelengths of light for your plant. Different kinds of bulbs emit different wavelengths of light, and plants use different wavelengths of light for different purposes. You need blue and red light if all you want is good foliage growth, but you need red and far red light if you want your plant to make flowers. Look at the packaging the bulb comes in to determine its light quality.

Standard cool-white daylight fluorescent tubes emit light in the blue and red range and are very suitable for vegetative growth. They do a very good job for foliage plants. The special fluorescent bulbs designed to promote plant growth and flowering, called grow lights, are expensive but are designed to emit the right quality of light (blue, red, and far red). They also avoid the heat load generated by incandescent, high-intensity discharge lamps, high pressure sodium, and metal halide lights. LED lights are a low-heat artificial light source, as well as being energy efficient.

A final consideration is the size of the plant you want to grow. Tall plants, like palms, other trees, and large shrubs, are very difficult (often impossible) to get close enough to your light source for the light to do much good due to the inverse square law discussed earlier.

Your best option for growing houseplants under artificial lights in your home is to concentrate on low-growing plants that can be positioned close to the bulbs. African violets, lady's slippers, and moth orchids are some of the very best choices for this purpose.

TEMPERATURE

Success with a particular houseplant depends on knowing the daily temperature regime (daytime high and nighttime low) that plant needs to flourish under your care. Fortunately, plants are fairly forgiving and will adjust to day or night temperatures within a range of about ten degrees Fahrenheit. The plant portrait of each houseplant specifies the appropriate temperature range, daytime and nighttime, for best success with that plant.

Night temperatures are critical for houseplants because plants cannot manufacture food (sugar) through photosynthesis when the sun is not shining. In order to maintain metabolism and growth at night the plant has to burn some of the food it made during the day. For plants, metabolizing food is called respiration. Respiration is the exact opposite process from photosynthesis and it is critically linked to temperature. As the temperature goes up metabolism goes up. As the nighttime temperature goes higher a plant will reach a point where it has burned up all the food it made during the day. At even higher temperatures it will burn up all its reserve food supply. Pretty soon the plant will be dead. This is why those irresistibly cute little miniature roses in 4-inch pots die within a couple weeks when you bring them home from the store. The warm nighttime temperature of our homes kills them. They are not only happy but exquisite if you plant them outdoors in the garden where nights are cold. They, like almost all temperate zone plants, are not houseplants.

High temperature. Plants that grow best in really warm temperatures generally do well with a daytime range of 75 to 85°F and a nighttime range of 65 to 75°F.

Moderate temperature. Plants that prefer moderate temperatures perform well with a daytime range of 70 to 80°F and a nighttime range of 60 to 70°F.

Low temperature. Plants that need low temperatures tolerate a daytime range of 65 to 75°F and a nighttime range of 55 to 65°F.

WATER

The goal of any watering practice or system is to keep the soil moist—neither soggy nor dry. Root rot as a result of overwatering is the number one killer of all plants in containers whether indoors or out. This fact, more than any other, tells us that appropriate watering is not as easy as it seems, and most people are too generous.

Not all plants are created equal with respect to their water needs. Some plants, bananas for example, really need a lot of water. Other plants, such as many cacti, would die swiftly if they were watered as much as a banana plant.

Never water your houseplants with cold water straight from the cold water faucet. Cold water is shocking to these tropical beauties. Always use cool, tepid (not cold, not hot) water. One technique is to fill a pitcher or jug with water and let it sit overnight to warm up to room temperature. Another is to turn on the hot water

just enough to warm the cold water slightly and take the chill off.

How to tell when to water. Determine when you need to water your plants with a simple finger test. The dry potting medium at the surface of the pot will be at room temperature. Stick your finger down into the potting medium, and you will eventually feel cool, moist soil with the tip of your finger. Use your finger to measure how thick the dry medium is at the surface of the pot.

If you don't trust your finger, or you just don't like to get it dirty, there are a number of devices available to determine when a plant needs to be watered. Some are battery-operated probes that you insert into the potting medium. These have an indicator needle on a gauge or a digital readout, either of which will help you determine the thickness of the dry potting medium. Other kinds of devices are little porous clay objects (some are shaped like little earthworms) that you insert into the potting medium. These turn dark when they are wet and light when they are dry.

The plant portraits will give you specific guidelines on water needs for each plant.

Ample water. Plants that prefer ample water need to be watered when the top of the potting medium is dry to a depth of 0.5 inch.

Moderate water. Plants that prefer moderate water need to be watered when the top of the potting medium is dry to a depth of 1 inch.

Low water. Plants that prefer low water need to be watered when the top of the potting medium is dry to a depth of 2 inches.

Frequency of watering. How frequently you need to water depends on plant requirements, on how porous your pots are, and other factors.

Unglazed clay (terracotta) pots are porous. Water evaporates through the walls of these pots very well so they dry out pretty quickly. In garden jargon these pots are said to breathe. Plastic pots, or glazed ceramic, glass, or metal pots do not breathe. Their walls are impervious to water so the potting medium stays moist much longer than in unglazed clay pots.

Ambient air temperature, humidity, and daylength also play a role with regard to frequency of watering. A houseplant's need for water goes up when the temperature goes up, or when it bursts into active growth, or begins to flower. On hot, dry summer days you need to water houseplants more frequently than on cool, moist winter days—even though the plants are inside the house and protected from temperature extremes.

Another factor to consider with regard to watering your houseplants is the potting medium itself. A general-purpose potting medium is designed to absorb and retain sufficient moisture, to allow free water to drain away adequately, and also to provide ample air for good root growth. Some potting media, African violet mixes for example, are designed to retain a little more moisture than a general-purpose potting medium. Other potting media, such as a cactus mix or orchid bark, are designed not to retain much water; they are said to drain well.

Provide drainage. As a general rule, never let a houseplant sit with the bottom of its pot in a puddle of water in its saucer for more than an hour or so. If the potting medium is moist (not soaking wet, not bone dry) then you're doing a good job. Water your plants until you see water begin to come out the drainage holes in the bottom of the pot, then stop watering. If the pot is propped up on pot feet or pebbles so that the bottom of the pot does not sit in a pool of water, you can let the water stand in the saucer. This standing water will help increase humidity. If your pot is not propped up on pot feet or pebbles, check back within 30 minutes to an hour. If there is any water left in the saucer, remove the saucer and discard the water. Put your plant back in the saucer and you're good to go until the next time you need to water.

Watering cans. A good watering can for most houseplants is small and has a very narrow spout. A bad watering can for houseplants is the big, 2- or 3-gallon, clunky one that you use outdoors in the garden, the one with the 3-inch-wide nozzle that has a couple dozen holes in it. Leave the clunky one in the garden and get a special one for your houseplants. It needs to be small and lightweight, with a narrow spout to control where the water goes. Stick the narrow nozzle of your little watering can down to the surface of the potting medium and pour the water on the medium, not the foliage. This is particularly important for African violets because their leaves are damaged if you drip water on them.

HUMIDITY

Water moves through a plant's body through a process called transpiration. The roots absorb water from the soil, then move it upward through the stem and out into the leaves. Water, as a vapor, moves out of the leaf into the air through special pores called stomates. Losing water through its leaves is a vital and necessary process for your plant. Just as your heart beats to pump blood to every cell in your body, so transpiration bathes every cell in a plant's body in nutrients carried by water.

If humidity is high a plant loses water more slowly from its leaves. If humidity is low a plant loses water rapidly from its leaves. Two other

Think of an orchid's natural habitat: on a sultry day it perches on a limb high in the canopy of a tropical rainforest. Mist your orchids daily to mimic this high-humidity home.

factors influence this process. First is the availability of water. If your potting medium is adequately moist then the plant is able to mine the soil with its roots for the water it needs. Conversely, if water is not available because you forgot to water and the medium is dry, then your plant can get into trouble quickly. The second factor is ambient air temperature. As the air temperature goes up humidity goes down; as the temperature goes down humidity goes up. Placing your plant too close to a hot air register or other heat source will suck the water right out of the leaves very quickly.

Depending on your climate, dry or humid, you may need to mist your indoor plants about once a week, as we did when we lived in Santa Fe, New Mexico. In the Pacific Northwest, where we live now, many of our plants do not need misting, even in the dry summer months.

POTTING MEDIA

When you purchase a bag of "potting soil" from your local garden center what you're actually getting is not soil. It's an artificial mixture of ingredients specifically designed to meet the needs of plants in containers and usually contains no actual soil at all. Garden soil, plain old dirt to some, does not promote good growth of container plants because it becomes more and more dense and airless over time. Garden soil is perfectly adequate—in the garden—where it benefits from the activities of worms, insects, fungi, and bacteria. But a pot is a special environment, not a garden, and any plant in a pot has special needs that cannot be met by ordinary garden soil alone.

Roots in a pot, like roots in a garden, must have access to oxygen or they die. Roots of most plants (other than orchids) are not green and are not capable of making food through photosynthesis. In order to stay alive and grow, roots have to metabolize the sugar manufactured by the leaves. This process, called respiration in plants, burns sugar to release energy and consumes oxygen in order to do so. Whenever the air (oxygen) in the medium surrounding the root system of your houseplant is depleted, whether due to long-term saturation by water or tight density of the medium, it is stressful and life-threatening to your plant.

The combination of primary ingredients in artificial "potting soil" includes inorganic mineral items like perlite and vermiculite that create air spaces in the medium and some sharp horticultural sand to promote drainage. It also contains organic material like bark fines to hold and retain moisture. Such a mix never becomes as dense and airless as garden soil in a pot. As the organic fraction of the medium breaks down and decomposes over time, however, the medium will tend to hold more moisture than is good for the plant. Then it's time to re-pot with fresh medium.

Potting mixes were invented in a time when seemingly inexhaustible quantities of sphagnum peat moss were available as a primary ingredient. Unfortunately those days are over and the sphagnum peat moss deposits have mostly been mined out. More responsible potting soil producers are now using the renewable and sustainable resource of bark fines obtained from tree farm timber harvesting, or coconut coir from coconut plantations instead of peat moss for the moisture-retaining organic component of their mixes.

Organic potting media. Aside from the primary ingredients just mentioned, most really good general-purpose organic potting soils contain other ingredients such as nutrients derived from organic fertilizers (manures, compost, worm castings), spores of mycorrhizal fungi, and CFUs (colony-forming units) of beneficial bacteria. The organic fertilizers in these mixes release their nutrients slowly and do not burn plant roots. Non-organic potting soils, which often have processed, water-soluble fertilizers included in the mix, are not recommended. For one thing, non-organic processed fertilizers are more concentrated than organic fertilizers and you run the risk of burning the roots of your plants. For another, these non-organic commercially prepared potting soils take a one-size-fits-all approach, and they're primarily made for annuals such as petunias, tomatoes, and the like, not for houseplants.

Special commercially prepared potting media are widely available for plants with special needs. Most of these are not organic, but you can make your own organic mix easily. Three kinds of houseplants benefit from special media that you can buy or make yourself.

Cactus and succulents. Mix 1 part sharp horticultural sand, 1 part perlite, and 1 part general-purpose organic potting medium. This well-drained mix works very well for cactus and succulents of all kinds.

African violets. Commercially prepared African violet potting media are often too dense and hold too much moisture for really good African violet growth. You can make your own by adding 1 part commercial African violet mix to 1 part general-purpose organic potting medium.

Orchids. Most orchids commonly grown as houseplants are potted in chunks of straight Douglas fir bark, or other kinds of tree bark with no bark fines or other moisture-holding components. Many orchids grow perfectly well in bark with nothing else added but weak fertilizers. They will die if potted in potting soil.

Orchid bark comes in three grades: coarse, medium, and fine. Coarse and medium bark are appropriate for most adult orchids. Use fine orchid bark for seedlings, miniatures, and other small plants. Bark media are extremely well drained, with very large pore spaces, and abundant oxygen around the roots.

Two kinds of orchids, however, cymbidiums and lady's slippers, do not fare well in straight orchid bark. You can mix 1 part fine orchid bark with 1 part general-purpose organic potting medium to make a well-drained medium appropriate for these semi-terrestrial orchids.

FERTILIZER

Commercial fertilizer packages often describe their contents as "plant food." This is a misnomer. Fertilizer contains mineral nutrients such as nitrogen, phosphorus, and potassium that plants require for growth, but any plant's actual food, what they actually eat, is the sugar they make from sunlight and carbon dioxide. When you breathe on your plants you are truly feeding them. They absorb the carbon dioxide from your breath, combine it with solar energy through photosynthesis, and manufacture sugar from it. When they metabolize the sugar it provides them with the fuel they need to grow new leaves, roots, stems, and flowers.

Plants need more than just sunlight, carbon dioxide, and water; they also require 12 essential mineral nutrients. In nature, plants obtain these nutrients from animal droppings, dead animals, and dead plant material. Houseplants have to obtain them from their more limited environment: if the organic potting medium you use has organic fertilizer and compost incorporated into it, your plant will get the nutrients it needs. The overwhelming majority of houseplants are not fussy about nutrients, but if the potting medium contains no fertilizer then you may need to add organic fertilizer. You may also need to add fertilizer later, after the plant has grown. Look to its portrait to determine a plant's fertilizer needs.

All fertilizers have three numbers on the front of the package (e.g., 6-12-4 or 10-10-10), which stand for the percentages of nitrogen (N), phosphorus (P), and potassium (K), in that order. These three essential nutrients are called primary or macronutrients because plants need them in relatively large quantities compared to the other nine.

Nitrogen (the first number) is vital for vegetative growth. A plant has to have nitrogen in order to grow new leaves, roots, stems, and so forth. High nitrogen promotes the lush growth of green leaves, so that any houseplant grown primarily for its attractive foliage, as opposed to flowers, needs a high-nitrogen fertilizer. Phosphorus (the middle number) is necessary for flowering and strong roots. Plants need phosphorus in order to initiate, develop, and maintain their flowers. This is why the percent of phosphorus is high in fertilizers designed for flowering bulbs. Any flowering houseplant grown primarily for its beautiful flowers, as opposed to its foliage, needs a fertilizer with a relatively high phosphorus component. Potassium (the last number) promotes strong stems and provides stress protection for plants. Your plant is better able to withstand extremes (too much or too little) of essential environmental variables such as light, temperature, and water if it's getting adequate potassium.

The secondary essential mineral nutrients are calcium, magnesium, and sulfur. They are not needed in quantities as large as the macronutrients, but they are still essential for healthy plants. Six micronutrients, needed in minute quantities, are boron, copper, iron, manganese, molybdenum, and zinc.

Plants require all 12 of the mineral nutrients just named in order to stay healthy. In addition to the 12, they also need the carbon, hydrogen, and oxygen they obtain from carbon dioxide and water in order to manufacture sugar. A good, high-quality, organic potting soil that contains organic fertilizer should supply all 12 of the essential mineral nutrients that your houseplant needs.

Nutrition Guidelines

Nutrient	Needed for . . .
Nitrogen	Vegetative growth, protein synthesis for new tissue.
Phosphorus	Flower and fruit production.
Potassium	Strong stems and stress protection.
Calcium	Essential for numerous metabolic and physiological processes.
Magnesium	Essential for growth and is a component of chlorophyll.
Sulfur	Vital for plant growth, especially roots and seed production.
Boron	Necessary component of cell walls and membrane function.
Copper	Necessary for photosynthesis and plant growth.
Iron	Necessary for photosynthesis.
Manganese	Important for carbohydrate and nitrogen metabolism.
Molybdenum	Important for nitrogen metabolism.
Zinc	Important for growth hormones and enzyme systems.

CONTAINERS

Your houseplants will come to you in a plethora of pot sizes. Smaller pots are measured by diameter in inches. For example, a 4-inch pot will be approximately that in diameter. Manufacturers differ enormously and some 4-inch pots are larger, 4.75 inches across, and some are smaller, 3.5 inches across. Some will be squat and others will be tall.

Larger pots are generally measured by volume. A 1-gallon pot is generally 8 inches in diameter by 7 inches tall. A 2-gallon pot is roughly 10×8 inches, a 3-gallon is about 11×9.5 inches, and a 5-gallon pot is approximately 14×10 inches. There literally are hundreds of variations in the sizes of the inexpensive, thin-walled plastic pots used by nurseries for plant production.

Most of the time when you purchase a houseplant it comes in a 4-inch or 1-gallon pot. Palm trees, citrus trees, and shrubs like hibiscus may be in a 2-gallon pot or even a 5-gallon pot. In any case, your plant will most likely arrive in an inexpensive, thin-walled, black or green plastic container.

Anything that holds a volume of potting medium and that has a drainage hole can be used for a houseplant container. If you want to grow your plant in an old boot, for example, you can do it; you just have to drill a hole in the boot to make sure you have adequate drainage. Wood boxes, tin cans, glass jars, terracotta, fine porcelain, brass, fiberglass, plastic—all these can be used as containers for houseplants. Whatever you use make sure there is at least one drainage hole. If there isn't then you'll either have to drill one or use the container as a cachepot, which is a decorative shell for the "real" pot.

A half-inch carbide bit and a ¾-horsepower electric drill are handy for drilling holes in ceramic containers, but be cautious because your fancy and expensive porcelain or

There are many sizes and shapes of pots, as well as materials from which they are made. Choose one that suits your taste and the plant's needs when you bring home your new plant.

These lovely ceramic pots all share one excellent attribute: they are wider at the top than at the bottom. Re-potting is much easier on you and the plant when the pot has this shape.

hand-thrown ceramic container is easily broken during the drilling process. You might be happier if you have the holes drilled professionally rather than attempting it yourself. It takes a lot of strength to bear down on the drill on a hard ceramic surface and the noise is absolutely deafening. Be sure to wear ear protection, goggles to protect your eyes, and gloves to protect your hands.

Pot shapes. One of the loveliest container shapes is where a wide-bodied pot swoops in to a narrow neck at its top. These are truly beautiful pots; however, they are possibly the worst choice you could make for a houseplant. The problem is that you must pull your plant out of its pot periodically. If the neck is narrower than the body then you either have to cut off the roots to get the plant out, or you have to break your pot. Much better choices are pots with straight sides or ones that flare out wide with a neck that is wider than the body. These shapes make it easy to remove your plant without damaging it or the pot.

Cachepots. If you just cannot stand the look of the ugly pot your plant is in, but your plant is not ready to up-pot into the gorgeous shiny new porcelain, brass, or hand-thrown container you purchased that perfectly complements your decor, then just plop the ugly pot into your pretty pot and call it done until your plant is ready to up-pot. The pretty pot that conceals the ugly pot is called a cachepot. If your cachepot is very large, too large for your plant even when your plant is ready for moving up, then up-pot your plant (when it's ready) to a larger but equally cheap and ugly pot and put it back in the decorative cachepot until your plant's big enough to handle the volume of soil in your cachepot.

If your beautiful cachepot does not have a drainage hole, you'll need to put 1 to 2 inches of clean pebbles in the bottom of the cachepot. Set your ugly pot on top of the pebbles so that the bottom of the ugly pot never has to sit in a pool of water. Water your plant carefully and never allow the water that drains out of the ugly pot to rise above the pebbles in the

This dumb cane still grows in one of those ugly plastic pots from the garden center. Until its owner has time to up-pot it, it resides in a cachepot.

POTTING YOUR PLANT

Most people want to replace their houseplant's original pot with something more attractive. After all, your companion plant should fit into your decor in a container that complements your home and those cheap, thin-walled plastic pots that come from the nursery don't quite reach the mark.

Up-potting. When you first get your plant, examine it to see if it would profit from being moved into a larger container (up-potting). Check by pulling the plant out of its pot and looking at the root ball. This will not harm the plant if you treat it gently.

If there are only a few roots visible on the sides of the root ball and the potting medium starts to fall apart when you poke it with your finger just push the plant back into its container and wait a year or so before up-potting. If you pull your plant out of its cheap plastic container and the root ball is covered by a healthy network of white roots strongly holding together the mass of potting medium in a compact ball, then you can go ahead and up-pot your plant into a larger container.

Another factor to consider is the rate at which plants grow. Some houseplants grow slowly by nature and some grow fast, but both will eventually need to be up-potted. When you're certain your plant is ready for a new, larger pot, use a tape measure to determine the diameter of the old original pot. It's important to know the size of the container whenever it comes time to move your plant up to a larger pot.

The new pot should be no more than 2 to 4 inches larger than the current pot. Why? Because a small plant with a small root system is physically incapable of mining a large volume of soil for moisture with the result that the potting

bottom of your cachepot. If you accidentally put in too much water then be sure to drain away the excess water so that your plant does not suffer from being waterlogged. Another technique for watering is to remove your plant from the cachepot, take it to the kitchen sink or into the shower, water it, let it drain, then put it back in the cachepot.

medium stays too wet too long and the roots rot. You have to move a plant up in increments until you get your plant into the size of pot you want it to live in for a very long time.

For a slow-growing plant the new pot should be 2 inches larger in diameter. For a fast-growing plant the new pot should be 4 inches larger. In other words, when you up-pot a slow-growing plant in a 4-inch pot, move it into a 6-inch pot. This will give you 1 inch of fresh potting medium packed around all sides of the root ball. When you up-pot a fast-growing plant in a 4-inch pot, put it into an 8-inch pot. This will give you 2 inches of fresh potting medium packed around all sides of the root ball. A really vigorous plant growing rapidly will quickly fill 2 inches of fresh potting medium with healthy roots, but a slow-growing plant cannot do so.

Keep in mind that some houseplants are destined to always be small, even when fully mature. An African violet comes to mind as a kind of plant that can never become large, like a tree. It will always be small even when fully mature and can live quite happily in a 4-inch pot. A rubber tree in a 4-inch pot, by contrast, will quickly outgrow the pot and need to be up-potted to a bigger container. Since the rubber tree is a forest giant in the wild, it can easily reach the ceiling in your home if you give it a large enough pot.

African violets stay small even when fully mature. Most varieties will never be more than about 6 inches tall and wide, so happily remain in 4-inch pots.

Re-potting. If your houseplant has reached the perfect size for your space (i.e., you do not want it to get much larger than it is), you don't want to move it into a larger pot. To restrict (or maintain) a plant's size you re-pot it and put it back into the same container, or a same-size container.

Pull the plant out of its container and examine the roots. You'll probably see a tangled mass of solid roots and you won't be able to see any potting medium. Using a clean, sterile, sharp knife, slice off 1 inch of the root ball on all sides and across the bottom. Pack the bottom of the pot with 1 inch of fresh potting medium and put your plant back in its pot, then pack the sides of the pot with 1 inch of fresh potting medium. In two to three years your plant will once again need to be re-potted and you'll just repeat this process.

PROPAGATION

Division, cuttings, and layering are tried and true methods of asexual propagation that make exact copies of your parent plant. Each plant portrait in this book tells you which propagation technique(s) can be used for that particular plant. You should be aware, however, that many cultivars are protected by plant patents. You may legally propagate as many patented plants as you desire, but for your own use only. It is illegal for you to sell them. Only the patent holder or licensee has the right to sell these plants.

Sterilize your tools. Propagation techniques involve cutting or wounding your plant with a knife or pruners. Whatever tool you use, be sure it is clean, sharp, and above all sterile before you start cutting your plant. The reason you have to sterilize your tools is because a large number of virus diseases and bacterial diseases infect plants, and the viruses and bacteria that cause them are routinely spread from plant to plant by pruners and knives. If you use a pruner on a plant that is infected with a virus, and then use the same pruner on a healthy plant without sterilizing it between plants, you'll probably infect your healthy plant.

Orchid collections worldwide are infected with cymbidium mosaic virus and ringspot virus, for example. Orchid fanciers routinely sterilize their pruners with a blow torch to kill any virus particles clinging to the blades. African violet fanciers sterilize their tools by soaking them in rubbing alcohol. Another technique is to soak your tools in a 10% bleach solution (1 part household bleach to 9 parts water). Bleach corrodes your tools badly but is very effective at killing pathogens. Still another technique is to use single-edge razor blades that can be discarded after use, or wrapped in aluminum foil and boiled in water for 20 minutes for re-use.

Divisions. Simple division is the easiest of all methods for making identical copies of your houseplants. You simply cut your plant into two or more pieces. That said, whenever you cut pieces off your plant you must reduce water loss or your divisions will desiccate and die. You accomplish this by removing one-third to one-half of the leaves from each division. Either cut off the leaves at the bottom of the stems, or cut leaves in half.

There are five types of divisions: rhizomes, tubers, stolons, pups, and keikis. For all divisions pot them in the same potting medium you used for the original plant. Keep humidity high and reduce water loss by putting a glass jar or plastic bag over each division until it is once again in active growth. Open up or remove this cover for an hour or so every day to let in air. Keep the divisions in a warm location in low light. Water cautiously till they're well rooted in their new location and actively making new leaves. When they are fully established, remove the cover and acclimatize them to their permanent location in the proper light and temperature conditions for that particular plant.

RHIZOMES. Some houseplants (many orchids, ferns, snake plant, cast-iron plant) have a rhizome, a specialized horizontal underground stem that sends up new shoots at regular intervals. Using a clean, sterilized, sharp knife or pruners you can cut this rhizome into two or more pieces, making sure each piece has its own roots, stems, and leaves. Gently pull the parent plant apart to disentangle the roots as you go.

TUBERS. Calla lily, caladium, and gloxinia have underground tubers. Use a clean, sterilized, sharp knife to cut the tuber into two or more pieces during the plant's dormant period.

STOLONS. A few plants, such as spider plant and creeping saxifrage, have specialized aboveground stems called runners or stolons that make plantlets (just like a strawberry plant). Using a clean, sterilized, sharp knife or pruners you can cut this runner into two or more pieces, making sure each piece has its own roots, stems, and leaves.

PUPS. Other houseplants (all bromeliads, many succulents, some cacti, a few palms) produce new shoots, or pups, around the base of the old mother plant. When these pups have enough roots they can be removed from their mother plant and planted in their own pots. Separate a pup from the parent plant with a clean, sterilized, sharp knife or pruners. Make sure to include a decent amount of roots.

KEIKIS. Moth orchids often produce a keiki (Hawaiian for "child") on their old flowering stems. These little plants develop leaves and roots while still attached to the old inflorescence. When they look large enough to survive on their own you can separate them from the mother plant with a clean, sterilized, sharp knife or pruners. Make sure to get all the roots.

Cuttings. Another easy method for propagation of houseplants is from cut pieces of stems or leaves. Most houseplants have stems that will sprout roots under the right conditions, however, palms are a notable exception and will be killed if you cut their tops off. Only a few plants are able to regenerate new plants from their leaves. Again, each plant portrait will tell you which propagation technique(s) can be used for that particular plant.

There are three types of cuttings: stem tip cuttings, stem cuttings, and leaf cuttings. For all cuttings pot them in the same potting medium you used for the original plant. Keep humidity high and reduce water loss by putting a glass jar or plastic bag over each cutting until it is once again in active growth. Open up or remove this cover for an hour or so every day to let in air. Keep the cuttings in a warm location in low light.

Water cautiously till they're well rooted in their new location and actively making new leaves.

Stem tip cuttings. Make a basic stem tip cutting by removing the top 6 to 8 inches from the tips of the stems. Always make your cut just below a node (the place where a leaf is, or was, attached to the stem) because the new root system will grow out of that node. Always use a clean, sterilized, sharp knife or pruners. Trim off all but the top two leaves of these cuttings and cut the remaining leaves in half in order to reduce water loss and prevent your cutting from suffering desiccation and death. Dip the bottom end of the cuttings in rooting hormones and plant them in moist sand. Alternatively, put cuttings in a jar of water. Many stems, but not all, will grow roots. Through the glass you can watch the roots develop. For both methods, when the leaves begin active growth again, pot them up.

Stem cuttings. Some plants will grow new roots and shoots from short, leafless pieces of stem.

Every time you harvest herbs from the garden or bring them home from the supermarket, put their stems in water. When they sprout enough roots, plant them in small pots that can be kept on the kitchen windowsill.

If one of these plants has gotten too tall, cut off the leafy top and treat it like a stem tip cutting. You'll be left with a bare stick or cane growing out of your pot. The bare cane will grow a new leafy top, but, if you'd like your plant to be even shorter, you can cut 6- to 8-inch-long sections from that cane and root them using the following directions. The stump you leave behind will grow a new top. Again, do not try this with a palm; you'll kill it.

Use a clean, sterilized, sharp knife or pruners to cut the topless cane off at the new height you want your original plant to become. Use a marker to mark the bottom of the cane you just lopped off (the opposite end from the leaves) so you can tell which is the bottom (toward the ground) and which is the top (toward the leaves). If your section of stem is long enough, cut it into 6- to 8-inch-long pieces, again marking the bottom end of each piece. The plant knows up from down. Roots will grow only from the bottom end and shoots will grow only from the top end, so be sure to plant it top end up and bottom end down. Let the pieces air dry for three days or so. Plant them in moist sand and the stems will grow new roots and shoots. When they are well rooted, pot them up in the same potting medium as the original plant.

TI. An alternative technique specifically for ti is to cut the stem into 2-inch-long pieces and plant the pieces on their sides in moist sand or in a 50/50 mix of perlite and vermiculite. Each piece will grow into a new plant. In the meantime, the stump of your original plant will have sprouted new shoots and be rejuvenated.

Leaf cuttings. A few plants are easily propagated by rooting their leaves. You can put several leaf cuttings in one pot or container filled with moist sand or a 50/50 mix of perlite and vermiculite. Keep humidity high and reduce water loss by putting a glass jar or plastic bag over each pot. Open up or remove this cover for an hour or so every day to let in air. Keep the leaf cuttings in a warm location in low light. It will take several weeks for roots to form. A gentle tug on a leaf cutting will reveal whether it has rooted or not. In a couple of months they will have made new little plantlets. At this point you can pot them up in individual pots using the same potting medium you used for the original plant. Four types of plants propagate especially well from leaf cuttings.

SNAKE PLANT. Cut a leaf off the parent plant using a clean, sterilized, sharp knife or pruners. Use a marker to mark the bottom of the leaf, the end closest to the potting soil. Now cut the leaf into 4-inch-long pieces, marking the bottom of each piece. The leaf remembers up from down, and if you plant a chunk of leaf upside down it will just die. Let your pieces of leaf air dry for a day or two, then plant them bottom end down in damp sand or a 50/50 mix of perlite and vermiculite.

AFRICAN VIOLETS, STREPTOCARPUS, GLOXINIA. Fill a pot with a 50/50 mix of perlite and vermiculite; water just till water seeps out the drainage holes. Cut middle-sized leaves from African violets (or their gesneriad cousins, streptocarpus and gloxinia) with a 1- to 2-inch stub of the petiole (leaf stalk) attached. Use a clean, sterilized, sharp knife or pruners. Insert the cut end of the petiole into rooting hormone and then into the damp mix of perlite and vermiculite you already prepared. You can put several leaf cuttings in one pot. The leaves will have rooted in 2 to 4 weeks and will begin to make baby plantlets shortly thereafter. When the baby plantlet's leaves are about 1 inch long, pot them up.

BEGONIAS. Begonias grown for their foliage and/or their flowers can be propagated exactly as for African violets, except the stub of the petiole needs to be shorter, 0.5 inch to 1 inch long.

JADE PLANT AND OTHER SUCCULENTS. Most succulents other than cacti root very well from their leaves. Remove leaves using a clean, sterilized, sharp knife or pruners and dip the cut ends in rooting hormone. Let them air dry for 3 days. Fill a pot with a 50/50 mix of perlite and vermiculite, and water just till water seeps out the drainage holes. Lay the dry leaves on the surface of the potting mix. Don't stick them into the medium; just lay them on top. Do not put succulents in a plastic bag or under a glass jar; they'll just rot. Keep the potting mix damp by watering around the leaves, but not on the leaves. Use a very small watering can with a pencil-thin spout. Keep the leaves dry. In about a month you'll see little roots sprouting from the end of the leaf along with a baby plantlet.

Layering. Layering is a technique that causes a stem to make roots while the stem is still attached to the mother plant. There are two ways to layer plants. Simple layering is quick and easy, air layering is time-consuming, tricky, and difficult.

Simple layering. Plants with long, flexible stems (like pothos and arrowhead plant) are particularly easy to propagate using simple layering. Plants with flexible specialized stems called stolons (like spider plant and creeping saxifrage) are also easily handled with this technique. All you need to do is select a container for your newly propagated plant to grow in and fill it with the potting medium appropriate for the plant in question. Moisten the potting medium with water, let it drain, and set the container close enough to your mother plant to allow you to pick up a healthy stem or stolon and lay it on the surface of the container.

STOLONS. If you're working with a stolon, there will be little plantlets at its nodes. Adjust the position of your pot and stolon to place one

Pothos has long, flexible stems and is the perfect candidate for simple layering to propagate new plants.

of these little plantlets in the center of your container. Use a U-shaped staple or piece of wire to pin the stolon to the potting medium with the little roots pushed down into the soil. The roots will be stimulated by the moist potting medium and will begin to grow. In a few weeks, when the little plant is well rooted and actively growing new leaves, you can cut the stolon and sever the connection between the little plant and the mother plant.

VINES. To propagate a vine, such as pothos, adjust the position of your pot to place the fourth leaf from the tip of the stem in the center of your container. The place where the leaf attaches to the stem is a node. There will usually be one or two fat little roots sticking out of the node on the side of the stem opposite the leaf. Push these little roots down into the soil. Use a U-shaped staple or piece of wire to pin the stem to the potting medium with the leaf pointing up. Cut the leaf off with a clean, sterilized, sharp knife or pruners and discard it.

You now have a length of stem with three leaves on it on the side of the node away from the mother plant. The stem is still connected to the mother plant. The roots at the node pinned to the potting medium will be stimulated by the moist medium and will begin to grow.

In a few weeks, the dormant bud at the node where the leaf you removed was attached to the stem will have grown out into a new stem and will be well rooted. At this point you cut the stem between the little plantlet and the mother plant to sever the tie between them. Now you have a new little plant with two growing stems, the original three-leaf stem tip plus the new stem that sprouted from the node.

Air layering. This is the most time-consuming and trickiest method of propagation for houseplants but is, nevertheless, a valuable tool for plants such as rubber tree and fiddle-leaf fig that are difficult or impossible to root using easier methods. As in simple layering, what you're attempting to do is to make a stem grow roots while it's still attached to the mother plant. But, unlike vines or stolons, these plants have rigid, non-flexible stems so it's very difficult to bend such a stem down to attach it to a container of potting medium without breaking it. The solution is to bring the potting medium up to the plant. Here are the 12 steps to successfully propagate plants by air layering:

1. Select a point 8 to 12 inches down from the tip of a healthy young stem and, using a clean, sterilized, sharp knife cut one-third of the way into the stem at an upward angle just below a node (the place where a leaf was attached to the stem). Do not cut more than one-third of the way through the stem, and support the stem above the wound so that it doesn't break off.

2. Remove a leaf or two if they are in your way.

3. When you wound them, rubber tree or fiddle-leaf fig will bleed milky white sap that dries to rubber. Wipe away the sap with a damp cloth.

4. Prop the wound open by inserting a toothpick sideways into the cut.

5. Put rooting hormones in the wound and wrap the wound with a couple handfuls of moistened, stringy, sphagnum moss.

6. While holding the moss in place, wrap the ball of moss in a cylinder of two layers of plastic.

7. Tape the top and bottom shut with electrical tape but leave the top of the package loose enough to add water to the inside.

8. Pour enough water inside every few days to keep the sphagnum moss moist.

9. In a month or two you'll see new roots forming inside the plastic, but sometimes it can take six to eight months for roots to form, so be patient.

10. When the new roots are about 2 inches long, remove the plastic wrapping, cut the stem off the parent plant just below the new little root ball. Do not remove the sphagnum moss from the root ball.

11. Pot up your new plant.

12. Keep it in a warm, shady location until it's adjusted to its new life independent from the original plant.

Seed. Some houseplants are easy to propagate from seed. This method takes a long time (years) to grow a decent-sized woody plant like a citrus tree, but it is much faster for herbaceous perennials like geraniums. Also, because seeds are the result of sexual reproduction, each seedling, like your own child, is a unique individual and different from its mother plant. If you want to make an identical copy of your plants then you need to propagate them asexually by division, cuttings, or layering.

Specialty seed companies offer seeds of many houseplants with clear instructions printed on the package or in their catalogs regarding the appropriate sowing medium, sowing depth, soil temperature, watering, and the light regime each kind of seed needs in order to germinate successfully.

Plant Portraits

Palms and
Palm-like Plants

Areca palm

Areca palms (*Dypsis lutescens*) are relatively fast-growing, multi-trunked, clumping true palms with many slender stems that sweep out and away from the center of the plant, creating an atmosphere of tropical abundance. The stems are smooth, yellow-green, and ringed by leaf scars, which gives them a bamboo-like appearance. The leaves are pinnately compound (feather-like), divided into 80 to 100 narrow, pointed leaflets, on both sides of the midrib. The midrib of the leaf curls in a graceful arch, and the leaflets are bright green, contrasting nicely with the golden yellow leaf stalks. These are popular houseplants, because they're pretty and inexpensive, but unfortunately, arecas really aren't the best palms to grow inside your home. They need a lot of light, they do not like fertilizer salt build-up in their potting medium, and they are sensitive to overwatering, all of which combine to make them relatively short-lived when grown indoors. Those that succeed get 8 feet tall and wide.

OPTIMUM HOUSEHOLD ENVIRONMENT

Read the Introduction for the specifics of each recommendation.

HIGH LIGHT. This palm really needs a lot of light. Full sun from a south window is best. It tolerates really bright indirect light but does best with direct sun. It is very difficult to grow under artificial lights.

LOW TEMPERATURE. Daytime 65 to 75°F, nighttime 55 to 65°F.

MODERATE WATER. Water whenever the top of the potting medium becomes dry to a depth of 1 inch.

HUMIDITY. Mist your areca palm twice a week with a spray bottle of water on a mist setting, or use a handheld mister. Put the pot in a saucer or tray of water, making sure the bottom of the pot never sits directly in the water by raising the pot up on pot feet or pebbles.

POTTING MEDIUM. Use any good organic, well-drained, general-purpose potting soil that incorporates organic fertilizer, mycorrhizal fungi, and other beneficial microbes.

FERTILIZER. Areca palms are fussy about nutrients. Their leaves turn yellow if they don't get what they need. Choose an organic fertilizer, in either a powder or liquid formulation, where the first number (nitrogen) is higher than the other two. Make sure that the fertilizer also incorporates kelp meal (seaweed), which provides magnesium, iron, and other nutrients. Apply once in early spring and again in June.

POTTING. When your plant needs up-potting, shift it to a container with a diameter 4 inches larger than the current pot. These palms can handle the larger size because they are fast growers. Up-pot again every two to three years until the plant is as big as you want it to get. A

Areca palm (aka golden cane palm, cane palm, Madagascar palm, yellow palm, butterfly palm).

large areca palm needs a large, heavy pot to prevent it from toppling over.

PROPAGATION. Areca palm is easy to propagate from seed.

COMMON PROBLEMS

Watch for yellowing leaves (page 257), mealybugs (page 262), and leaf spot fungus (page 269).

Banana

Lush, large, and beautiful, the various species of banana plants, including hardy banana (*Musa basjoo*) and *Ensete ventricosum*, instantly create a tropical ambiance in any home. These are big, bold, rock stars—plants that stand out in any crowd. These plants are so charismatic, their mere presence can transport you to a South Sea island. Bananas are sometimes called banana trees, but they're really giant herbs, not trees at all, because they lack woody stems. Their trunk-like "stems" are actually pseudostems, made up of the tightly wrapped bases of leaves. *Musa acuminata*, *M. balbisiana*, and the hybrids between them produce edible fruits; cultivars of the Dwarf Cavendish group usually reach 6 to 8 feet tall, but the smallest of them, 'Super Dwarf Cavendish', gets only 2 to 4 feet tall and wide, making it the perfect size for many situations inside the home.

The foliage is the most attractive part of any banana plant. The big, wide, green leaves are simple, entire, and very beautiful. 'Super Dwarf Cavendish' has leaves perhaps 2 feet long and 8 inches wide, much smaller than standard but just as gorgeous. Some cultivars have foliage with purple-red blotches or stripes, and other cultivars have variegated leaves with sophisticated patches of pure white, pale green, and dark green. Banana leaves are easily shredded by the wind, so if your plant spends its summers

Banana plant (aka plantain, fiber banana, Japanese banana, ensete).

outdoors protect it from the wind. The flowers are tiny, neither large nor colorful. They form on stalks that emerge from the center of the crown of foliage as soon as a pseudostem is old enough to bloom—at about 18 months. The first flowers to form are male, later flowers are female and develop into the familiar ripe fruits we all know and love. Bananas don't need to be pollinated to make fruit. As soon as the fruit ripens, the pseudostem dies, and the perennial rhizome in the soil sends up new shoots called pups.

OPTIMUM HOUSEHOLD ENVIRONMENT

Read the Introduction for the specifics of each recommendation.

HIGH LIGHT. Banana likes a lot of light, especially if you'd like it to fruit for you. It does best in a south window in full sun. It survives and is lovely in medium light from an east or west window, but with only a half-day of light it is unlikely to make fruit.

HIGH TEMPERATURE. Daytime 75 to 85°F, nighttime 65 to 75°F. This tropical plant likes it hot, especially if you hope to get some fruit from it. To grow banana as a non-fruiting ornamental foliage plant, just provide moderate temperatures: daytime 70 to 80°F, nighttime 60 to 70°F.

AMPLE WATER. Water whenever the top of the potting medium becomes dry to a depth of 0.5 inch.

HUMIDITY. Mist your banana plant daily with a spray bottle of water on a mist setting, or use a handheld mister. Put the pot in a saucer or tray of water, making sure the bottom of the pot never sits directly in the water by raising the pot up on pot feet or pebbles.

POTTING MEDIUM. Use any good organic, well-drained, general-purpose potting medium that incorporates organic fertilizer, mycorrhizal fungi, and other beneficial microbes.

FERTILIZER. Use any balanced organic fertilizer, in either a powder or liquid formulation. Apply dry fertilizer every month year-round. Apply liquid fertilizer at half-strength every two weeks.

POTTING. Given enough light, heat, water, and nutrients your banana grows rapidly and needs to be up-potted to a larger container before the first year is up. Shift it to a container with a diameter 4 inches larger than the current pot. Up-pot again every year until the plant is as big as you want it to get.

PROPAGATION. Bananas are easy to propagate by potting up the pups whenever you are re-potting the main plant. Don't be alarmed when the pseudostem dies after it flowers. The rhizome always makes new pups for you, and your plant does not die.

COMMON PROBLEMS

Watch for yellowing leaf edges (page 257), scale insects (page 262), and root rot (page 272).

Chinese fan palm

Chinese fan palm (*Livistona chinensis*) is well known for its outdoor hardiness (to zone 8), but more and more it is used in interiorscaping, especially in shopping malls and other public buildings. It does well in pots, and as a houseplant, it grows very slowly to an eventual 8 feet. It has a single, large, straight trunk, which can be as much as 18 inches in diameter. Its bright evergreen leaves are palmate (fan-shaped) and up to 6 feet long. Individual leaflets have long, tapered, ribbon-like tips that droop at the ends, giving this palm an attractive, shimmery, weeping look. Leaf stalks (petioles) are armed with stout, sharp thorns, so find a location where passersby cannot bump into it.

OPTIMUM HOUSEHOLD ENVIRONMENT

Read the Introduction for the specifics of each recommendation.

HIGH LIGHT. Chinese fan palm does best where it gets the full light of a south window. It also does well in medium light from a west window with half a day of full sun, especially when it is young, because it likes the heat of the afternoon sun and because young plants are more tolerant of partial shade.

MODERATE TEMPERATURE. Daytime 70 to 80°F, nighttime 60 to 70°F.

LOW WATER. Water whenever the top of the

Chinese fan palm (aka Chinese fountain palm, fountain palm).

potting medium becomes dry to a depth of 2 inches.

HUMIDITY. Mist your Chinese fan palm twice a week with a spray bottle of water on a mist setting, or use a handheld mister. Put the pot in a saucer or tray of water, making sure the bottom of the pot never sits directly in the water by raising the pot up on pot feet or pebbles.

POTTING MEDIUM. Use any good organic, well-drained, general-purpose potting soil that incorporates organic fertilizer, mycorrhizal fungi, and other beneficial microbes.

FERTILIZER. Use any organic fertilizer, in either a powder or liquid formulation, where the first number (nitrogen) is higher than the other two. Apply once in early spring and again in June.

POTTING. When your plant needs up-potting, shift it to a container with a diameter 2 inches larger than the current pot. This plant grows very slowly so avoid putting it in too large a pot.

PROPAGATION. Chinese fan palm is easy to propagate from seed.

COMMON PROBLEMS

Watch for brown leaf tips (page 246), spider mites (page 263), and root rot (page 272).

Corn plant

Corn plant (*Dracaena fragrans*) is ubiquitous in the interiorscaping of hospitals, hotels, and other public buildings because it's big, bold, and beautiful. It's extremely easy to grow well, and it tolerates a wide range of light, temperature, and water conditions. Its forgiving, low-maintenance nature and ability to rid indoor air of pollutants make it extremely popular in the home as well. Indoors, corn plant is usually slow-growing and handsome, with two or three slender trunks and a swirling rosette of evergreen foliage at the top. You'll rarely see it more than 8 feet tall as a houseplant. The leaves are usually 18 to 24 inches long, strap-shaped, and glossy. The wild form of the plant has leaves that are uniformly bright green, but numerous cultivars are available with leaves striped in chartreuse or white. Corn plant rarely flowers as a houseplant, but if it ever does you may not notice the flowers at first because they're not very showy. The flowers are borne in long, branched clusters of underwhelming, 1-inch-wide blossoms with skinny petals. The best thing about the flowers, by far, is the fragrance—a strong, lovely perfume.

Corn plant (aka cornstalk dracaena, dracaena).

OPTIMUM HOUSEHOLD ENVIRONMENT

Read the Introduction for the specifics of each recommendation.

MEDIUM LIGHT. Corn plant performs at its very best with a half-day of full sun from an east or west window. It endures the high light of full sun from a south window or the low light (permanent shade) of a north window; however, it cannot reach its full potential under those conditions.

LOW TEMPERATURE. Daytime 65 to 75°F, nighttime 55 to 65°F.

MODERATE WATER. Water whenever the top of the potting medium becomes dry to a depth of 1 inch.

HUMIDITY. Corn plant prospers with slightly higher humidity than the average home offers. Mist your corn plant several times a week with a spray bottle of water on a mist setting, or use a handheld mister. Put the pot in a saucer or tray of water, making sure the bottom of the pot never sits directly in the water by raising the pot up on pot feet or pebbles.

POTTING MEDIUM. Use any good organic, well-drained potting soil that incorporates organic fertilizer, mycorrhizal fungi, and other beneficial microbes.

FERTILIZER. Use any organic fertilizer, in either a powder or liquid formulation, where the first number (nitrogen) is higher than the other two. Apply once in early spring and again in June.

POTTING. When your plant needs up-potting, shift it to a container with a diameter 2 inches larger than the current pot. This plant grows slowly so avoid putting it in too large a pot.

PROPAGATION. Corn plant is easy to propagate from stem cuttings and stem tip cuttings.

COMMON PROBLEMS

Watch for brown leaf tips (page 246), mealybugs (page 262), and root rot (page 272).

Dragon tree

Dragon tree (*Dracaena reflexa* var. *angustifolia*) is one of the most popular of all houseplants. It's beautiful, inexpensive, and widely available, and many people believe it somehow brings good fortune. This easy-to-grow, low-maintenance, shrubby plant looks like a Dr. Seuss tree with crooked stems topped by a troll's hairdo of long, stiff, narrow leaves. The stems are thin but strong. The leaves are 1 to 2 inches wide and 12 to 24 inches long, or even longer, and taper to a

Dragon tree (aka Madagascar dragon tree, red-edge dracaena, marginata, money plant, money tree, pleomele, song of India, rainbow plant).

Dragon tree, variegated form.

narrow point at the tip. All the ribbon-like leaves occur in a clump at the top of each stem. They curve gracefully out and away from the center of the plant and eventually droop down. As a houseplant, the plant grows slowly to about 6 feet tall.

OPTIMUM HOUSEHOLD ENVIRONMENT

Read the Introduction for the specifics of each recommendation.

MEDIUM LIGHT. A half-day of sun from an east window is optimum because hot, intense sunlight burns the leaves, especially of cultivars with variegated foliage like 'Tricolor' and 'Colorama'.

LOW TEMPERATURE. Daytime 65 to 75°F, nighttime 55 to 65°F.

MODERATE WATER. Water whenever the top of the potting medium becomes dry to a depth of 1 inch.

HUMIDITY. Dragon tree tolerates dry air very well, but it grows better with slightly higher humidity if the air in your house is significantly drier than average. Mist your dragon tree twice a week with a spray bottle of water on a mist setting, or use a handheld mister. Put the pot in a saucer or tray of water, making sure the bottom of the pot never sits directly in the water by raising the pot up on pot feet or pebbles.

POTTING MEDIUM. Use any good organic, well-drained potting soil that incorporates organic fertilizer, mycorrhizal fungi, and other beneficial microbes.

FERTILIZER. Use any organic fertilizer, in either a powder or liquid formulation, where the first number (nitrogen) is higher than the other two. Apply once in early spring and again in June.

POTTING. When your plant needs up-potting, shift it to a container with a diameter 2 inches larger than the current pot. This plant grows slowly so avoid putting it in too large a pot.

PROPAGATION. Dragon tree is easy to propagate from stem cuttings and stem tip cuttings.

COMMON PROBLEMS

Watch for brown leaf tips (page 246), spider mites (page 263), and root rot (page 272).

Dumb cane

Dumb cane (*Dieffenbachia amoena*, *D. seguine*, and hybrids between these and other species) is among the most popular houseplants, because, like many aroids, it has beautiful foliage and is readily available, inexpensive, and easy to grow. It's a shrubby plant that typically gets 6 feet tall in the older cultivars. Many modern cultivars, selected for their short stature, grow only to 1 foot. Dumb cane's soft but sturdy stems tend to grow straight up and support numerous leaves arranged in a spiral. The stems are reminiscent of corn stalks: they are pithy inside, not hard and woody like a tree. The large leaves, 12 to 18 inches long and 6 to 9 inches wide, are patterned and flecked with areas of white, light green, and darker green. Some cultivars have leaves that are mostly white with dark green edges, some have white streaks on dark green leaves, and others have random flecks of different colors scattered across the surface of the leaves.

❶ This plant is toxic to people and pets and should be sited in an out-of-the-way place. Its tissues contain calcium oxalate crystals, and if leaves are chewed the crystals penetrate the soft tissues of lips, throat, and tongue (hence the common name, as in "deaf, dumb, and blind"), causing painful swelling, drooling, and vomiting. If you suspect a person or pet has ingested parts of this plant, or if a person or pet exhibits serious symptoms such as difficulty breathing, call your local emergency hotline, poison control center, or vet.

Dumb cane (aka mother-in-law plant).

OPTIMUM HOUSEHOLD ENVIRONMENT

Read the Introduction for the specifics of each recommendation.

MEDIUM LIGHT. Dumb cane does best in an east or west window filtered by gauzy curtains. It tolerates the low light of a north window.

MODERATE TEMPERATURE. Daytime 70 to 80°F, nighttime 60 to 70°F.

MODERATE WATER. Water whenever the top of the potting medium becomes dry to a depth of 1 inch.

HUMIDITY. Mist your dumb cane twice a week with a spray bottle of water on a mist setting, or use a handheld mister. Put the pot in a saucer or tray of water, making sure the bottom of the pot never sits directly in the water by raising the pot up on pot feet or pebbles.

POTTING MEDIUM. Use any good organic, well-drained potting soil that incorporates organic fertilizer, mycorrhizal fungi, and other beneficial microbes.

FERTILIZER. Use any organic fertilizer, in either a powder or liquid formulation, where the first number (nitrogen) is higher than the other two. Apply once a month.

POTTING. When your plant needs up-potting, shift it to a container with a diameter 2 inches larger than the current pot. This plant grows slowly so avoid putting it in too large a pot.

PROPAGATION. Dumb cane is easy to propagate from stem cuttings and stem tip cuttings.

COMMON PROBLEMS

Watch for brown leaf tips (page 246), mealybugs (page 262), and leaf spot fungus (page 269).

European fan palm

European fan palm (*Chamaerops humilis*) grows slowly as a houseplant, to about 4 feet tall. The plant is typically clump-forming, developing suckers from the base of the main trunk, an unusual trait among true palms. The cluster of stems eventually curves gracefully out and away from the center—each stem completely clothed in old, persistent leaf bases that form a spiny, basketweave network of brown and black fibers. As implied by the common name, the leaves are fan-shaped (palmate) rather than feather-like (pinnate). The stiff leaves are small by palm standards (about 24 inches wide on 15-inch-long petioles) and vary in color from bright green to silvery blue. The leaf petioles (stalks) have sharp spines on the edges so handle carefully and with gloves. The plant sheds the oldest leaves from the bottom of the crown as it grows taller, developing the typical palm silhouette of a leafless trunk with a crown of foliage at the top. This tough little palm is one of two (the other is Chinese fan palm) that are hardy enough to grow outdoors in zone 8. As a houseplant, it really appreciates a summer vacation outdoors on the deck or patio. If it has been getting full sun indoors you can move it into full sun outdoors, otherwise give it filtered sunlight. At the end of summer be sure to examine it thoroughly for scale and other insect pests and clean it prior to bringing it back indoors.

OPTIMUM HOUSEHOLD ENVIRONMENT

Read the Introduction for the specifics of each recommendation.

MEDIUM LIGHT. A half-day of full sun from an east window is perfect for this plant. It also does well with high light filtered through a sheer curtain. It can also take high light from a south window but needs to be acclimated carefully to those conditions or the leaves burn.

MODERATE TEMPERATURE. Daytime 70 to 80°F, nighttime 60 to 70°F. European fan palm needs cool nights from 50 to 60°F in winter.

MODERATE WATER. Water whenever the top of the potting medium becomes dry to a depth of 1 inch. Water less in winter, waiting till the top of the potting medium is dry to a depth of 2 inches.

HUMIDITY. This plant is very tolerant of the dry air in the average home.

POTTING MEDIUM. Use any good organic, well-drained potting soil that incorporates organic fertilizer, mycorrhizal fungi, and other beneficial microbes.

FERTILIZER. Use any organic fertilizer, in either a powder or liquid formulation, where the first number (nitrogen) is higher than the other two. Apply dry fertilizer once in early spring and again in June. Apply liquid fertilizer at half-strength every two weeks in spring and summer. Stop feeding your plant in fall and winter.

POTTING. After two to three years, when your plant has grown enough to need up-potting, shift it to a container with a diameter 4 inches larger than the current pot. Select a deep pot rather than a shallow one. Up-pot again every two to three years until the plant is as big as you want it to get. The deep roots are a bit fragile, so handle them carefully when up-potting. And be sure to protect yourself from this palm's spiny stems and leaves by wearing gloves.

PROPAGATION. European fan palm is easy to propagate from seed. You can also carefully remove a sucker from the base of the plant's trunk and plant it in its own pot. Give it filtered light until it is well rooted and established.

COMMON PROBLEMS
Watch for scale insects (page 262).

European fan palm (aka Mediterranean fan palm).

Kentia palm

Both species, *Howea forsteriana* and *H. belmoreana*, are large, single-trunked, slow-growing palms cultivated everywhere as large houseplants. Kentias were especially fashionable in the Victorian era and remain among the most popular indoor palms in the world. Today they are often a prominent feature of large open lobbies and atriums of public buildings, shopping malls, and private homes. Indoors in containers, they'll be 8 to 10 feet tall and 5 to 6 feet wide—pretty impressively big by normal houseplant standards. The slender trunk of these trees is smooth, green, and ringed with whitish leaf scars. The large, dark green leaves are pinnately compound (feather-like), 3 feet long and 1 foot wide. New leaves at the top of the crown are upright but the lowermost leaves are held horizontally, making the crown of the tree very wide. The 60 or more individual leaflets of each leaf are long, pointed, and droop gracefully, pointing down toward the ground on both sides of the midrib.

Usually, when you purchase a kentia palm, it looks like the plant has multiple trunks, but it does not. Nurserymen put two to five single-trunked plants in each pot because it gives the product a lusher, full appearance and makes it more attractive to customers. Should you decide to separate these plants, do it carefully because the roots are brittle and easily damaged.

Kentia palm (aka sentry palm, thatch palm, paradise palm, curly palm, Belmore sentry palm).

OPTIMUM HOUSEHOLD ENVIRONMENT

Read the Introduction for the specifics of each recommendation.

MEDIUM LIGHT. Kentia palms do not like full sun—the leaves burn and develop black patches where the sun has killed the tissue. Sheer, gauzy curtains to diffuse the light on a south, east, or west window work well. These palms tolerate shade but don't thrive in it.

LOW TEMPERATURE. Daytime 65 to 75°F, nighttime 55 to 65°F. Kentia palms like cool nights but don't let the nighttime temperature drop below 50°F.

MODERATE WATER. Water whenever the top of the potting medium becomes dry to a depth of 1 inch. Water less often in winter but never let the plant go completely dry.

HUMIDITY. Mist your plant several times a week

with a spray bottle of water on a mist setting, or use a handheld mister. Put the pot in a saucer or tray of water, making sure the bottom of the pot never sits directly in the water by raising the pot up on pot feet or pebbles. Consider putting a humidifier in the room.

POTTING MEDIUM. Use any good organic, well-drained potting soil that incorporates organic fertilizer, mycorrhizal fungi, and other beneficial microbes.

FERTILIZER. Use any organic fertilizer, in either a powder or liquid formulation, where the first number (nitrogen) is higher than the other two. Apply dry fertilizer once a month. Apply liquid fertilizer at half-strength every two weeks in spring and summer. Stop feeding your plant in fall and winter.

POTTING. Even large kentia palms do very well in small pots. After two or more years, when your plant has grown enough to need up-potting, shift it to a container with a diameter 4 inches larger than the current pot. Up-pot again every three years until the plant is as big as you want it to get. Its roots are fragile so handle with care.

PROPAGATION. Kentia palms are only propagated from seeds, which are hard to get. It is impossible to grow new plants from cuttings and, as with many palms, if you cut off the growing tip you'll kill the tree.

COMMON PROBLEMS

Watch for brown leaf tips (page 246), scale insects (page 262), and root rot (page 272).

····················

Lady palm

The beautiful lady palm (*Rhapis excelsa*) enjoys great popularity in Europe and America. Its elegance adds a distinctly Asian note to your interiorscape. Like a classic movie star, it tolerates neglect and poor light with panache and

Lady palm (aka broadleaf lady palm).

goes right on being attractive. Widely used as an interiorscaping subject, this slow-growing palm is a common sight in offices, malls, and other public buildings, and its easy, forgiving nature makes it a choice houseplant for large rooms. The plant is a small, clump-forming, multi-stemmed palm to 6 feet tall and wide with slender, 1-inch-thick stems completely wrapped in brown fibers. With age the fibers enclosing the trunks drop off to reveal the jointed, bamboo-like trunks. Each palmate (fan-shaped), dark green, glossy leaf has numerous leaflets radiating out like the fingers of your widespread hand. Some cultivars have variegated leaves. The slender leaf-stalks arise from a fibrous, net-like, brown sheath that envelops the trunks.

OPTIMUM HOUSEHOLD ENVIRONMENT

Read the Introduction for the specifics of each recommendation.

MEDIUM LIGHT. In spring and summer, while the plant is in active growth, it does best in filtered or dappled bright light as from a south, east, or west window. But it cannot tolerate full sun unless the light is filtered by Venetian blinds or gauzy curtains. In winter, when the plant is not growing as much, it gets along with low light.

LOW TEMPERATURE. Daytime 65 to 75°F, nighttime 55 to 65°F. In winter, make sure the nighttime temperature does not go below 55°F and keep your lady palm away from cold drafts and heat vents.

MODERATE WATER. Through the growing season, water whenever the top of the potting medium becomes dry to a depth of 1 inch. In winter, water whenever the top of the potting medium becomes dry to a depth of 2 inches.

HUMIDITY. Mist your plant several times a week with a spray bottle of water on a mist setting, or use a handheld mister. Put the pot in a saucer or tray of water, making sure the bottom of the pot never sits directly in the water by raising the pot up on pot feet or pebbles. Consider putting a humidifier in the room.

POTTING MEDIUM. Use any good organic, well-drained potting soil that incorporates organic fertilizer, mycorrhizal fungi, and other beneficial microbes.

FERTILIZER. Use any organic fertilizer, in either a powder or liquid formulation, where the first number (nitrogen) is higher than the other two. Apply once a month through the growing season. Stop feeding your plant in fall and winter.

POTTING. Lady palms like to be slightly rootbound. Wait two to three years to shift it to a larger container. Choose a pot with a diameter 4 inches larger than the current pot. Up-pot again every three or four years until your lady palm is as big as you want it to get.

PROPAGATION. Lady palm develops new upright stems from its rhizome, making it easy to propagate by division.

COMMON PROBLEMS

Watch for brown leaf tips (page 246), scale insects (page 262), and leaf spot fungus (page 269).

Parlor palm

Parlor palms (*Chamaedorea elegans* and *C. seifrizii*) are deservedly the most popular and widely grown indoor palms in the world. These beautiful, elegant little true palms are well adapted to indoor culture as houseplants. They were extremely popular during the Victorian era and remain so today. Indoors, both grow very slowly to about 4 feet tall. *Chamaedorea elegans* has a single trunk, which is green, slender (1 inch thick), and cane-like, with rings (leaf scars) that

Parlor palm (aka neanthe bella palm, bamboo palm, reed palm).

make it appear jointed like bamboo. *Chamae-dorea seifrizii* is a clumping species that forms multiple trunks from underground runners. The leaves of these palms are pinnately compound (feather-like), 1 to 2 feet long, with many narrow leaflets on both sides of the midrib. Foliage color is usually a mid- to dark green. When the plants are more than three years old they may flower and make seeds. These seeds are usually not fertile so just cut off the flower stalks when they start to turn brown. Most of the time, when you acquire a parlor palm it is *C. elegans*, or a hybrid between *C. elegans* and *C. seifrizii*. Regardless of the label, the cultural requirements of any of these parlor palms are basically the same. The single biggest difference is that some are single-trunked and some are multi-trunked.

OPTIMUM HOUSEHOLD ENVIRONMENT

Read the Introduction for the specifics of each recommendation.

MEDIUM LIGHT. Bright but indirect light such as from an east or west window with sheer curtains to filter and soften the light is perfect for parlor palms. They tolerate low light in that they don't just give up the ghost and die in the dark; however, they will not be as strong and healthy in shade as they would be with more light.

MODERATE TEMPERATURE. Daytime 70 to 80°F, nighttime 60 to 70°F.

MODERATE WATER. Water whenever the top of the potting medium becomes dry to a depth of 1 inch.

HUMIDITY. Mist your plant several times a week with a spray bottle of water on a mist setting, or use a handheld mister. Put the pot in a saucer or tray of water, making sure the bottom of the pot never sits directly in the water by raising the pot up on pot feet or pebbles. Consider putting a humidifier in the room.

POTTING MEDIUM. Use any good organic, well-drained potting soil that incorporates organic fertilizer, mycorrhizal fungi, and other beneficial microbes.

FERTILIZER. Use any organic fertilizer, in either a powder or liquid formulation, where the first number (nitrogen) is higher than the other two. Apply at half-strength once a month through the growing season. Stop feeding your plant in fall and winter.

POTTING. When your plant needs up-potting, shift it to a container with a diameter 4 inches larger than the current pot. Up-pot again every two to three years until the plant is as big as you want it to get.

PROPAGATION. Single-trunked parlor palms (*Chamaedorea elegans*) are easy to propagate from seed. This is how professional growers propagate them because they cannot be divided or grown from cuttings. Growers usually put two or three seedlings into a pot to make the product look more attractive. Parlor palms that are naturally multi-trunked (*C. seifrizii*) can be divided by cutting the rhizome to make two or more plants, each with its own stem, leaves, and roots.

COMMON PROBLEMS

Watch for brown leaf tips (page 246), spider mites (page 263), and root rot (page 272).

Pony-tail palm

Many people know and love pony-tail palm (*Beaucarnea recurvata*), another plant that looks like it came straight from a story by Dr. Seuss. Grown worldwide as an ornamental, it also succeeds quite well indoors in a large pot, growing to 8 feet in 20 years. The base of the trunk is enormously swollen. This bulbous base is a water storage feature of this drought-tolerant desert dweller. This makes a large plant, say 4 feet tall or so, extremely heavy. You'll probably want eventually to put this one's pot on wheels.

The 3-foot-long leaves are very long, thin, flexible, and ribbon-like. They dangle like a bright green mop from the top of the tree's trunk. It does look a bit like hair, from a distance, and the name pony-tail is rather descriptive.

OPTIMUM HOUSEHOLD ENVIRONMENT

Read the Introduction for the specifics of each recommendation.

HIGH LIGHT. Full sun from a south window is the best light regime, with medium light from a west window next best. Pony-tail palm is a semi-succulent, drought-tolerant, desert-adapted plant so give it as much bright light as possible.

MODERATE TEMPERATURE. Daytime 70 to 80°F, nighttime 60 to 70°F.

LOW WATER. Water whenever the top of the potting medium becomes dry to a depth of 2 inches. Pony-tail palm wants dryish soil. Wet, soggy soil kills it. Water it infrequently in winter.

HUMIDITY. Pony-tail palm prefers low humidity so you don't need to mist it.

POTTING MEDIUM. Use a good organic, fast-draining potting soil designed for cactus and succulents that includes mycorrhizal fungi and other beneficial microbes.

FERTILIZER. Use any organic fertilizer, in either a powder or liquid formulation, where the first number (nitrogen) is higher than the other two. Feed your plant once a month through the growing season. Stop feeding it in fall and winter.

POTTING. The large swollen base of pony-tail palm gets big fairly rapidly. When your plant's base has grown to within 2 inches of the edge of the pot it needs up-potting. Shift it to a container with a diameter 4 inches larger than the current pot. Up-pot again every two to three years until the plant is as big as you want it to get. Pots that are wide and shallow work well for this plant.

PROPAGATION. Pony-tail palm is primarily

Pony-tail palm (aka beaucarnea, elephant's foot, bottle palm, nolina).

propagated by seed available from specialist suppliers. It is unlikely ever to bloom and make seeds for you when grown indoors in a container.

COMMON PROBLEMS

Watch for brown leaf tips (page 246), spider mites (page 263), and stem rot (page 275).

Pygmy date palm

Pygmy date palm (*Phoenix roebelenii*) is grown everywhere as an ornamental in the interiorscaping of public buildings and as a houseplant in private homes, where it reaches only about 3 feet in height. The plant's stout little stems are encased in fibrous brown leaf bases in an attractive basketweave pattern. The leaves are 2 to 4 feet long and pinnately compound (feather-like), with narrow leaflets to 6 inches long and 0.5 inch wide on both sides of the midrib. At the bottom quarter of each leaf stalk these little leaflets become stout, needle-sharp spines. Wear gloves when trimming off the lower leaves of this plant. It actually produces 0.5-inch-long dates when grown outdoors, nothing as big as real dates from its cousin, *P. dactylifera*, but dates nonetheless—tiny and quite yummy in date nut bread.

Pygmy date palm (aka miniature date palm).

OPTIMUM HOUSEHOLD ENVIRONMENT

Read the Introduction for the specifics of each recommendation.

HIGH LIGHT. Pygmy date palm prefers bright light and even tolerates full sun.

MODERATE TEMPERATURE. Daytime 70 to 80°F, nighttime 60 to 70°F.

MODERATE WATER. Water whenever the top of the potting medium becomes dry to a depth of 1 inch. Water less often in fall and winter.

HUMIDITY. Pygmy date palm seems not to mind dry air and does not need to be misted.

POTTING MEDIUM. Use any good organic, general-purpose potting soil that incorporates organic fertilizer, mycorrhizal fungi, and other beneficial microbes.

FERTILIZER. Pygmy date palm is fussy about micronutrients. Choose a balanced organic fertilizer that supplies magnesium and manganese, in addition to nitrogen, phosphorus, and potassium (N-P-K). Apply fertilizer once a month through the growing season. Stop feeding your plant in fall and winter.

POTTING. When your plant needs up-potting, shift it to a container with a diameter 4 inches larger than the current pot. Up-pot again every two years until the plant is as big as you want it to get. Pygmy date palm does well when slightly rootbound. When you need to re-pot this plant remember the sharp spines on the leaves and be sure to wear gloves.

PROPAGATION. Pygmy date palm is easy to propagate from seed.

COMMON PROBLEMS

Watch for yellow patches on leaves (page 258), scale insects (page 262), and leaf spot fungus (page 269).

Ti

Graceful and elegant, ti (*Cordyline fruticosa*) is beloved for its beautiful evergreen foliage in a wide variety of colors. A shrub, the plant has thin, strong, woody stems that, when grown as a houseplant, reach 4 to 5 feet tall. The strap-shaped 2-foot-long and 4-inch-wide leaves have pointed tips and grow in a spiral around the upper third of the stems. Ti sheds its oldest leaves as it grows, becoming a slender stalk with a tuft of foliage at the top. The foliage can be uniformly green, or variegated with red, pink, purple, and/or white patches. Flowers are small and rarely seen when the plant is grown as a houseplant. Fruits are red berries. The starchy rhizomes of this asparagus relative are sweet when cooked and, when fermented, are the main ingredient of okolehao, a Hawaiian liquor.

OPTIMUM HOUSEHOLD ENVIRONMENT

Read the Introduction for the specifics of each recommendation.

MEDIUM LIGHT. Give ti full sun for a half-day for best success, ideally in an east or west window, or a south window with sheer curtains to filter the light.

MODERATE TEMPERATURE. Daytime 70 to 80°F, nighttime 60 to 70°F.

MODERATE WATER. Water whenever the top of the potting medium becomes dry to a depth of 1 inch.

HUMIDITY. Mist your ti daily with a spray bottle of water on a mist setting, or use a handheld mister. Put the pot in a saucer or tray of water, making sure the bottom of the pot never sits directly in the water by raising the pot up on pot feet or pebbles. Consider putting a humidifier in the room.

POTTING MEDIUM. Use any good organic, well-drained potting soil that incorporates

Ti (aka Hawaiian ti, cabbage palm, good luck tree, palm lily).

organic fertilizer, mycorrhizal fungi, and other beneficial microbes.

FERTILIZER. Use any organic fertilizer, in either a powder or liquid formulation, where the first number (nitrogen) is higher than the other two. Look for one that also contains kelp meal or seaweed extracts, which add micronutrients. Apply dry fertilizer once a month. Apply liquid fertilizer at half-strength every two weeks. Stop fertilizing ti in winter.

POTTING. When ti needs up-potting, shift it to a container with a diameter 4 inches larger than the current pot. Ti is happy in a smallish pot so you do not need to up-pot very often.

PROPAGATION. Ti is easy to propagate from stem tip cuttings and stem cuttings.

COMMON PROBLEMS

Watch for brown leaf tips (page 246), spider mites (page 263), and root rot (page 272).

Trees and Shrubs

Citrus

All citrus plants are species in or hybrids derived from the genera *Citrus* and *Fortunella*. Most are ancient accidental hybrids, which were discovered growing wild by humans a very long time ago—so long ago that no one remembers exactly where they came from. Botanists are certain, however, that lemon is a natural hybrid between pummelo (*C. maxima*) and citron (*C. medica*). A more recently discovered natural hybrid is the Meyer lemon, a cross between lemon and the sweet orange, which itself is an ancient natural hybrid between pummelo and mandarin (*C. reticulata*). All citrus are renowned for the powerful and sensuous fragrance of their flowers as well as for their delicious, vitamin-rich fruit, and all have beautiful evergreen foliage. Trees bloom sporadically throughout the year but tend to flower more profusely in springtime. Flowers are star-shaped, five-petaled, and white, about 1.5 inches across, and often have a purplish blush in the bud. They are borne in small clusters along the branches. The fruits are rich in vitamin C, and zest from the rind is laden with savory aromatic oils that find wide application in cuisine, alcoholic beverages, and even cleaning solutions.

The most successful citrus to grow as houseplants—lemon, Meyer lemon, lime, and kumquat—are small in stature. But sweet orange, one of the larger trees, may also be grown indoors. All reliably bloom and set fruit when given appropriate environmental conditions in your home. In the average home it is difficult to provide the abundant sunlight and warmth an orange tree needs to produce sweet fruit. Limes and lemons have sour fruits, need less sunlight and warmth, and fruit regularly in your home given a south window. The plants are self-fertile, and many of the flowers set fruit. In fact they regularly produce too many of them. If that

(top) Lime (aka Tahitian lime).   (bottom) Meyer lemon.

happens, nip the tiny fruitlets off your plant and allow only a few to mature. Otherwise the tree exhausts itself and becomes weakened as it attempts to mature a heavy crop.

Many citrus species are spiny, some strongly so. If yours is one of the more thorny types be sure to place it in a location in your home where it cannot snag passersby.

OPTIMUM HOUSEHOLD ENVIRONMENT

Read the Introduction for the specifics of each recommendation.

HIGH LIGHT. All citrus want as much sunlight as you can give them. A south window is best for maximum sunlight all year long. If you do not have a south window then the medium light of an east or west window suffices, but with only a half-day of light, your tree will produce fewer fruits.

LOW TEMPERATURE. Daytime 65 to 75°F, nighttime 55 to 65°F. A summer vacation outdoors is a convenient way to provide cooler nights and abundant daylight for your trees, but be certain to bring them back indoors before the first frost of autumn. You can put them out again in the spring after all danger of frost has passed. Flower buds and fruits are damaged below 32°F but the plants are not killed. Plants are killed outright at or below 25°F.

MODERATE WATER. Water whenever the top of the potting medium becomes dry to a depth of 1 inch. Citrus are very sensitive to waterlogged soils and can develop root rot and die if the medium is too wet for too long. Be certain your container is propped up on pot feet or pebbles so that the pot never sits in water in the pot's saucer.

HUMIDITY. Depending on the dryness of your home, mist your plants occasionally (perhaps once a week) with a spray bottle of water.

POTTING MEDIUM. Use a good-quality, organic potting soil that is light, airy, and water-retentive. Excellent choices are those that include mycorrhizal fungi and other beneficial microbes in the mix.

FERTILIZER. Any organic fertilizer especially designed for use with citrus works well for your lemons and limes. Those that are blended with humic acid are the best choices. Citrus need a lot of nitrogen so make sure the nutrients are 7-3-3 or something close to that. Follow the recommendations on the package and feed your citrus in spring and in fall.

POTTING. When your citrus needs up-potting, shift it to a container with a diameter 4 inches larger than the current pot.

COMMON PROBLEMS

Watch for yellow patches on leaves (page 258), aphids (page 260), and root rot (page 272).

Coontie

Coontie (*Zamia pumila*) is a small, tough, very slow growing woody cycad. Because these plants thrive in sun or shade, have high drought tolerance, moderate salt tolerance, and are cold hardy to zone 9, coonties are widely used in outdoor landscaping. All these virtues combine to make them excellent houseplants as well, less than 2 feet tall and wide indoors in containers. Coonties are frequent bonsai subjects because they can remain the same size for years.

Cycads are ancient gymnosperms—conifers, like ginkgos and pine trees. Like all cycads, coontie is dioecious, meaning there are male plants and there are female plants. In their cones, male plants produce only pollen, and female plants produce only seeds, which are bright orange. Coontie has thick, short, fleshy, tuberous stems that multiply underground to form large clumps. Leaves are dark green, stiff, glossy, fine-textured,

Coontie (aka Florida arrowroot, comfort root, Seminole bread).

evergreen, and fern-like. Each leaf is pinnately compound (feather-like) and up to 2 feet long. Individual plants are variable in leaflet shape; some plants have wide and flat leaflets and some have narrow ones. Several leaves are borne clustered at the tops of the short stems. New foliage is covered with short, rusty-brown hairs.

❶ Leaves, seeds and stems of coontie are poisonous, causing severe liver failure in people and pets. The seeds are the most toxic part of coontie, but all parts are poisonous, and the plant should be kept in an out-of-the-way place. If you suspect a person or pet has ingested parts of this plant, call your local emergency hotline, poison control center, or vet.

OPTIMUM HOUSEHOLD ENVIRONMENT

Read the Introduction for the specifics of each recommendation.

MEDIUM LIGHT. Coontie does best with full sun, filtered by sheer curtains, from a south, east, or west window. It tolerates low or high light, but it grows better with medium filtered light.

LOW TEMPERATURE. Daytime 65 to 75°F, nighttime 55 to 65°F.

LOW WATER. Water whenever the top of the potting medium becomes dry to a depth of 2 inches.

HUMIDITY. Coontie does not generally suffer from dry air and does not need to be misted.

POTTING MEDIUM. Use any good organic, cactus and succulent potting soil that incorporates organic fertilizer, mycorrhizal fungi, and other beneficial microbes.

FERTILIZER. Use any organic fertilizer, in either a powder or liquid formulation, where the first number (nitrogen) is higher than the other two. Apply dry fertilizer once in early spring and again in June. Apply liquid fertilizer at half-strength every two weeks in spring and summer. Stop feeding in fall and winter.

POTTING. When coontie needs up-potting, shift

it to a container with a diameter 2 inches larger than the current pot. Up-pot again every two to three years until it is as big as you want it to get. Plants grow very slowly and do not mind being somewhat rootbound.

PROPAGATION. Coontie is easy to propagate from seed and from pups.

COMMON PROBLEMS

Watch for scale insects (page 262) and root rot (page 272).

Croton

A well-grown croton (*Codiaeum variegatum*) is a brilliant focal point in any room. It's an ever-green, or rather ever-colorful, shrub, and many of the hundreds of croton cultivars are choice houseplants. They are well worth the effort to keep them bright and happy. As a houseplant croton can reach 5 to 6 feet tall under ideal conditions, but usually it is much smaller, to about 3 feet. Stems are slender, woody, and much branched, making a compact, rounded mound of

Croton (aka garden croton, variegated croton).

a shrub. The gorgeous foliage is the main reason for growing croton. The leaves are large, usually about 6 inches long and 3 to 4 inches wide, but really, all bets are off with croton leaves. It seems as though they can be any size, shape, or color. They can be 8 inches long and 1 inch wide, or twisted and curled, lobed like an oak leaf, or not lobed at all. As to color, they can be green, white, purple, orange, yellow, red, pink, or any imaginable blend of those colors. Colors occur in round spots, irregular blotches, or follow along the veins of the leaf. The colors change with the age of the leaf and with the amount of sunlight it gets. Bright filtered light gives you the most vibrant colors.

Croton, like some other houseplants, resents being moved. Sometimes, when you bring your gorgeous plant home from the garden center, it has a hissy fit and throws all its leaves on the ground. If that happens, once you get over your shock and disappointment, just give it TLC and it soon rewards you with a fresh batch of brilliant foliage. The new leaves are likely to be completely different from what you purchased, but as they age they color up properly, given enough light.

❶ This plant is toxic to people and pets and should be kept in an out-of-the-way place. The bark, roots, leaves, and sap contain 5-deoxyingenol, a chemical that causes burning of the mouth and eczema in sensitive individuals; however, croton is not listed by the ASPCA as toxic to cats or dogs. If you suspect a person or pet has ingested parts of this plant, call your local emergency hotline, poison control center, or vet.

OPTIMUM HOUSEHOLD ENVIRONMENT

Read the Introduction for the specifics of each recommendation.

MEDIUM LIGHT. Croton wants bright, filtered, dappled light, as from sheer curtains on a south, east, or west window. It does not like full sun, and the leaves burn and turn black, especially in yellow portions of the foliage, if it is in full direct sun for too long. The vibrant colors of the foliage fade if it isn't getting enough light so do not keep it in low light.

LOW TEMPERATURE. Daytime 65 to 75°F. Croton defoliates if the nighttime temperature drops below 55°F so try to keep the temperature above 60°F and avoid cold drafts.

MODERATE WATER. Water whenever the top of the potting medium becomes dry to a depth of 1 inch.

HUMIDITY. Mist your plant several times a week with a spray bottle of water on a mist setting, or use a handheld mister. You can also set the pot on top of a tray filled with gravel and water. Just be sure the pot is raised up above the surface level of the water.

POTTING MEDIUM. Use any good organic, well-drained potting soil that incorporates organic fertilizer, mycorrhizal fungi, and other beneficial microbes.

FERTILIZER. Use any organic fertilizer, in either a powder or liquid formulation, where the first number (nitrogen) is higher than the other two. Apply dry fertilizer once in early spring and again in June. Apply liquid fertilizer at half-strength every two weeks in spring and summer. Stop feeding in fall and winter.

POTTING. When croton needs up-potting, shift it to a container with a diameter 4 inches larger than the current pot. Up-pot again every two to three years until the plant is as big as you want it to get.

PROPAGATION. Croton is easy to propagate from stem tip cuttings.

COMMON PROBLEMS

Watch for leaves changing color (page 249), spider mites (page 263), and root rot (page 272).

False aralia

False aralia (*Schefflera elegantissima*) is tall, upright, and bushy, with very attractive seven- to 11-fingered evergreen palmately compound leaves. The beautiful leaflets are nearly black, knobby, and spidery thin—so thin that false aralia is considered a see-through plant, whose lacy foliage is never so dense as to block the light. Indoors in a pot, false aralia is a tree or large shrub with woody stems to 5 feet tall, rarely 7 to 10 feet tall. It grows slowly and eventually drops the oldest leaves near its base, revealing the trunk. The coppery-red new foliage matures to a dark black-green. False aralia produces two kinds of leaves, juvenile and adult. Juvenile leaves have small, narrow leaflets to 3 inches long and 0.5 inch wide and are found on young plants or on branches near the base of mature plants. Adult leaves are large, with leaflets 9 to 12 inches long and 3 inches wide. Leaflets are coarsely toothed and knobby, spreading out from the petiole like the fingers of your widespread hand. If your mature false aralia suddenly starts producing small juvenile leaves at the top of the plant, then it is under stress and needs more nutrients and water.

This is another species that pitches a fit and drops its leaves to the floor when you bring it home from the store. It wants a permanent home and soon grows new leaves in its new location. Giving it a summer vacation outdoors is probably not a good idea; it loses too many leaves.

OPTIMUM HOUSEHOLD ENVIRONMENT

Read the Introduction for the specifics of each recommendation.

MEDIUM LIGHT. Filtered light from an east or west window with sheer curtains works best for false aralia. Avoid full, direct, hot sun because the

False aralia (aka spider aralia, threadleaf aralia, finger aralia).

plant's root system is restricted by the pot and cannot deliver water to the foliage fast enough to keep the leaf tips and edges from dying and turning brown.

MODERATE TEMPERATURE. Daytime 70 to 80°F, nighttime 60 to 70°F. False aralia may shed its leaves if the temperature drops below 60°F.

MODERATE WATER. Water whenever the top of the potting medium becomes dry to a depth of 1 inch. Never allow false aralia to go completely dry.

HUMIDITY. High humidity is important to false aralia. Mist daily with a spray bottle of water. Put the pot in a saucer or tray of water, making sure the bottom of the pot never sits directly in the water by raising the pot up on pot feet or pebbles. Consider putting a humidifier in the room.

POTTING MEDIUM. Use any good organic, general-purpose potting soil that incorporates organic fertilizer, mycorrhizal fungi, and other beneficial microbes.

FERTILIZER. Use any organic fertilizer, in either a powder or liquid formulation, where the first number (nitrogen) is higher than the other two. Apply dry fertilizer once in early spring and again in June. Apply liquid fertilizer at half-strength every two weeks in spring and summer. Stop feeding in fall and winter.

POTTING. When false aralia needs up-potting, shift it to a container with a diameter 4 inches larger than the current pot. Keep it in a heavy clay or ceramic pot to prevent it from toppling over as it gets taller.

PROPAGATION. False aralia is easy to propagate from stem tip cuttings.

COMMON PROBLEMS
Watch for leaf drop (page 249) and spider mites (page 263).

Fiddle-leaf fig

A big, bold, dramatic houseplant that makes a beautiful addition to any room, fiddle-leaf fig (*Ficus lyrata*) is easy to grow and low maintenance. You frequently see it as a large specimen plant or focal point in offices, malls, or other large public buildings that can provide sufficient indirect light. Full sun is far too intense for fiddle-leaf fig. When grown as a houseplant, this broadleaf evergreen tree does not produce fruit and rarely exceeds 8 to 10 feet. You can trim it to encourage side branches and develop a bushy, full, rounded look. Or you can trim off side branches and lower leaves to expose the trunk and encourage a tall, erect, tree-like shape. The big, handsome leaves are 15 inches long and 10 inches wide. Dark, glossy green and shaped like a lyre or violin ("fiddle"), the leaves have a leathery texture, prominent veins, and a wavy margin. The dwarf 'Little Fiddle' gets only 6 feet tall with leaves half the size of standard varieties. The variegated 'Ivonne', with leaves splashed in white and pale green, is spectacular.

Fiddle-leaf fig (aka banjo fig).

OPTIMUM HOUSEHOLD ENVIRONMENT

Read the Introduction for the specifics of each recommendation.

MEDIUM LIGHT. Give fiddle-leaf fig bright, filtered light and it grows fairly rapidly. It tolerates a couple hours of direct sun from an east window but direct sun all day long from a south window is too much for it. Filter the light (and heat) from a south or west window with sheer curtains or Venetian blinds. In too much shade it grows very slowly.

MODERATE TEMPERATURE. Daytime 70 to 80°F, nighttime 60 to 70°F.

MODERATE WATER. Water whenever the top of the potting medium becomes dry to a depth of 1 inch.

HUMIDITY. Mist your fiddle-leaf fig twice a week with a spray bottle of water on a mist setting, or use a handheld mister. Put the pot in a saucer or tray of water, making sure the bottom of the pot never sits directly in the water by raising the pot up on pot feet or pebbles. Consider putting a humidifier in the room.

POTTING MEDIUM. Use any good organic, well-drained potting soil that incorporates organic fertilizer, mycorrhizal fungi, and other beneficial microbes.

FERTILIZER. Use any organic fertilizer, in either a powder or liquid formulation, where the first number (nitrogen) is higher than the other two. Apply dry fertilizer once in early spring and again in June. Apply liquid fertilizer at half-strength every two weeks in spring and summer. Stop feeding in fall and winter.

POTTING. When fiddle-leaf fig needs up-potting, shift it to a container with a diameter 4 inches larger than the current pot. Up-pot again every year until it is as big as you want it to get. Keep it in a heavy ceramic pot to prevent it from toppling over.

PROPAGATION. Fiddle-leaf fig is difficult to propagate but it can be accomplished by air layering.

COMMON PROBLEMS

Watch for leaf drop (page 249), spider mites (page 263), and leaf spot fungus (page 269).

Flowering maple

Flowering maple (*Abutilon ×hybridum*) is a fast-growing, broadleaf evergreen shrub with long twiggy stems that bend and arch under the weight of the flowers. It acquired its common name because the leaves have the same shape as maple leaves and because it has pretty flowers. The plants typically grown as houseplants are a popular group of hybrids of garden origin, possibly between *A. darwinii* and *A. pictum*. They grow 2 to 4 feet tall and wide and develop a sprawling habit if you let them. Cut back in the spring, shortening the branches by a third, to keep plants compact. You can also pinch the growing tips off the stems during the growing season to force them to grow side branches. The thin, light green leaves clothe the bush closely, making it fairly dense. Leaves of some cultivars are flecked with gold and yellow patches, as shown in the photo. The gold flecking is caused by a virus and is considered a desirable feature. The viral infection seems not to harm the plant significantly. Variegated cultivars with patches of white and green are not virus-infected. The bell- or trumpet-shaped flowers dangle on thin stalks and come in red, orange, yellow, white, pink, and multicolor blends. They are as much as 3 inches across and have five overlapping petals. In many cultivars the flowers open wide, becoming almost flat as they mature. Flowers are produced continuously all year long but are more abundant in spring and summer. They are edible and sweet, sometimes used in salads.

Flowering maple (aka parlor maple, Chinese bell flower, Chinese lantern, Indian mallow, velvetleaf).

Read the Introduction for the specifics of
each recommendation.

MEDIUM LIGHT. Flowering maple can tolerate a
few hours of direct sun but is at its best in cool
morning sun from an east window. In order to
flower this plant needs intense bright light. It
does not do well in the heat, however, and the
hot afternoon sun of a west window may cause
it to wilt. Bright light filtered through sheer
curtains of a south or west window also allows
flowering maple to flower well but be sure it is
well hydrated.

LOW TEMPERATURE. 65 to 75°F day and night.

MODERATE WATER. Water whenever the top of the
potting medium becomes dry to a depth of 1 inch.

HUMIDITY. Mist flowering maple several times a
week with a spray bottle of water on a mist setting, or use a handheld mister. Put the pot in a
saucer or tray of water, making sure the bottom
of the pot never sits directly in the water by raising the pot up on pot feet or pebbles. Consider
putting a humidifier in the room.

POTTING MEDIUM. Use any good organic,
well-drained potting soil that incorporates
organic fertilizer, mycorrhizal fungi, and other
beneficial microbes. Don't add lime because
flowering maple prefers acidic soils.

FERTILIZER. Use any organic fertilizer, in either a
powder or liquid formulation, where the second
number (phosphorus) is higher than the other
two to promote flowering. Apply once a month.
Stop feeding your plant in winter.

POTTING. When flowering maple needs up-
potting, shift it to a container with a diameter
4 inches larger than the current pot.

PROPAGATION. Flowering maple is easy to propagate from stem tip cuttings.

COMMON PROBLEMS

Watch for leaf drop (page 249), whiteflies (page
265), and rust fungus (page 273).

Gardenia

The touchy gardenia (*Gardenia jasminoides*)
is almost worth growing for the pretty leaves
alone. But it's the intensely fragrant pure white
flowers that lure you to it. Their heady, tropical,
unforgettable scent fills a room, making gardenia absolutely irresistible despite its demanding
nature. Indoors, in a pot, this woody, broadleaf
evergreen shrub grows 2 to 4 feet high and wide.
If your gardenia grows too tall, prune it back
to a more manageable size. Pruning stimulates
the growth of new side branches and promotes
flowering. The very attractive leaves are dark
green, glossy, and prominently veined, which

Gardenia (aka Cape jasmine, Cape jessamine).

gives them an undulating rippled effect. Flowers are 2 to 3 inches wide and may be single (five petals) or double (many petals). Plants bloom most profusely in spring, and often again in fall. The color contrast between the lovely green of the foliage and the pure white of the flowers is quite beautiful.

Gardenia has a reputation as a finicky houseplant. If your plant's flower buds slowly turn yellow and fall off and then the leaves turn yellow and drop, your plant is telling you that it's either too cold, or the soil isn't acid enough, or the air is too dry, or it's not getting enough light. And then it's up to you to figure out exactly what the problem is and to fix it.

OPTIMUM HOUSEHOLD ENVIRONMENT

Read the Introduction for the specifics of each recommendation.

MEDIUM LIGHT. Bright indirect light filtered by sheer curtains on a south, east, or west window. Avoid direct sun because it can cause the plant to wilt or burn the leaves.

MODERATE TEMPERATURE. Daytime 70 to 80°F, nighttime 60 to 70°F. Gardenia appreciates a nighttime temperature drop of about ten degrees, but temperatures lower than 60°F may cause it to drop its leaves and flower buds. Avoid cold drafts and blasts of hot air from a furnace.

MODERATE WATER. Water whenever the top of the potting medium becomes dry to a depth of 1 inch.

HUMIDITY. Gardenia likes constantly high humidity. Mist it daily with a spray bottle of water on a mist setting, or use a handheld mister. Put the pot in a saucer or tray of water, making sure the bottom of the pot never sits directly in the water by raising the pot up on pot feet or pebbles. Consider putting a humidifier in the room.

POTTING MEDIUM. Use any good organic, well-drained potting soil that incorporates organic fertilizer, mycorrhizal fungi, and other beneficial microbes. Do not add lime to the potting mix; gardenia wants acid soil.

FERTILIZER. Feed gardenia with an acidic organic fertilizer designed for acid-loving plants. A teaspoon of horticultural sulfur scratched into the surface of the potting soil makes the soil acidic enough for good growth. Gardenias also respond well to frequent applications of coffee grounds, though exactly why they respond so dramatically is a bit of a mystery, as research has shown that coffee grounds do not acidify the soil. Other than pH, gardenia is not fussy. Any balanced organic fertilizer, in either a powder or liquid formulation, should work well. Apply dry fertilizer once in early spring and again in June. Apply liquid fertilizer at half-strength every two weeks in spring and summer. Stop feeding in fall and winter.

POTTING. When your gardenia needs up-potting, shift it to a container with a diameter 4 inches larger than the current pot.

PROPAGATION. Gardenia is easy to propagate from stem tip cuttings taken in early spring.

COMMON PROBLEMS

Watch for flower bud drop (page 248), aphids (page 260), and root rot (page 272).

Hibiscus

Hibiscus (*Hibiscus rosa-sinensis*) is the state flower of Hawaii, and almost every advertisement for a vacation in that paradise features a beautiful Hawaiian woman with a brilliant Technicolor hibiscus flower tucked behind her ear. Those gorgeous, evocatively tropical flowers, the biggest of any plant grown as a houseplant, are the best reason for bringing this plant into your home. As a houseplant, this woody, evergreen, multi-trunked shrub gets 5 to 6 feet

(top) Hibiscus (aka Hawaiian rose, rose mallow, Chinese hibiscus, China rose, shoe flower).

(left) Hibiscus, blended form.

tall and wide. Glossy, dark green leaves, 6 inches long and 4 inches wide, contrast beautifully with the vibrant flowers. In many cultivars the leaves are toothed along the edges. Flowers are huge, 4 to 8 inches in diameter with overlapping petals that unfurl as the buds open to become wide and flat. They come in screaming scarlet, fluorescent orange, hot pink, intense yellow, pure white, and multicolor blends. Each flower lasts only a day, or two at most, but they are produced continuously year-round. Hibiscus flowers are edible and widely used, dried, as a tea, for their delightfully acidic flavor.

OPTIMUM HOUSEHOLD ENVIRONMENT

Read the Introduction for the specifics of each recommendation.

HIGH LIGHT. Hibiscus needs abundant bright light in order to flower. It does well with a full day of bright indirect light filtered through sheer curtains. In too little light hibiscus grows lots of leaves, but no flowers.

HIGH TEMPERATURE. Daytime 75 to 85°F, nighttime 65 to 75°F. Temperatures below 50°F can kill hibiscus.

MODERATE WATER. Water whenever the top of the potting medium becomes dry to a depth of 1 inch.

HUMIDITY. Mist hibiscus twice a week with a spray bottle of water on a mist setting, or use a handheld mister. Put the pot in a saucer or tray of water, making sure the bottom of the pot never sits directly in the water by raising the pot up on pot feet or pebbles.

POTTING MEDIUM. Use any good organic, well-drained, general-purpose potting soil that incorporates organic fertilizer, mycorrhizal fungi, and other beneficial microbes.

FERTILIZER. Hibiscus is a little fussy about nutrients. Many cultivars suffer if they get too much phosphorus. Choose an organic fertilizer specially formulated for hibiscus with the ratio of N-P-K any multiple of 2-1-3. Use either a powder or a liquid formulation and apply once in early spring and again in June.

POTTING. When hibiscus needs up-potting, shift it to a container with a diameter 4 inches larger than the current pot.

PROPAGATION. Hibiscus is easy to propagate from stem tip cuttings.

COMMON PROBLEMS

Watch for flower bud drop (page 248), whiteflies (page 265), and gray mold (page 268).

Japanese aralia

Japanese aralia (*Fatsia japonica*) was introduced into cultivation in the western world in the early 1800s and has been a popular houseplant ever since. It adds tropical flair to any room. This big, bold, burly foliage plant is especially

Japanese aralia (aka fatsia, glossy leaved paper plant, false castor oil plant, fig leaf palm).

desirable because it does well in those difficult shady corners that are anathema to so many other houseplants. Japanese aralia has thick stems and grows pretty fast to 6 feet tall and 3 to 4 feet wide, so give it plenty of space and it rewards you quickly and handsomely with its superb architectural presence. The huge, exotic, tropical-looking leaves are 12 inches across, deep green, and glossy. Each leathery, fan-shaped (palmate) leaf is deeply divided into seven to nine lobes, like a giant maple leaf. The leaf stalks (petioles) are also 12 inches long and carry the leaves well. 'Variegata', a very handsome form of the species, has creamy white patches on the leaves.

OPTIMUM HOUSEHOLD ENVIRONMENT

Read the Introduction for the specifics of each recommendation.

MEDIUM LIGHT. Give Japanese aralia bright indirect light to partial shade, and limited direct sun. It succeeds well in the bright indirect light of a north window. It tolerates a few hours of sun from an east window in the cool of the morning. But the intense light and heat of a south or west window is not for this plant. Too much light burns the leaves.

LOW TEMPERATURE. Daytime 65 to 75°F, nighttime 55 to 65°F. Japanese aralia appreciates a rest with a cold period, a daytime temperature drop to about 50°F, in the winter time.

MODERATE WATER. Water whenever the top of the potting medium becomes dry to a depth of 1 inch.

HUMIDITY. Mist your Japanese aralia twice a week with a spray bottle of water on a mist setting, or use a handheld mister. Put the pot in a saucer or tray of water, making sure the bottom of the pot never sits directly in the water by raising the pot up on pot feet or pebbles. Consider putting a humidifier in the room.

POTTING MEDIUM. Use any good organic, well-drained potting soil that incorporates organic fertilizer, mycorrhizal fungi, and other beneficial microbes.

FERTILIZER. Use any organic fertilizer, in either a powder or liquid formulation, where the first number (nitrogen) is higher than the other two. Apply dry fertilizer once in early spring and again in June. Apply liquid fertilizer at half-strength every two weeks in spring and summer. Stop feeding in fall and winter.

POTTING. When Japanese aralia needs up-potting, shift it to a container with a diameter 4 inches larger than the current pot. Up-pot again every year until it is as big as you want it to get. After it has reached the size you want, prune it back by a third every year in the spring and use the trimmings to make cuttings. Pruning it causes it to grow side branches and become bushy.

PROPAGATION. Japanese aralia is easy to propagate from stem tip cuttings.

COMMON PROBLEMS

Watch for brown leaf tips (page 246), mealybugs (page 262), and root rot (page 272).

Norfolk Island pine

Every November markets are flooded with millions of tiny living Christmas trees in 4-inch pots. The trees are sprinkled with glitter, sometimes sprayed with green paint, and decorated with ribbons and little glass bulbs. These little seedlings of Norfolk Island pine (*Araucaria heterophylla*) may or may not survive the mass merchandising process. A better, and longer-lived, option is to buy a larger specimen from your local independent garden center. They're often available in various sizes, from compact tabletop forms to tall, tree-sized floor plants. In Hawaii,

Norfolk Island pine (aka suicide tree, star pine, triangle tree, living Christmas tree).

Norfolk Island pine, adult leaves.

Norfolk Island pines are grown outdoors and used as cut Christmas trees for the holidays. They're big enough to reach the ceiling, easy to decorate the wide spaces between the branches, and they last a long time. If you're lucky enough to share your home with one of these large companion trees year-round, it's a simple matter to temporarily glitz it up for the holidays and use it as your permanent living Christmas tree year after year.

As a houseplant, this single-trunked conifer slowly forms a beautifully symmetrical pyramid 6 to 7 feet tall. The branches are whorled (formed in a ring around the trunk), with wide spaces on the trunk between each ring. Leaves change shape as they mature, thus the epithet *heterophylla* ("different leaves"). Juvenile leaves on young branches are 0.5-inch-long, soft, bright green needles. Adult leaves are spine-tipped, stiff, flat scales, 0.25 inch long and wide, that overlap and give the branches a braided, rope-like appearance. Norfolk Island pine has a weak root system and topples over in hurricanes. Obviously, you won't have to worry about that in your living room, but be aware when re-potting that its root system is delicate.

OPTIMUM HOUSEHOLD ENVIRONMENT

Read the Introduction for the specifics of each recommendation.

HIGH LIGHT. Abundant light from a large south window is ideal. Medium light from an east or west window that provides at least two, preferably more, hours of direct sun is acceptable. A cool sunroom is perfect. Give the tree a quarter turn every week to preserve its conical shape and pagoda-like branching pattern and prevent it from leaning into the light.

LOW TEMPERATURE. Daytime 65 to 75°F, nighttime 55 to 65°F.

MODERATE WATER. Water whenever the top of the potting medium becomes dry to a depth of 1 inch.

HUMIDITY. Mist Norfolk Island pine two or three times a week with a spray bottle of water on a mist setting, or use a handheld mister. Put the pot in a saucer or tray of water, making sure the bottom of the pot never sits directly in the water by raising the pot up on pot feet or pebbles. Consider putting a humidifier in the room.

POTTING MEDIUM. Use any good organic, general-purpose potting soil that incorporates organic fertilizer, mycorrhizal fungi, and other beneficial microbes.

FERTILIZER. Norfolk Island pine is a little fussy about nutrients. Use any organic fertilizer, in either a powder or liquid formulation, where the first number (nitrogen) is higher than the other two and that also supplies nutrients such as iron, manganese, and magnesium. Apply dry fertilizer once in early spring and again in June. Apply liquid fertilizer at half-strength every two weeks in spring and summer. Stop feeding in fall and winter.

POTTING. When Norfolk Island pine needs up-potting, shift it to a container with a diameter 2 inches larger than the current pot. Handle it gently because the roots are fragile. Up-pot again every two years until it is as big as you want it to get. Keep this tree in a heavy ceramic pot to prevent it from toppling over.

PROPAGATION. Norfolk Island pine is easy to propagate from seed.

COMMON PROBLEMS

Watch for needle drop (page 252), scale insects (page 262), and root rot (page 272).

Rubber tree

Rubber tree is indeed a tree, and it does in fact produce rubber; however, it is actually a fig, *Ficus elastica*, and in common with the rest of the species in the banyan group of figs, it readily grows aerial roots from its branches. As a houseplant, rubber tree is grown for its beautiful, smooth, glossy, oval leaves 4 to 14 inches long and 2 to 6 inches wide. The evergreen leaves are thick and leathery, and several cultivars have reddish, variegated, or tricolor foliage. Rubber tree grows slowly if it isn't getting the right combination of light, warmth, and water, faster with more favorable conditions. Very old plants growing in pots may get as tall as 12 feet but take years to do so. The fruit is a small fig, about 0.3 inch, but this tree is extremely unlikely to ever flower indoors.

OPTIMUM HOUSEHOLD ENVIRONMENT

Read the Introduction for the specifics of each recommendation.

MEDIUM LIGHT. Bright or moderate, indirect light but no direct sun serves rubber tree well.

East or west windows filtered by sheer curtains are perfect.

MODERATE TEMPERATURE. Daytime 70 to 80°F, nighttime 60 to 70°F.

MODERATE WATER. Water whenever the top of the potting medium becomes dry to a depth of 1 inch.

HUMIDITY. Mist your rubber tree twice a week with a spray bottle of water on a mist setting, or use a handheld mister. Put the pot in a saucer or tray of water, making sure the bottom of the pot never sits directly in the water by raising the pot up on pot feet or pebbles.

POTTING MEDIUM. Use any good organic, general-purpose potting soil that incorporates organic fertilizer, mycorrhizal fungi, and other beneficial microbes.

FERTILIZER. Use any organic fertilizer, in either a powder or liquid formulation, where the first number (nitrogen) is higher than the other two. Apply once a month. Stop feeding in winter.

POTTING. When rubber tree needs up-potting,

(left) Rubber tree, variegated form.

(above) Rubber tree (aka rubber fig, rubber bush, rubber plant, Indian rubber bush).

shift it to a container with a diameter 4 inches larger than the current pot.

PROPAGATION. Rubber tree is difficult to propagate but it can be done by air layering.

COMMON PROBLEMS

Watch for leaf drop (page 249), scale insects (page 262), and root rot (page 272).

Sago palm

This extremely slow growing, very tough plant will live in your home for many years, providing a distinctly Asian accent. Sago palm (*Cycas revoluta*) looks like a palm, but isn't, and looks like a fern, but isn't. It's a cycad, an ancient family of plants that reached their heyday during the age of dinosaurs. Their seeds are borne in cones, marking them as gymnosperms, like ginkgos and pine trees. Young plants are fern-like, 2 to 3 feet tall. The short trunk is 1 inch thick in young plants and as much as 8 inches thick in older ones, at which point it looks a little bit like a shaggy brown pineapple, clothed in fibrous brown leaf bases in an attractive basketweave pattern. Leaves are pinnately compound (feather-like), 2 to 3 feet long, and are borne in a rosette at the top of the trunk. They look soft, but they're surprisingly stiff to the touch. Glossy and dark green, the hard foliage almost feels plastic. The individual leaflets are very narrow

Sago palm (aka king sago, sago cycad, Japanese sago palm).

and have strongly recurved edges. Young plants make only one or two new fronds each spring. It can take five or six years to grow a full crown of foliage. Older specimens add a whole rosette of new leaves to the crown each spring. Like all cycads, sago palm is dioecious, meaning plants are either male or female. Female plants produce seeds in structures called megasporophylls, and male plants produce pollen-bearing cones (strobili).

❶ This plant (especially its seeds) is poisonous to people and pets, with a fatality rate of 50 to 75%. Fortunately, it is extremely unlikely that your sago palm could ever make seeds, and the stiff leaves are very difficult to chew. Nevertheless, if you suspect a victim has been poisoned, call your local emergency hotline, poison control center, or vet.

OPTIMUM HOUSEHOLD ENVIRONMENT

Read the Introduction for the specifics of each recommendation.

MEDIUM LIGHT. Sheer curtains filtering the light from a south, east, or west window provide just the right environment.

LOW TEMPERATURE. Daytime 65 to 75°F, nighttime 55 to 65°F.

LOW WATER. Water whenever the top of the potting medium becomes dry to a depth of 2 inches.

HUMIDITY. Mist twice a week with a spray bottle of water on a mist setting, or use a handheld mister. Put the pot in a saucer or tray of water, making sure the bottom of the pot never sits directly in the water by raising the pot up on pot feet or pebbles.

POTTING MEDIUM. Use any good organic, general-purpose potting soil that incorporates organic fertilizer, mycorrhizal fungi, and other beneficial microbes.

FERTILIZER. Use any organic fertilizer, in either a powder or liquid formulation, where the first number (nitrogen) is higher than the other two. Apply once a month. Stop feeding in winter.

POTTING. When sago palm needs up-potting, shift it to a container with a diameter 2 inches larger than the current pot. Up-pot again every three years or so until it is as big as you want it to get.

PROPAGATION. Sago palm is easy to propagate from seed. Seeds are vermilion but are rarely produced indoors.

COMMON PROBLEMS

Watch for scale insects (page 262) and root rot (page 272).

Tree ivy

It's pretty rare for plants from different genera to cross successfully, but tree ivy is just such an intergeneric hybrid, first created in 1912, at the Lizé Frères tree nursery in Nantes, France. One parent is Japanese aralia and the other is ivy. A shrub (*Fatsia*) crossed to a vine (*Hedera*) equals

Tree ivy (aka aralia ivy, fatshedera, fat-headed Lizzy, botanical wonder).

×*Fatshedera lizei*, a hybrid that can't quite make up its mind whether it's a shrub or a vine. Tree ivy's stems tend to grow in a straight line, easily 8 feet long, and flop about unless tied to a support of some kind. The stems are somewhat flexible when young but get brittle and break easily when mature. If you intend to train it to a support, do it while the stems are young and pliable. You can also prune away the tips of the stems to make them grow side branches, which gives you a shorter, bushier houseplant. The leaves of tree ivy are evergreen, like both its parents, and intermediate in size between them. They are palmate (fan-shaped) and look like maple leaves or giant ivy leaves, to 10 inches across, with three to five lobes. The foliage is glossy, leathery, and bright green. The leaves of variegated cultivars have a central yellow-green blotch ('Annemieke') or pure white borders ('Variegata').

OPTIMUM HOUSEHOLD ENVIRONMENT

Read the Introduction for the specifics of each recommendation.

MEDIUM LIGHT. Sheer curtains filtering the sunlight from south, east, or west windows provide the right quality of light during the growing season.

LOW TEMPERATURE. Daytime 65 to 75°F, nighttime 55 to 65°F.

AMPLE WATER. Water whenever the top of the potting medium becomes dry to a depth of 0.5 inch.

HUMIDITY. Mist tree ivy two or three times a week with a spray bottle of water on a mist setting, or use a handheld mister. Put the pot in a saucer or tray of water, making sure the bottom of the pot never sits directly in the water by raising the pot up on pot feet or pebbles.

POTTING MEDIUM. Use any good organic, well-drained potting soil that incorporates organic fertilizer, mycorrhizal fungi, and other beneficial microbes.

FERTILIZER. Use any organic fertilizer, in either a powder or liquid formulation, where the first number (nitrogen) is higher than the other two. Apply once a month. Stop feeding in winter.

POTTING. When tree ivy needs up-potting, shift it to a container with a diameter 4 inches larger than the current pot. Up-pot again every year in the spring until it is as big as you want it to get. Provide newly up-potted plants with cool shade for a week in order to avoid post-repotting collapse.

PROPAGATION. Tree ivy is easy to propagate from stem tip cuttings.

COMMON PROBLEMS

Watch for post-repotting collapse (page 253), spider mites (page 263), and root rot (page 272).

Umbrella tree

Each large, attractive leaf of umbrella tree (*Schefflera actinophylla*) and dwarf umbrella tree (*S. arboricola*) has seven to 11 or more leaflets all attached to the same point at the tip of the petiole (leaf stalk). The leaflets radiate from the center and droop like the ribs of a shiny green umbrella. The resemblance to umbrellas ends there, however, because the leaflets are not joined side to side. Umbrella tree is a "houseplant gone wild"—an invasive weed in both Hawaii and Florida. Dwarf umbrella tree seems not to be nearly as invasive. Both species are excellent houseplants, however, and indoors, in a container, they rarely get more than 6 to 8 feet tall. Both plants have sturdy, woody trunks and branches, palmately compound (fan-shaped) leaves, and smooth, broadly oval leaflets. Umbrella tree leaflets get 10 inches long; the leaflets of dwarf umbrella tree are much

Umbrella tree (aka Queensland umbrella tree, umbrella plant, octopus tree, schefflera).

smaller, only 3 inches long. Individual flowers are tiny, bright red in umbrella tree, yellow in dwarf umbrella tree, but it's unlikely that either species would bloom inside the house.

OPTIMUM HOUSEHOLD ENVIRONMENT

Read the Introduction for the specifics of each recommendation.

MEDIUM LIGHT. Both species want dappled or filtered light but no direct sun.

MODERATE TEMPERATURE. Daytime 70 to 80°F, nighttime 60 to 70°F.

MODERATE WATER. Water whenever the top of the potting medium becomes dry to a depth of 1 inch.

HUMIDITY. Mist twice a week with a spray bottle of water on a mist setting, or use a handheld mister. Put the pot in a saucer or tray of water, making sure the bottom of the pot never sits directly in the water by raising the pot up on pot feet or pebbles. Consider putting a humidifier in the room.

POTTING MEDIUM. Use any good organic, well-drained potting soil that incorporates organic fertilizer, mycorrhizal fungi, and other beneficial microbes.

FERTILIZER. Use any organic fertilizer, in either a powder or liquid formulation, where the first number (nitrogen) is higher than the other two. Apply once a month. Stop feeding in winter.

POTTING. When your tree needs up-potting, shift

(top) Weeping fig (aka Benjamin fig, Benjamin tree, ficus tree, ficus).

(above) Weeping fig, variegated form.

it to a container with a diameter 4 inches larger than the current pot.

PROPAGATION. Umbrella trees are easy to propagate from stem tip cuttings.

COMMON PROBLEMS

Watch for plant sprawl (page 253), mealybugs (page 262), and root rot (page 272).

Weeping fig

Weeping fig (*Ficus benjamina*), a fast-growing, broadleaf evergreen with gracefully drooping branchlets, well deserves a place of honor in any home. It's one of the most popular houseplants in the world—relatively low-maintenance, readily available, and very beautiful—but it is unlikely to produce its edible, tiny, true figs indoors. As a houseplant this tree, either single- or multi-trunked, grows to 8 feet tall. The trunk is pale brown and eventually sturdy, but very flexible when young. Growers sometimes braid the trunks of young specimens together and put all three trees in the same pot. The branches are thin and delicate, arching out and drooping down to give a weeping effect. Like all figs, weeping fig has milky white sap that dries to rubber. The lovely leaves of this tree are dark green, 4-inch-long, glossy ovals with long, pointed drip tips. Many plants from humid tropical rainforests have leaves with long drip tips that help the leaf shed the abundant rainfall. The edges of the leaves undulate, giving each leaf a slight rippled effect. The leaves dangle from the pendulous branchlets, pointing down toward the ground. Several cultivars have foliage with white or yellow markings.

Weeping fig does not like to be moved about and protests by throwing its leaves on the ground. Find the perfect spot for it and leave it there. If you've just purchased your fig and brought it home from the garden center don't be surprised if it drops its leaves. If you're up-potting an older specimen expect it to lose quite a few leaves. Be patient with it because it will grow new leaves fairly quickly.

OPTIMUM HOUSEHOLD ENVIRONMENT

Read the Introduction for the specifics of each recommendation.

MEDIUM LIGHT. The light from a south, east, or west window, filtered by sheer curtains, is just right for weeping fig.

LOW TEMPERATURE. 65 to 75°F day and night.

LOW WATER. Water whenever the top of the potting medium becomes dry to a depth of 2 inches.

HUMIDITY. Mist weeping fig occasionally with a spray bottle of water on a mist setting, or use a handheld mister. Put the pot in a saucer or tray of water, making sure the bottom of the pot never sits directly in the water by raising the pot up on pot feet or pebbles.

POTTING MEDIUM. Use any good organic, well-drained potting soil that incorporates organic fertilizer, mycorrhizal fungi, and other beneficial microbes.

FERTILIZER. Use any organic fertilizer, in either a powder or liquid formulation, where the first number (nitrogen) is higher than the other two. Apply once a month. Stop feeding in winter.

POTTING. When weeping fig needs up-potting, shift it to a container with a diameter 4 inches larger than the current pot. Up-pot again every two to three years until it is as big as you want it to get.

PROPAGATION. Weeping fig is easy to propagate from stem tip cuttings taken in the spring.

COMMON PROBLEMS

Watch for leaf drop (page 249), scale insects (page 262), and leaf spot fungus (page 269).

Zebra plant

Zebra plant (*Aphelandra squarrosa*) is an almost irresistibly gorgeous woody, broadleaf evergreen shrub. The striped foliage alone is a traffic-stopper, and when it's in bloom it knocks your socks off. But it's a cranky little devil—a real challenge to keep it alive in your home for more than a couple of years, much less coax it into bloom. Still, lots of people just have to have it and, if you give it exactly what it needs, it rewards you handsomely. As a houseplant, it rarely exceeds 2 feet tall and wide, and many people prune it to 12 to 18 inches. The amazing leaves are big, showy, and oval, 6 to 9 inches long by 3 to 4 inches wide, with pointed tips. Their rich, glossy, deep enamel green contrasts beautifully with the broad strokes of glistening pure white that cover their veins like stripes on a zebra. The waxy inflorescence bears bright yellow bracts all along its length, with one tubular yellow flower peeking out from each. Flower spikes reach 8 inches in length at the tips of the stems and last as long as six weeks, from late summer into fall.

OPTIMUM HOUSEHOLD ENVIRONMENT

Read the Introduction for the specifics of each recommendation.

MEDIUM LIGHT. Sheer curtains over south, east, or west windows provide bright light that won't burn the leaves. So, no direct sun.

HIGH TEMPERATURE. Daytime 75 to 85°F, nighttime 65 to 75°F.

MODERATE WATER. Water whenever the top of the potting medium becomes dry to a depth of 1 inch.

HUMIDITY. Zebra plant requires high humidity to grow well. Mist daily with a spray bottle of water on a mist setting, or use a handheld mister. Put the pot in a saucer or tray of water, making sure the bottom of the pot never sits directly in the water

Zebra plant (aka saffron spike).

by raising the pot up on pot feet or pebbles. Consider putting a humidifier in the room.

POTTING MEDIUM. Use any good organic, well-drained potting soil that incorporates organic fertilizer, mycorrhizal fungi, and other beneficial microbes.

FERTILIZER. Use any organic fertilizer, in either a powder or liquid formulation, where the first number (nitrogen) is higher than the other two. Apply dry fertilizer once in early spring and again in June. Apply liquid fertilizer at half-strength every two weeks in spring and summer. Stop feeding in fall and winter.

POTTING. When your plant needs up-potting, shift it to a container with a diameter 2 inches larger than the current pot. Up-pot again every year until the plant is as big as you want it to get.

PROPAGATION. Zebra plant is easy to propagate from stem tip cuttings.

COMMON PROBLEMS
Watch for brown leaf tips (page 246), aphids (page 260), and root rot (page 272).

Herbaceous Perennials

African violet

African violets (*Saintpaulia* spp.) are easily, and deservedly, the most popular houseplant in the world. People love them because they flower all year long, the jewel-like blossoms come in a rainbow of luscious colors, and the plants are small, compact, and easy to grow. They are charming even when not in bloom. The hundreds of available cultivars differ in plant size, flower color and type, and leaf size, color, and type. All stand ready to add their boisterous attributes to any windowsill. African violets bear a superficial resemblance to true violets, but they are not violets. They are gesneriads, first collected by Baron Walter von Saint Paul-Illaire in Tanzania in 1892. The generic name honors him.

African violet stems are very short, only 3 to 4 inches in the standard varieties, with a saucer-like cluster of leaves arranged in a rosette at the tips of the stems. Plant size is determined by the diameter of this rosette: micro-miniature (less than 3 inches across), miniature (3 to 6 inches across), standard (8 to 16 inches across), and large (more than 16 inches across). Leaves have long, rather succulent petioles (leaf stalks) with a heart-shaped blade at the tip. The blade is thick and softly furry, like little kitten paws. The leaves near the bottom of the rosette have the longest petioles and the leaves near the top of the rosette have the shortest petioles. In this way no leaf is shaded by the leaf above it, an arrangement known as imbricated.

There are many different foliage types in African violets. The standard plain green leaf is called a "boy" leaf, named for 'Blue Boy', the most famous of the early varieties. A "girl" leaf, named for 'Blue Girl', is green with wavy edges and a white spot at the base of the leaf blade. Variegated leaves are blotched or spotted with yellow, cream, or white. And then there are oak

African violet.

leaf types, fringed leaf types, and quilted leaf types, among others. Many cultivars are grown as much for the size, color, and shape of the leaves as they are for the lovely little flowers.

The flowers, borne in clusters on stalks that arise from the middle of the rosette, stand above the leaves. A well-grown plant in full flower is a perfect little nosegay. Flowers come in a huge array of colors including blue, pink, white, purple, magenta, red, and two-tone blends. As with leaf types, flower types abound. Single flowers have five petals with the top two smaller than the bottom three, and look most like true violets. Semi-double flowers have more than five petals, and double flowers have at least ten petals. Frilled/ruffled flowers have petals with wavy edges, picotees have dark edges on pastel petals, and star flowers have five equally spaced petals, all the same size.

OPTIMUM HOUSEHOLD ENVIRONMENT

Read the Introduction for the specifics of each recommendation.

MEDIUM LIGHT. Provide filtered or dappled light and no direct sun. These low-growing plants also do really well under fluorescent lights with the lights about 12 inches above them.

MODERATE TEMPERATURE. Daytime 70 to 80°F, nighttime 60 to 70°F.

MODERATE WATER. Water whenever the top of the potting medium becomes dry to a depth of 1 inch. Avoid getting water on the leaves or flowers.

HUMIDITY. African violets like high humidity but don't mist them because their hairy leaves stay too wet too long. If your home is dry you can raise the humidity by putting the pot in a saucer or tray of water, making sure the bottom of the pot never sits directly in the water. Raise the pot up on pot feet or pebbles. Never let your African violet sit in water and become waterlogged.

POTTING MEDIUM. Use any good organic, well-drained, special-purpose potting soil designed for African violets. The best kinds will incorporate organic fertilizer, mycorrhizal fungi, and other beneficial microbes.

FERTILIZER. For standard African violets, use a balanced organic fertilizer, that is, one where the N-P-K numbers are approximately the same (e.g., 14-12-14). Miniature African violets like a slightly different formula (e.g., 7-9-5). Use either a powder or a liquid formulation and apply every three months year-round. Alternatively, dilute liquid fertilizer to half-strength and apply some every time you water your plant.

POTTING. When your plant needs up-potting, shift it to a container with a diameter 1 inch larger than the current pot. African violets prefer small, shallow pots so avoid putting them in too large a pot. Their small root systems are incapable of mining a large volume of soil for moisture.

PROPAGATION. African violet is easy to propagate from leaf cuttings.

COMMON PROBLEMS

Watch for whitish spots on leaves (page 256), mealybugs (page 262), and gray mold (page 268).

Aluminum plant

Aluminum plant (*Pilea cadierei*) is an easy-to-grow tropical houseplant, welcome everywhere for its striking evergreen foliage. Plants get 12 inches tall by 8 inches wide; they live in good condition for up to five years and can be maintained indefinitely by rooting tip cuttings of their somewhat fleshy and succulent stems. It's the fantastic 3-inch-long leaves that make this plant worth growing. Each oval leaf has raised patches that give it a quilted texture, and each patch seems to have been brushed

Aluminum plant (aka watermelon pilea).

with shiny, silvery aluminum. These pale streaks on a darker green background resemble watermelon rind. Aluminum plant rarely flowers as a houseplant. If it does flower, the individual flowers are extremely tiny and not at all showy or pretty. Just pinch them off so the plant doesn't waste energy producing flowers and seeds you don't want at the expense of those pretty leaves that you do want. It's also a good idea to pinch off the stem tips, or take tip cuttings, to make the plant bushy.

OPTIMUM HOUSEHOLD ENVIRONMENT

Read the Introduction for the specifics of each recommendation.

MEDIUM LIGHT. Provide a half-day of filtered light as from an east or west window with sheer curtains. Direct sun will burn the foliage.

MODERATE TEMPERATURE. Daytime 70 to 80°F, nighttime 60 to 70°F.

MODERATE WATER. Water whenever the top of the potting medium becomes dry to a depth of 1 inch.

HUMIDITY. Aluminum plant prefers moderate to high humidity. If the air in your home is drier than average, mist your plant twice a week with a spray bottle of water on a mist setting, or use a handheld mister. Put the pot in a saucer or tray of water, making sure the bottom of the pot never sits directly in the water by raising the pot up on pot feet or pebbles.

POTTING MEDIUM. Use any good organic, well-drained, cactus potting soil that incorporates sand along with organic fertilizer, mycorrhizal fungi, and other beneficial microbes.

FERTILIZER. Use any balanced organic fertilizer. Apply at half-strength every two weeks through the growing season.

POTTING. Pull the plant out of its pot and check the root system every spring. The root system of aluminum plant can break pots if it gets rootbound. When your plant needs up-potting, shift it to a container with a diameter 2 inches larger than the current pot.

PROPAGATION. Aluminum plant is easy to propagate from stem tip cuttings.

COMMON PROBLEMS

Watch for leggy growth (page 251), spider mites (page 263), and root rot (page 272).

Angel wing begonia

Angel wing begonias are easy, gorgeous year-round houseplants that bloom profusely with drooping clusters of small brightly colored flowers. The original was a hybrid between *Begonia aconitifolia* and *B. coccinea* created by California plant breeder Eva Kenworthy Gray in 1926. Since that cross, many more have been made with several other species, and hundreds of beautiful angel wing begonias are now available. The beautiful leaves are asymmetrical at the base, shaped like wings, and carried along the length of the green stems, which are thin but strong, and knobby, reminiscent of bamboo. Although some plants grow quite tall, all can be kept shorter through judicious pruning. In general, modern hybrids are much shorter and compact; some are even suitable for hanging baskets. They are grouped into three classes: Superba Canes, Mallet Canes, and All Other Canes.

Superba Canes can easily reach 8 to 10 feet tall and have leaves that are deeply cleft, lobed, or fringed. Most also have silver polka-dots on the upper surface of the leaves, but in a few the leaves are entirely silver.

Mallet Canes are hybrids involving *Begonia rex*, which gives the foliage unusual coloring and texture. The original hybrid of this type, 'Arthur Mallet', has given its name to all other angel wing begonias of similar heritage. Most begonias

Angel wing begonia (aka cane begonia, dragon-wing begonia).

Angel wing begonia, flower.

in this group have very colorful leaves that are thin-textured and sparsely hairy.

Begonia ×corallina falls into the All Others class. It grows 3 to 4 feet tall on average. The edges of the beautiful leaves are smooth and entire (i.e., they aren't toothed, serrated, or lobed). The green, bronze, or brownish upper surface of the leaves is usually spangled with shiny metallic silver polka dots. Sometimes the silver spots are absent. The underside of leaves is typically red.

Flowers give angel wing begonias additional appeal—small red, pink, or white blossoms cascade from the stems. Interestingly, the flowers are edible and are both sweet and tart.

OPTIMUM HOUSEHOLD ENVIRONMENT

Read the Introduction for the specifics of each recommendation.

MEDIUM LIGHT. Bright, indirect morning light from an east window with sheer curtains is ideal. These begonias cannot handle direct sun.

MODERATE TEMPERATURE. Daytime 70 to 80°F, nighttime 60 to 70°F. Begonias are easily damaged by temperatures below 55°F so protect them from cold drafts.

MODERATE WATER. Water whenever the top of the potting medium becomes dry to a depth of 1 inch.

HUMIDITY. Mist your plant several times a week

with a spray bottle of water on a mist setting, or use a handheld mister. Put the pot in a saucer or tray of water, making sure the bottom of the pot never sits directly in the water by raising the pot up on pot feet or pebbles.

POTTING MEDIUM. Use any good organic, well-drained, general-purpose potting soil that incorporates organic fertilizer, mycorrhizal fungi, and other beneficial microbes.

FERTILIZER. Use any liquid organic fertilizer where the second number (phosphorus) is higher than the other two to promote flowering. Apply at half-strength every two weeks during the growing season.

POTTING. In the spring, when your plant needs up-potting, shift it to a container with a diameter 2 inches larger than the current pot. Angel wing begonias have a fibrous root system and grow best in a small pot. Putting them in too large a pot can lead to problems associated with overwatering, such as leaf drop and root rot.

PROPAGATION. Angel wing begonia is easy to propagate from leaf cuttings and stem tip cuttings.

COMMON PROBLEMS

Watch for leaf drop (page 249), mealybugs (page 262), and gray mold (page 268).

Bird's nest philodendron

Philodendrons are the unsung heroes of the houseplant world. Not only are they perfectly comfortable living in the same environments as humans, they are lovely to look at and very tolerant of being relocated. Move them from room to room or take them outside for a summer vacation and they won't sulk and throw all their leaves on the ground like some other

Bird's nest philodendron.

houseplants. They will simply enjoy their new location. Bird's nest philodendron is the name applied to a group of mostly man-made hybrids derived from several different *Philodendron* species, including *P. auriculatum* and *P. deflexum*. It is so forgiving and commonplace as to be almost invisible, but newer and more colorful hybrids are introduced regularly, changing the face of this underappreciated workhorse companion. Most grow to about 2 feet tall and wide. Leaves are 8 to 12 inches long and shaped like stretched-out spear points or arrowheads. They are one-third to one-half as wide as they are long and glossy to waxy deep green. Many cultivars have foliage in colors other than green. Some have leaves that open coppery orange and then change to green as they mature. Others have leaves that are bright chartreuse or dark burgundy with red veins. Some leaves are almost black at maturity. All these colorful leaves resemble a crown, or a bouquet, that seems almost to erupt from the soil itself. However, they are all attached to a very short stem at their bases. It is very rare for bird's nest philodendron to flower indoors. If it does you will see a small, scoop-shaped spathe surrounding a finger-like spadix covered with minute flowers. Female flowers near the base of the spadix form berries after fertilization.

🛈 This plant is toxic to people and pets and should be kept in an out-of-the-way place. Its tissues contain calcium oxalate crystals, and if leaves are chewed the crystals penetrate the soft tissues of lips, tongue, and throat, causing painful swelling, drooling, and vomiting. If you suspect a person or pet has ingested parts of this plant, or if a person or pet exhibits serious symptoms such as difficulty breathing, call your local emergency hotline, poison control center, or vet.

OPTIMUM HOUSEHOLD ENVIRONMENT

Read the Introduction for the specifics of each recommendation.

MEDIUM LIGHT. Filtered light. Artificial light also works well for these forgiving plants. They also tolerate low light.

MODERATE TEMPERATURE. Daytime 70 to 80°F, nighttime 60 to 70°F.

MODERATE WATER. Water whenever the top of the potting medium becomes dry to a depth of 1 inch.

HUMIDITY. Mist your plant occasionally with a spray bottle of water on a mist setting, or use a handheld mister. Put the pot in a saucer or tray of water, making sure the bottom of the pot never sits directly in the water by raising the pot up on pot feet or pebbles.

POTTING MEDIUM. Use any good organic, well-drained, general-purpose potting soil that incorporates organic fertilizer, mycorrhizal fungi, and other beneficial microbes.

FERTILIZER. Use any organic fertilizer, in either a powder or liquid formulation, where the first number (nitrogen) is higher than the other two. Make sure that the fertilizer also incorporates micronutrients. Apply once a month through the growing season, every other month in winter.

POTTING. When your plant needs up-potting, shift it to a container with a diameter 2 inches larger than the current pot. Re-pot in spring or early summer every two years.

PROPAGATION. Bird's nest philodendron is easy to propagate from stem tip cuttings or by air layering.

COMMON PROBLEMS

Watch for yellowing leaves (page 257), aphids (page 260), and root rot (page 272).

Calla lily

As with all aroids, the colorful part of the calla lily (*Zantedeschia* spp.) is the scoop-shaped spathe surrounding a finger-like spadix covered with minute flowers. Hundreds of these barely visible flowers are packed onto the spadix. The big, bright spathe and the gorgeous foliage are the reasons we love these plants. Georgia O'Keeffe loved them too. She featured the elegant and sophisticated white calla lily (*Zantedeschia aethiopica*) in many of her sensuous paintings. This is a big plant, to 3 feet tall and wide when grown indoors. Modern hybrids developed from *Z. rehmannii* and *Z. elliottiana* are smaller plants, to 12 inches high and wide as houseplants. Their very colorful spathes can be deep purple, lavender, cream, orange, light and deep pink, or bright yellow.

All calla lilies have a bulb-like underground rhizome that is perennial. Leaves and flowers sprout directly from the eyes in the tops of these rhizomes so there is no aboveground stem. White calla lily is nearly evergreen and does not go dormant. All the small colorful species

White calla lily (aka arum lily, altar lily, lily of the Nile).

Calla lily hybrids.

In late summer the small callas prepare for dormancy by ceasing to grow and flower. The leaves slowly turn yellow and fade away as the plant prepares to go to sleep and pulls all its resources down into the underground rhizome. Remove old flowers and fading leaves. Stop fertilizing the plant and reduce watering until it is completely dormant. When dormancy is complete, stop watering entirely. Place the plant in cool shade until you re-pot it in mid-winter. After re-potting, move the plant to warmth and light in early spring and begin to water again to encourage it to break dormancy and begin active growth.

Many people find that calla lilies in their second or subsequent years as houseplants are not as vigorous and floriferous as they were in their first year, so they regard them as temporary houseplants and discard them when they go dormant.

❶ This plant is toxic to people and pets and should be kept in an out-of-the-way place. Its tissues contain calcium oxalate crystals, and

and hybrids have a growth habit much like any temporary houseplant with bulbs: they go completely dormant in the autumn. Leaves of white calla lily are arrow-shaped, 18 inches long and 10 inches wide. They are usually not spotted, but some cultivars have silvery white spots on the leaves. Leaves of the smaller hybrids are also arrow-shaped, 10 to 12 inches long and 2.5 to 6 inches wide. Many have white spots on the leaves.

if leaves are chewed the crystals penetrate the soft tissues of lips, tongue, and throat, causing painful swelling, drooling, and vomiting. If you suspect a person or pet has ingested parts of this plant, or if a person or pet exhibits serious symptoms such as difficulty breathing, call your local emergency hotline, poison control center, or vet.

OPTIMUM HOUSEHOLD ENVIRONMENT

Read the Introduction for the specifics of each recommendation.

MEDIUM LIGHT. These plants dislike direct sunlight and will be at their best in filtered or dappled light.

LOW TEMPERATURE. Daytime 65 to 75°F, nighttime 55 to 65°F.

AMPLE WATER. Callas like lots of water when they are in active growth and flowering. Water whenever the top of the potting medium becomes dry to a depth of 0.5 inch. Stop watering during their dormant period.

HUMIDITY. Calla lilies like high humidity. Mist your plant every other day with a spray bottle of water on a mist setting, or use a handheld mister. Put the pot in a saucer or tray of water, making sure the bottom of the pot never sits directly in the water by raising the pot up on pot feet or pebbles.

POTTING MEDIUM. Use any good organic, well-drained, general-purpose potting soil that incorporates organic fertilizer, mycorrhizal fungi, and other beneficial microbes.

FERTILIZER. Use any balanced organic fertilizer. Apply once a month through the growing season. Do not fertilize during the dormant period.

POTTING. In mid-winter your small calla needs re-potting before it begins a new cycle of growth and flowering. Remove the bulb-like rhizome from the old spent soil and pot it up with fresh potting medium. For the white and the small, if the rhizome appears to be rootbound, up-pot to a container with a diameter 4 inches larger than the current pot.

PROPAGATION. Calla lilies are easy to propagate by dividing the rhizome when re-potting.

COMMON PROBLEMS

Watch for loss of vigor (page 252), aphids (page 260), and soft rot (page 274).

Cast-iron plant

Cast-iron plant (*Aspidistra elatior*) is practically indestructible, as its common name suggests. This tough-as-nails, easy-to-grow plant was very popular and quite common in the Victorian era. In modern times, however, it's harder to find and can be pricey: it grows very slowly and so it's expensive for growers to get it to marketable size. This plant has no stems above the soil line, just leaves that seem to sprout directly from the potting medium. Well-grown, older plants have as many as 12 to 18 leaves that arch gracefully. Leaves are 2 feet long, 4 inches wide, deep green and glossy. Some cultivars have variegated leaves with creamy white stripes or small creamy spots. These grow even more slowly than the green-leafed original. You may be surprised one day to find a flower peeking up out of the dirt. Only mature plants flower and even then only rarely. They produce one small purplish brown flower at a time, right at the surface of the potting medium.

OPTIMUM HOUSEHOLD ENVIRONMENT

Read the Introduction for the specifics of each recommendation.

LOW LIGHT. This plant does very well in the dim ambient light of a north window. It also does well in artificial light. It cannot tolerate direct sun.

Cast-iron plant (aka barroom plant, saloon plant).

MODERATE TEMPERATURE. Daytime 70 to 80°F, nighttime 60 to 70°F. Unlike most houseplants, cast-iron plant is very forgiving in its temperature requirements and readily adapts to a wide range of temperatures, from 45 to 85°F.

LOW WATER. For most of the year, water whenever the top of the potting medium becomes dry to a depth of 2 inches. But when the plant is in active growth in late spring and early summer, water whenever the top of the potting medium becomes dry to a depth of 1 inch.

HUMIDITY. Cast-iron plant does well in dry air and needs no supplemental humidity.

POTTING MEDIUM. Use any good organic, well-drained, general-purpose potting soil that incorporates organic fertilizer, mycorrhizal fungi, and other beneficial microbes.

FERTILIZER. Use any balanced organic fertilizer. Apply once a month through the growing season. If your plant develops slits in the leaves, it's getting too much fertilizer.

POTTING. When your plant needs up-potting, shift it to a container with a diameter 2 inches larger than the current pot. This very slow grower will need to be up-potted only every three to five years.

PROPAGATION. Cast-iron plant is easy to propagate by division of the rhizome.

COMMON PROBLEMS

Watch for yellowing leaves (page 257) and scale insects (page 262).

Chinese evergreen

In addition to their beauty, Chinese evergreens (*Aglaonema commutatum, A. modestum, A. pictum*) are undemanding; thus, they are widely grown in public spaces such as shopping malls, hospitals, and hotels. The plant's small size and proven ability to purify indoor air make it a perfect companion for the home and office as well. Crowns of deep green foliage—mottled, marbled, and painted with splashes of pale silvery green—are typical for these handsome, easy-to-grow plants. Some newer cultivars have bright red, pink, and creamy white markings on the leaves. Stems are short—it is the crown of beautiful foliage that gives the plant its height and width. Many older cultivars become 2 to 3 feet tall and wide as they mature, but newer cultivars are bred to be very short and compact, about 1 foot tall and wide. Stems can become trunk-like with age as the oldest leaves are shed. Leaf size and shape varies widely; typical leaves are 6 to 10 inches long and 3 to 4 inches wide, but some cultivars have very narrow foliage, only 1 to 2 inches wide. The inflorescence is a small, pale green, scoop-shaped spathe surrounding a finger-like spadix covered with tiny flowers. Female flowers near the base of the spadix form red berries after fertilization.

❶ This plant is toxic to people and pets and should be kept in an out-of-the-way place. Its tissues contain calcium oxalate crystals, and if leaves are chewed the crystals penetrate the soft tissues of lips, tongue, and throat, causing painful swelling, drooling, and vomiting. If you suspect a person or pet has ingested parts of this plant, or if a person or pet exhibits serious symptoms such as difficulty breathing, call your local emergency hotline, poison control center, or vet.

(top) Chinese evergreen (aka aglaonema, painted drop tongue, poison dart plant).

(above) Chinese evergreen, narrow-leaved form.

OPTIMUM HOUSEHOLD ENVIRONMENT

Read the Introduction for the specifics of each recommendation.

LOW OR MEDIUM LIGHT. Cultivars with darker green foliage do best near a north window. Those with lighter, more extensive variegation of the foliage need the brighter light of an east window with curtains to filter the light. All varieties do well under artificial light. Chinese evergreen is intolerant of direct sun.

MODERATE TEMPERATURE. Daytime 70 to 80°F, nighttime 60 to 70°F. This plant is sensitive to cold air so avoid drafty locations and temperatures below 60°F.

MODERATE WATER. Water whenever the top of the potting medium becomes dry to a depth of 1 inch.

HUMIDITY. These plants tolerate moderately dry air very well. But if the air in your home is very dry, then mist your plant twice a week with a spray bottle of water on a mist setting, or use a handheld mister.

POTTING MEDIUM. Use any good organic, well-drained, general-purpose potting soil that incorporates organic fertilizer, mycorrhizal fungi, and other beneficial microbes.

FERTILIZER. Use any balanced organic fertilizer. Apply once a month through the growing season, every two months in winter.

POTTING. When your plant needs up-potting, every two years or so, shift it to a container with a diameter 2 inches larger than the current pot. These plants prefer being a little rootbound. Re-potting can be done any time of year.

PROPAGATION. Chinese evergreen is easy to propagate from stem tip cuttings.

COMMON PROBLEMS

Watch for leaves changing color (page 249), scale insects (page 262), and bacterial leaf spot (page 267).

Clivia

The slow-growing clivia (*Clivia miniata*) has 2-foot-long, 2-inch-wide, dark evergreen, strap-shaped leaves. These arch out gracefully, seemingly direct from the potting medium. There are stems, but they are short and completely covered by the foliage. Underground, the plant has long, ropy rhizomes. Mature, well-grown specimens of clivia can be 2 to 3 feet high and wide. The beautiful leaves grow in fans, making the plants appealing even when not in flower. As the plant grows, the oldest leaves closest to the ground will wither and turn brown. This is normal. Just remove the dead leaves as they occur.

Clusters of ten to 20 brilliantly colorful flowers float above the foliage on thick stalks (peduncles). Each flower is a wide-open bell

Clivia (aka Natal lily, bush lily).

with flaring petals that are joined at the base. Flower color varies from orange, salmon, red, and yellow to white in the various cultivars and hybrids. A plant more than three years old will flower if you give it a cool rest in autumn. Move it into low light in a cool room (50 to 65°F is ideal), and water sparingly for three months (e.g., October through December). After three months of rest, bring it back into active growth by moving it into a warm room and gradually increasing water. Six to 12 weeks later, the plant will flower. When the blooms fade, cut the flower stalks off at the base; otherwise the plant will put its energy into making seeds.

OPTIMUM HOUSEHOLD ENVIRONMENT

Read the Introduction for the specifics of each recommendation.

MEDIUM LIGHT. Cool morning light from an east window with sheer curtains is best. Direct sun can easily burn the leaves.

MODERATE TEMPERATURE. Daytime 70 to 80°F, nighttime 60 to 70°F, during the growing season. During the autumn resting period, give it cool daytime temperature of 50 to 65°F for three months.

MODERATE WATER. Water whenever the top of the potting medium becomes dry to a depth of 1 inch through the growing season. Gradually decrease watering during the autumn resting period by watering only when the potting medium is dry to a depth of 2 inches.

HUMIDITY. Clivia tolerates dry air very well. Avoid misting this plant.

POTTING MEDIUM. Use any good organic, well-drained potting medium designed for semi-terrestrial orchids, one that incorporates organic fertilizer, mycorrhizal fungi, and other beneficial microbes.

FERTILIZER. Use any organic fertilizer, in either a powder or liquid formulation, where the second number (phosphorus) is higher than the other two to promote flowering. Apply once a month through the growing season. Do not feed in the autumn rest period and winter.

POTTING. When your plant needs up-potting, shift it to a container with a diameter 2 inches larger than the current pot. Clivia prefers being somewhat rootbound, so re-pot only every three to five years or so. Put it in a heavy pot that is relatively shallow to keep it from toppling over.

PROPAGATION. Clivia is easy to propagate by separating pups from the main plant after the flower stalks fade.

COMMON PROBLEMS

Watch for yellowing leaves (page 257), spider mites (page 263), and root rot (page 272).

Coleus

The appeal of coleus (*Solenostemon scutellarioides*) lies in its fantastic, bizarre, amazing foliage. Three or four brilliant kaleidoscopic colors of green, yellow, red, pink, orange, magenta, white—even black—adorn each soft, velvety leaf in discrete patches or intricate lace-like patterns. The basic shape of a typical coleus leaf is ovate (egg-shaped), wide at the base and narrow at the tip, but there are hundreds of cultivars, several of which have earned the Royal Horticultural Society's Award of Garden Merit. Leaves of most cultivars are 3 to 4 inches long and 2 to 3 inches wide. Some cultivars have long, narrow leaves, others have short, wide leaves. Some cultivars have leaves with scalloped edges, others have lobed or fringed edges. Easy and fast-growing, these bushy evergreen perennials get 2 to 3 feet tall and wide. Stems get woody at the base as they age. The flowers are unremarkable—small, pale purplish blue, borne in spiky inflorescences at the tip of each stem.

Coleus (aka painted nettle, flame nettle, painted leaf, poor man's croton).

Most growers pinch off the flower buds to keep the plant vigorous and encourage additional fabulous foliage. Making flowers and subsequent seed production saps the energy of the plant.

OPTIMUM HOUSEHOLD ENVIRONMENT

Read the Introduction for the specifics of each recommendation.

MEDIUM LIGHT. Coleus prefers light from an east or west window filtered by sheer curtains. Direct sun at midday will bleach the color of the leaves or even burn them badly.

MODERATE TEMPERATURE. Daytime 70 to 80°F, nighttime 60 to 70°F.

AMPLE WATER. During the growing season, water whenever the top of the potting medium becomes dry to a depth of 0.5 inch. In winter, water whenever the top of the potting medium becomes dry to a depth of 1 inch.

HUMIDITY. Keep humidity high by misting your plant several times a week with a spray bottle of water on a mist setting, or use a handheld mister. Put the pot in a saucer or tray of water, making sure the bottom of the pot never sits directly in the water by raising the pot up on pot feet or pebbles.

POTTING MEDIUM. Use any good organic, well-drained, general-purpose potting soil that incorporates organic fertilizer, mycorrhizal fungi, and other beneficial microbes.

FERTILIZER. Use any organic fertilizer, in either a powder or liquid formulation, where the first number (nitrogen) is higher than the other two. Apply dry fertilizer once in early spring and again in June. Apply liquid fertilizer at half-strength once a week through the growing season.

POTTING. When your plant needs up-potting, shift it to a container with a diameter 4 inches larger than the current pot. Coleus generally does not need a pot larger than 8 inches in diameter.

PROPAGATION. Coleus is easy to propagate from stem tip cuttings rooted in water. It is also easy to grow from seed, but each seedling will be a unique individual that does not duplicate the original plant.

COMMON PROBLEMS

Watch for sunburn (page 256), mealybugs (page 262), and gray mold (page 268).

Creeping saxifrage

Creeping saxifrage (*Saxifraga stolonifera*) is a perennial that keeps on giving. Plant one out in your garden and before you know it, you will have thousands of them. As a houseplant, it is just as generous but much more controllable—though you'll still have to watch out for it

Creeping saxifrage (aka Aaron's beard, creeping rockfoil, roving sailor, strawberry begonia, strawberry geranium, strawberry saxifrage).

crawling into bed with its neighbors. This saxifrage has very attractive leaves reminiscent of begonia/geranium foliage, and it grows just like a strawberry, sending out runners in every direction that take root and grow new plantlets. Plants spread rapidly, forming mats from 6 to 8 inches tall and 12 inches wide. Leaves are nearly round, about 4 inches across, and dark green, with beautiful silver veins and pink to purple-red undersides. Some cultivars have maroon leaves. The starry, delicate, 1-inch-wide flowers are white with tiny pink to red freckles on the three small, pointed upper petals. The two lower petals are four times longer than the upper petals, pure white, and pointed. Flowers appear in May and June and are carried on 2-foot-long stalks in loose, open clusters well above the foliage. Grown in a hanging basket, creeping saxifrage will have lots of red runners cascading down around the sides of the pot. These form new little plantlets at their tips, and the overall effect is lovely. Even in a pot sitting on a windowsill, the runners will form little plantlets that sit on the sill all around the feet of the mother plant.

OPTIMUM HOUSEHOLD ENVIRONMENT

Read the Introduction for the specifics of each recommendation.

MEDIUM LIGHT. This plant does well with dappled or filtered light. Keep it out of direct sun because the foliage burns easily in hot sun.

LOW TEMPERATURE. Daytime 65 to 75°F, nighttime 55 to 65°F.

MODERATE WATER. Water whenever the top of

the potting medium becomes dry to a depth of 1 inch.

HUMIDITY. Creeping saxifrage does well with average humidity, but if the air in your home is drier than normal raise the humidity by putting the pot in a saucer or tray of water, making sure the bottom of the pot never sits directly in the water by raising the pot up on pot feet or pebbles.

POTTING MEDIUM. Use any good organic, well-drained, general-purpose potting soil that incorporates organic fertilizer, mycorrhizal fungi, and other beneficial microbes.

FERTILIZER. Use any liquid organic fertilizer where the second number (phosphorus) is higher than the other two to promote flowering. Apply at half-strength once a month through the growing season.

POTTING. This plant grows fast and does not like to be rootbound, so you should probably up-pot or re-pot it once a year. Up-pot to a container with a diameter 4 inches larger than the current pot.

PROPAGATION. Creeping saxifrage is easy to propagate by layering the stolons.

COMMON PROBLEMS
Watch for sunburn (page 256), aphids (page 260), and root rot (page 272).

False shamrock

Don't confuse false shamrock (*Oxalis triangularis*) with either its weedy relative, *O. corniculata*, or true Irish shamrock (*Trifolium dubium*), both of which have yellow flowers. False shamrock is neither invasive nor weedy, and its dainty flowers are white or pale pink. It is endemic to Brazil—a very long way from Ireland. Leaves sprout directly from odd-looking, scaly little underground bulbs, forming a mound of foliage 6 to 10 inches high and wide. Each leaf has three triangular leaflets at the top of a thin stalk (petiole). In the most popular cultivars these leaflets are dark purple with a bright purple center. In other varieties the leaflets are green on the upper surface and purple on the lower surface, or green with a silver edge. No matter what color the leaves are, they all move. The three leaflets of each leaf fold down at night and open up in daylight. The starry flowers, with five wide-spreading petals, are carried in clusters on long stalks above the foliage. The dramatic contrast between the dark foliage and the pale flowers is another attractive aspect of this plant.

False shamrock goes dormant from time to time, particularly when it's finished flowering in the autumn. Like many other bulbs, the plant just wants to go to sleep for a while and will resume growth after it has a period of rest. When this happens you might think your

False shamrock (aka shamrock, Irish shamrock, purple shamrock, lucky shamrock, love plant, woodsorrel).

plant is dying. It isn't. Just reduce watering, let the plant dry out, and all the leaves will die back. After a month or so of dormancy, it will start into active growth again. At that point, resume watering and your plant will soon be in flower again.

 The leaves are edible in small doses by adults. They add a fresh, acidic taste and deep purple color to green salads. But don't eat too much because these plants contain soluble oxalates that can cause mild to severe poisoning if sufficient quantities are consumed. Keep this plant out of the reach of children and pets. Symptoms to watch for include drooling, vomiting, diarrhea, lethargy, and weakness. If you suspect a child or pet is in difficulty, call your local emergency hotline, poison control center, or vet.

OPTIMUM HOUSEHOLD ENVIRONMENT

Read the Introduction for the specifics of each recommendation.

MEDIUM LIGHT. Provide dappled or filtered light.

LOW TEMPERATURE. 65 to 75°F day and night.

MODERATE WATER. While your plant is in active growth, water whenever the top of the potting medium becomes dry to a depth of 1 inch.

HUMIDITY. This plant is very tolerant of the dry air in the average home. If your home is really dry, however, mist your plant twice a week with a spray bottle of water on a mist setting, or use a handheld mister. Put the pot in a saucer or tray of water, making sure the bottom of the pot never sits directly in the water by raising the pot up on pot feet or pebbles.

POTTING MEDIUM. Use any good organic, well-drained, general-purpose potting soil that incorporates organic fertilizer, mycorrhizal fungi, and other beneficial microbes.

FERTILIZER. Use any organic fertilizer, in either a powder or liquid formulation, where the second number (phosphorus) is higher than the other

two to promote flowering. Apply dry fertilizer once a month during the growing season. Apply liquid fertilizer at half-strength every two weeks through the growing season.

POTTING. When your plant needs up-potting, shift it to a container with a diameter 2 inches larger than the current pot.

PROPAGATION. False shamrock is easy to propagate by division of the bulbs while the plant is dormant.

COMMON PROBLEMS

Watch for premature dormancy (page 254), spider mites (page 263), and leaf spot fungus (page 269).

Flamingo flower

What's not to love about a plant that grows slowly, likes the warmth and reduced light of our homes, and whose flowers last for months? Flamingo flowers (*Anthurium* spp.) are, in many ways, perfect flowering houseplants, and even when not in bloom, their heart-shaped foliage is appealing. Indeed, some species, *A. crystallinum* in particular, are grown primarily for their attractive leaves. The leaves of all anthuriums are leathery, evergreen, and glossy. They are held erect on stiff peduncles and slowly swivel to face the light. The showy part of flamingo flower's inflorescence is the big colorful, scoop-shaped spathe, which surrounds a finger-like spadix covered with minute flowers. Flower colors include bright red, scarlet, orange, pink, lavender, purple, and white. Multicolored flowers with green on the "ears" of the spathe are called *obake* ("ghost," in Japanese). The flowers are very stiff and feel almost like plastic. This heavy construction is one reason they last so long, whether on the plant (for months, literally) or as cut flowers (easily three or four weeks in the vase).

Flamingo flower (aka boy flower, anthurium, pigtail anthurium, painted flamingo, flamingo lily, painter's palette, tailflower, laceleaf).

The large flowers of *Anthurium andraeanum*, which are so frequently used in tropical floral arrangements, are borne on big plants to 3 feet tall and wide. The pigtail (*A. scherzerianum*), only 18 inches high and wide, got its common name because its spadix is coiled in a spiral like the tail of a pig. Modern small-flowered hybrids derived from *A. amnicola* are about the same size as pigtail, but have a straight rather than curly spadix.

❶ This plant is toxic to people and pets and should be kept in an out-of-the-way place. Its tissues contain calcium oxalate crystals, and if leaves are chewed the crystals penetrate the soft tissues of lips, tongue, and throat, causing painful swelling, drooling, and vomiting. If you suspect a person or pet has ingested parts of this plant, or if a person or pet exhibits serious symptoms such as difficulty breathing, call your local emergency hotline, poison control center, or vet.

OPTIMUM HOUSEHOLD ENVIRONMENT

Read the Introduction for the specifics of each recommendation.

MEDIUM LIGHT. These plants flower well with bright light from an east window filtered by sheer curtains. They also do well in low light from a north window or skylight. They should never be exposed to direct sun unless they have been cautiously acclimated because their heavy foliage burns quickly.

MODERATE TEMPERATURE. Daytime 70 to 80°F, nighttime 60 to 70°F. These plants will suffer if the temperature drops below 60°F.

AMPLE WATER. Water whenever the top of the potting medium becomes dry to a depth of 0.5 inch.

HUMIDITY. Flamingo flower loves high humidity. Mist your plant daily with a spray bottle of water on a mist setting, or use a handheld mister. Put the pot in a saucer or tray of water, making sure the bottom of the pot never sits directly in the water by raising the pot up on pot feet or pebbles.

POTTING MEDIUM. Use any good organic, well-drained potting medium designed for semi-terrestrial orchids, one that incorporates organic fertilizer, mycorrhizal fungi, and other beneficial microbes.

FERTILIZER. Use any balanced liquid organic fertilizer. Apply at half-strength every two weeks throughout the year because these plants tend to flower at any time of year.

POTTING. When your plant needs up-potting, shift it to a container with a diameter 2 inches larger than the current pot.

PROPAGATION. Flamingo flower is easy to propagate from stem tip cuttings and stem cuttings.

COMMON PROBLEMS

Watch for sunburn (page 256), mealybugs (page 262), and anthurium blight (page 266).

Geranium

The geraniums we grow as houseplants in the United States are species and cultivars of the genus *Pelargonium*. All are evergreen perennials whose original home was South Africa, so they are all frost-tender. These include scented-leaf geraniums (various species with strongly aromatic foliage), zonal geraniums (*P. ×hortorum*), ivy geranium (*P. peltatum*), and Lady Washington (or regal) geraniums (*P. ×domesticum*). Because cold weather kills them, many people grow them outdoors as annual bedding plants. But you can keep them alive and well, and flowering to boot, all winter long inside your home.

Zonal geraniums grow into shrubby plants, 1 to 3 feet tall and wide, with stems that are woody at the base and succulent at the tips. They have circular or kidney-shaped foliage that is velvety soft and hairy. Most cultivars have a circular red-brown zone in the middle of the leaf, but some have entirely green leaves. Fancy-leaved cultivars are grown for their brightly colored—yellow, orange, red, brown—foliage alone. But most of the 500 or so cultivars of zonal geraniums are grown for their beautiful flowers. The 1-inch-wide, five-petaled flowers come in every possible tint and shade of red, scarlet, rose, pink, salmon, orange, mauve, lavender, violet, and white. Flowers are borne in tight, ball-like clusters of 30 to 50 blossoms.

Ivy geraniums are vine-like plants with thin, trailing stems that can get as long as 6 feet. They are typically grown in hanging baskets because of their prostrate, spreading habit. The 2- to 3-inch-wide leaves, smooth, waxy, and palmately lobed, bear a superficial resemblance to leaves

(top right) Geranium (aka garden geranium, pelargonium, storksbill).

(right) Geranium, flowers.

of ivy (*Hedera helix*). The 1-inch-wide flowers have two upper petals that are slightly smaller than the three lower petals, giving each flower an asymmetrical look. Flowers are pink, red, or white, streaked with darker lines, and borne in small clusters of two to nine blossoms.

Lady Washington geraniums are shrubby plants with woody stems; they grow 3 feet tall and wide. Their 2- to 4-inch-wide dark green leaves are heart- or kidney-shaped, crinkled, and have pointed teeth along the margins. The flowers, however, are the glory of this striking type. They are large, to 3.5 inches across, very showy, and colorful. Flower colors range from white through pink, red, lavender, and purple. The petals have brilliant blotches and streaks of darker colors.

The foliage of scented-leaf geraniums is strongly aromatic. The lightest touch of any leaf is enough to release the powerful fragrance it contains: rose (*Pelargonium capitatum, P. graveolens*), lemon (*P. crispum*), apple (*P. odoratissimum*), strawberry (*P. ×scarboroviae*), and peppermint (*P. tomentosum*). The scented geraniums are a varied lot as you might expect with so many different species involved. Most grow 1 to 3 feet high and wide. Many have deeply divided palmately lobed, ferny foliage that is gray-green or silvery; some have round, green leaves. The leaves range in size from minute to 4 inches wide. Flowers are small, usually white or rosy pink, but are secondary in importance to the scented leaves. Scented geranium leaves have a variety of medicinal and culinary uses and are perhaps best known for their contribution to desserts in the form of cakes, jellies, and flavored drinks. The essential oils of certain cultivars ('Attar of Roses', 'Sweet Mimosa', and 'Paton's Unique', among others) exhibit antibacterial and antifungal properties.

OPTIMUM HOUSEHOLD ENVIRONMENT

Read the Introduction for the specifics of each recommendation.

HIGH LIGHT. Put geraniums in full sun in a south window. They need strong light in order to flower well.

LOW TEMPERATURE. Daytime 65 to 75°F, nighttime 55 to 65°F.

MODERATE WATER. Water whenever the top of the potting medium becomes dry to a depth of 1 inch.

HUMIDITY. These plants grow well in average room humidity. They don't need to be misted.

POTTING MEDIUM. Use any good organic, well-drained, general-purpose potting soil that incorporates organic fertilizer, mycorrhizal fungi, and other beneficial microbes.

FERTILIZER. Use any liquid organic fertilizer where the second number (phosphorus) is higher than the other two to promote flowering. For foliage types, choose a fertilizer where the first number (nitrogen) is higher. Apply at half-strength once a month through the growing season.

POTTING. When your plant needs up-potting, shift it to a container with a diameter 4 inches larger than the current pot. Put ivy geraniums in hanging baskets and all other types into regular pots.

PROPAGATION. All geraniums are easy to propagate from stem tip cuttings.

COMMON PROBLEMS

Watch for edema (page 247), whiteflies (page 265), and gray mold (page 268).

Gloxinia

Spectacular flowers, in eye-catching colors and as velvety soft as a horse's nose, almost guarantee impulse purchases of gloxinia (*Sinningia speciosa*). How could anyone pass this houseplant up when it is in full gorgeous bloom? Gloxinias strongly resemble their cousins, African violets, except that their flowers are bigger, as much as 4 inches across. Flowers come in bright red, pink, purple, and white, sometimes with white edges and sometimes with spots or lines of contrasting colors on the petals. The softly furry leaves form a compact basal rosette near ground level, and the flowers emerge from the center of the whorl of leaves. Leaves are large, 8 to 12 inches long, with shallow crenellations along the edges. They are often green above and purple on the undersides. Mature gloxinia plants get 6 to 12 inches tall and wide. Modern hybrids with such species as *S. pusilla* or *S. concinna* have been developed to obtain smaller versions of this

Gloxinia (aka florist gloxinia).

large-flowered beauty and an extended range of colorful flowers.

These plants sprout from small underground tubers. They tend to bloom all summer and then they die to the ground in the autumn. When this happens, don't panic—your plant is not really dying. It is just going to sleep for the winter. When your gloxinia goes dormant, move its pot to a dark, cool place (50 to 60°F), stop watering and fertilizing, and allow it to dry out over winter. In late winter re-pot the tubers in fresh potting medium, bring them back into the light, and resume watering. The plants will resume growth and soon be flowering again.

OPTIMUM HOUSEHOLD ENVIRONMENT

Read the Introduction for the specifics of each recommendation.

MEDIUM LIGHT. Provide filtered or dappled light, no direct sun. These low-growing plants also do really well under artificial lights with the lights about 12 inches above them.

MODERATE TEMPERATURE. Daytime 70 to 80°F, nighttime 60 to 70°F.

MODERATE WATER. Water throughout the growing season whenever the top of the potting medium becomes dry to a depth of 1 inch. Avoid getting water directly on the leaves. Do not water when the plant is dormant.

HUMIDITY. Gloxinia appreciates humidity but do not mist the foliage. Put the pot in a saucer or tray of water, making sure the bottom of the pot never sits directly in the water by raising the pot up on pot feet or pebbles.

POTTING MEDIUM. Use any good organic, well-drained, African violet potting soil that incorporates organic fertilizer, mycorrhizal fungi, and other beneficial microbes.

FERTILIZER. Choose an acidic liquid organic fertilizer designed for acid-loving plants where the second number (phosphorus) is higher than the other two to promote flowering. Apply at half-strength every two weeks through the growing season. Do not fertilize when the plant is dormant.

POTTING. When your plant needs up-potting, shift it to a container with a diameter 2 inches larger than the current pot. Re-pot in late winter when the plant is dormant.

PROPAGATION. Gloxinia is easy to propagate from leaf cuttings.

COMMON PROBLEMS

Watch for whitish spots on leaves (page 256), spider mites (page 263), and root rot (page 272).

Goldfish plant

All goldfish plants—*Nematanthus wettsteinii*, *Columnea gloriosa*, and *Neomortonia nummularia*—are trailing evergreen perennials that grow very well in hanging baskets. The small leaves are thick and waxy, glossy in some, fuzzy in others. Leaf color is usually a crisp bright green but can be dark green, variegated, or even purplish. Many cultivars have a red blotch on the undersides of the leaves. All these plants have small flowers in shades of bright orange, red, or yellow. Most look rather like little pot-bellied goldfish with tiny, round, open mouths. Some lack the pot-bellied pouch on the underside and are simple tubes with five petals that flare open at the mouth. Still others have flowers that flare out into a hood at the tip. Plants are shrubby, with lax, spreading stems that get as much as 3 feet long. Young goldfish plants in small pots generally grow upright, but as they age, the stems get longer, tumbling out and down from the plant's center. Pinching off the tips of the stems causes them to branch into a bushier form that produces more of the charming flowers.

Goldfish plant (aka candy-corn plant, guppy plant, dolphin plant).

OPTIMUM HOUSEHOLD ENVIRONMENT

Read the Introduction for the specifics of each recommendation.

MEDIUM LIGHT. Give these plants light filtered by sheer curtains or a half-day of sun from an east window. They also do very well under artificial light.

MODERATE TEMPERATURE. Daytime 70 to 80°F, nighttime 60 to 70°F.

AMPLE WATER. Through the growing season, water whenever the top of the potting medium becomes dry to a depth of 0.5 inch. In winter cut back and water whenever the top of the potting medium becomes dry to a depth of 1 inch.

HUMIDITY. Goldfish plant likes high humidity.

Mist your plant daily with a spray bottle of water on a mist setting, or use a handheld mister. Put the pot in a saucer or tray of water, making sure the bottom of the pot never sits directly in the water by raising the pot up on pot feet or pebbles. Alternatively, use a humidifier in the room to bring the humidity up to higher levels.

POTTING MEDIUM. Use any good organic, well-drained potting medium designed for semi-terrestrial orchids, one that incorporates organic fertilizer, mycorrhizal fungi, and other beneficial microbes.

FERTILIZER. Use any organic fertilizer, in either a powder or liquid formulation, where the second number (phosphorus) is higher than the other two to promote flowering. Apply at half-strength every two weeks through the growing season.

POTTING. When your plant needs up-potting, in two to three years, shift it to a container with a diameter 2 inches larger than the current pot. To keep it in a same-size container, re-pot in spring and prune the roots lightly.

PROPAGATION. Goldfish plant is easy to propagate from stem tip cuttings. Newly rooted cuttings will not flower until they are a year old.

COMMON PROBLEMS
Watch for leaf drop (page 249), mealybugs (page 262), and root rot (page 272).

Lipstick plant

Lipstick plant (*Aeschynanthus radicans*) is a vine-like evergreen perennial that grows to perfection in hanging baskets. The 2-foot-long stems arch gracefully out and down, away from the center of the plant. Cutting the stems back by not more than one-third encourages side branching and makes for a bushier form that will produce more flowers. The flowers begin as bright scarlet buds poking out of velvety purple-black calyx tubes—together, the pairing looks for all the world like red lipstick in a

Goldfish plant.

Lipstick plant (aka lipstick vine, basket vine).

Lipstick plant.

MEDIUM LIGHT. Lipstick plant does best in bright, strong light filtered by sheer curtains. It cannot tolerate direct sun.

HIGH TEMPERATURE. Daytime 75 to 85°F, nighttime 65 to 75°F, during the spring and summer growing season. In winter, give it cooler temperatures to 55 to 65°F and this will stimulate flower production. Do not expose it to temperatures below 55°F because this will cause the leaves to drop off.

AMPLE WATER. Through the growing season, water whenever the top of the potting medium becomes dry to a depth of 0.5 inch. Reduce watering in winter and water whenever the top of the potting medium becomes dry to a depth of 1 inch.

HUMIDITY. Lipstick plant likes high humidity. Mist your plant daily with a spray bottle of water on a mist setting, or use a handheld mister. Better yet, use a humidifier in the room. Put the pot in a saucer or tray of water, making sure the bottom of the pot never sits directly in the water by raising the pot up on pot feet or pebbles.

POTTING MEDIUM. Use any good organic, well-drained potting medium designed for semi-terrestrial orchids, one that incorporates organic fertilizer, mycorrhizal fungi, and other beneficial microbes.

FERTILIZER. Use any liquid organic fertilizer where the second number (phosphorus) is higher than the other two to promote flowering. Apply at half-strength once a month through the growing season.

POTTING. When your plant needs up-potting, shift it to a container with a diameter 2 inches larger than the current pot. This plant will flower best when kept slightly rootbound.

PROPAGATION. Lipstick plant is easy to propagate from stem tip cuttings.

dark lipstick tube. As the flowers mature they extend far beyond the tube, and the petals flare at the tips, opening up the flower so that it no longer looks like lipstick. But while the buds are developing the common name is a dead ringer for this plant. The leaves are thick, glossy, 2 to 4 inches long, bright green, and very attractive. The leaves are opposite (a pair of leaves at every node) and handsomely arranged. Some cultivars have variegated foliage in green and white. Some people consider this plant worth growing for the foliage alone, but for most of us, it is most desirable when it's in full bloom.

OPTIMUM HOUSEHOLD ENVIRONMENT

Read the Introduction for the specifics of each recommendation.

COMMON PROBLEMS

Watch for leaf drop (page 249), mealybugs (page 262), and root rot (page 272).

Lucky bamboo

Lucky bamboo (*Dracaena braunii*) isn't really a bamboo and it's a good thing. Real bamboo doesn't make a good houseplant, whereas lucky bamboo is nearly indestructible inside our homes. It is often found in dimly lit restaurants, on the front desk of hotel lobbies, even in the dentist's office—all because of the widely held belief that the plant brings happiness and prosperity. Maybe that's why you'll often see it right beside the cash register. As a houseplant, especially when grown in water, this extremely slow grower will live comfortably on a desk or table for many years. Its green stems merely look jointed, like real bamboo, because they are ringed by attractive white leaf scars. The light to medium green strap-shaped leaves are 6 to 10 inches long, 1 to 2 inches wide at their bases, and pointed at the tips. Some cultivars have beautifully variegated leaves bordered in pure white. Flowers are insignificant.

Lucky bamboo is most often sold as pieces of stem in short, medium, or long lengths stuck into a vase of water. The stems may or may not have roots. The pieces of stem may be straight, or, more frequently they have been coerced by growers in Taiwan and China into interesting twisted shapes, spirals, circles, or braids. Lucky bamboo does not naturally grow in circles. It is forced to do so by being kept on its side in a box with a shifting light source. As it slowly grows toward whatever side has the light, the stem turns a tiny bit every day. Eventually it will have grown into a complete circle or spiral. Once this intensive training stops, the plant resumes its normal growth habit, and new stems grow straight up from the decoratively twisted portion of the plant.

Lucky bamboo will grow for years in a vase with an inch or so of chlorine-free water in the

Lucky bamboo (aka Belgian evergreen, Chinese water bamboo, curly bamboo, friendship bamboo, Goddess of Mercy plant, ribbon dracaena, ribbon plant, Sander's dracaena).

bottom along with a few marbles or pebbles to stabilize the plant. Change the water once a week and keep it free of fallen leaves, which will rot and infect your plant. The chlorine in tap water causes the leaves to turn yellow and drop, so use bottled or filtered water. Give it a drop or two of liquid fertilizer and it will be happy. You can also grow this plant in potting medium in a container, just as you would any other houseplant.

OPTIMUM HOUSEHOLD ENVIRONMENT

Read the Introduction for the specifics of each recommendation.

LOW LIGHT. Bright but indirect light from a north window or skylight works very well for lucky bamboo. Some even survive windowless bathrooms! This cannot be recommended as a general policy, but it just goes to show how tough this plant is. Avoid direct sunlight; it will burn the foliage.

MODERATE TEMPERATURE. Daytime 70 to 80°F, nighttime 60 to 70°F.

MODERATE WATER. If you're growing lucky bamboo in potting medium, water whenever the top of the potting medium becomes dry to a depth of 1 inch. If you're growing it in water, keep the water about 1 inch deep and change it every week. Use filtered water. This plant is sensitive to the chlorine in tap water.

HUMIDITY. Mist your plant twice a week with a spray bottle of water on a mist setting, or use a handheld mister. Put the pot in a saucer or tray of water, making sure the bottom of the pot never sits directly in the water by raising the pot up on pot feet or pebbles.

POTTING MEDIUM. Use any good organic, well-drained, general-purpose potting soil that incorporates organic fertilizer, mycorrhizal fungi, and other beneficial microbes.

FERTILIZER. Use any organic fertilizer where the first number (nitrogen) is higher than the other two. For plants in potting medium, use either a powder or a liquid formulation. For plants grown in water, use one drop of fertilizer in the vase of water every other month.

POTTING. Lucky bamboo grows very slowly and can live in the same container for years. When your plant needs up-potting, shift it to a container with a diameter 2 inches larger than the current pot.

PROPAGATION. Lucky bamboo is easy to propagate from stem tip cuttings and stem cuttings.

COMMON PROBLEMS

Watch for brown leaf tips (page 246), mealybugs (page 262), and root rot (page 272).

Nerve plant

Nerve plant (*Fittonia albivenis*) is a creeping houseplant grown for its dramatic evergreen foliage. Each leaf displays an intricate, lace-like network of veins in white, magenta-pink, or red that contrasts beautifully with the dark olive-green background. The resulting intense color patterns invite closer inspection. It's a small plant, only 6 inches high and 12 inches wide, with egg-shaped leaves to 4.5 inches long. Flowers rarely appear and are not showy if

Nerve plant (aka mosaic plant, painted net leaf, silver net leaf).

they do. Most people just cut the flower spikes off the plants because the spikes actually detract from the attractive foliage. There are two different groups of nerve plant. The Verschaffeltii Group has dark green leaves with pink to red veins. The Argyroneura Group has dark green leaves with white veins.

Nerve plant, like a temperamental opera star, needs attentive coddling to perform. This little diva is at its best in the constant moisture and high humidity of dish gardens and terrariums. Treat it like a common, ordinary houseplant, kept in a pot by itself sitting on a table, and it may have a hissy fit, reacting badly to the dry air of your home. It is possible to have this plant do well for you outside of a terrarium, but you will need to be extra attentive in meeting its demands for humidity and water.

OPTIMUM HOUSEHOLD ENVIRONMENT

Read the Introduction for the specifics of each recommendation.

MEDIUM LIGHT. Bright filtered light, or artificial light, is best for nerve plant.

LOW TEMPERATURE. Daytime 65 to 75°F, nighttime 55 to 65°F.

AMPLE WATER. Water whenever the top of the potting medium becomes dry to a depth of 0.5 inch. This plant will faint or collapse completely if it dries out at all so keep it well watered. Just make sure it also has good drainage.

HUMIDITY. Nerve plant needs high humidity and is very successful in a terrarium. If your plant is not in a terrarium, mist it daily with a spray bottle of water on a mist setting, or use a handheld mister. Put the pot in a saucer or tray of water, making sure the bottom of the pot never sits directly in the water by raising the pot up on pot feet or pebbles. Consider putting a humidifier in the room.

POTTING MEDIUM. Use any good organic, well-drained, general-purpose potting soil that incorporates organic fertilizer, mycorrhizal fungi, and other beneficial microbes.

FERTILIZER. Use any organic fertilizer, in either a powder or liquid formulation, where the first number (nitrogen) is higher than the other two. Apply once a month.

POTTING. When your plant needs up-potting, shift it to a container with a diameter 2 inches larger than the current pot.

PROPAGATION. Nerve plant is easy to propagate from stem tip cuttings.

COMMON PROBLEMS

Watch for plant collapse (page 252), aphids (page 260), and root rot (page 272).

Peace lily

Peace lilies (*Spathiphyllum* spp.), like so many aroids, are among the easiest and most reliable of all houseplants, blooming regularly with minimum fuss and tolerating a certain amount of benign neglect with aplomb. If your plant wilts because you forgot to water it, it will bounce right back after a good soaking. Dozens of cultivars are available. Some grow into large robust plants to 2 to 3 feet tall and wide. Others are miniatures that stay under 1 foot tall and wide.

Peace lilies have no aboveground stems. The cluster of evergreen leaves arises like a crown directly from underground rhizomes. The leaves are borne on long, thin stalks from 6 to 24 inches long depending on the cultivar. The oval, pointed leaf blades are glossy deep green and attractively ribbed with prominent veins. In larger cultivars the blades can be 10 inches wide; smaller cultivars have correspondingly smaller blades to 3 inches wide. Plants generally flower in spring. A showy leaf-like spathe surrounds a finger-like spadix, covered with tiny, almost

Peace lily (aka closet plant, white sails).

microscopic flowers. The spathe is usually white but may also be green or pale yellowish on the backside. The spathes are held well above the foliage on long, thin stalks.

❗ This plant is toxic to people and pets and should be kept in an out-of-the-way place. Its tissues contain calcium oxalate crystals, and if leaves are chewed the crystals penetrate the soft tissues of lips, tongue, and throat, causing painful swelling, drooling, and vomiting. If you suspect a person or pet has ingested parts of this plant, or if a person or pet exhibits serious symptoms such as difficulty breathing, call your local emergency hotline, poison control center, or vet.

OPTIMUM HOUSEHOLD ENVIRONMENT

Read the Introduction for the specifics of each recommendation.

MEDIUM LIGHT. Peace lily thrives in bright filtered light. It cannot tolerate full sun. It will even do well in low light from a north window or skylight.

MODERATE TEMPERATURE. Daytime 70 to 80°F, nighttime 60 to 70°F.

MODERATE WATER. Water whenever the top of the potting medium becomes dry to a depth of 1 inch. Peace lilies can be sensitive to the chlorine in tap water so filtered or bottled water is a better choice.

HUMIDITY. Mist your plant regularly with a spray bottle of water on a mist setting, or use a hand-held mister. Put the pot in a saucer or tray of water, making sure the bottom of the pot never sits directly in the water by raising the pot up on pot feet or pebbles.

POTTING MEDIUM. Use any good organic, well-drained, general-purpose potting soil that incorporates organic fertilizer, mycorrhizal fungi, and other beneficial microbes.

FERTILIZER. Use any balanced organic fertilizer. Apply at half-strength once a month through the growing season.

POTTING. When your plant needs up-potting, shift it to a container with a diameter 4 inches larger than the current pot.

PROPAGATION. Peace lily is easy to propagate by division of the rhizome.

COMMON PROBLEMS
Watch for sunburn (page 256), mealybugs (page 262), and root rot (page 272).

Peacock plant

The aptly named peacock plant struts its striking evergreen foliage with panache. Commonly grown species include *Calathea lancifolia, C. makoyana, C. rufibarba,* and *C. zebrina.* These tropical beauties and their numerous hybrids can be a little demanding with their water and humidity needs but are well worth the effort. Plants form clumps from 2 to 4.5 feet tall and wide. The slender stems bear large, distinctively patterned leaves, pale green on dark green or vice versa, that spiral around the stem. Although the leaves are very beautiful, they are also very tough. In some varieties the leaf blades are oval, 4 to 8 inches long and 6 inches wide. Other varieties have narrow, lance-shaped leaves up to 16 inches long with rippled, undulating leaf

Peacock plant (aka calathea, prayer plant, rattlesnake plant, zebra plant).

margins. On all peacock plants, newly emerging leaves are rolled into a cylinder and each handsome, attractively variegated leaf has a red-purple underside. Flowers are insignificant in most species and hybrids.

OPTIMUM HOUSEHOLD ENVIRONMENT
Read the Introduction for the specifics of each recommendation.

MEDIUM LIGHT. Filtered light is best for peacock plant. Avoid direct sun as the leaves are easily burned.

MODERATE TEMPERATURE. Daytime 70 to 80°F, nighttime 60 to 70°F.

AMPLE WATER. Water whenever the top of the potting medium becomes dry to a depth of 0.5 inch. Use filtered or even distilled water because peacock plant is sensitive to fluoride, chlorine, and salts in tap water. Although this plant wants a lot of water, it also requires good drainage and will not tolerate waterlogged soil.

HUMIDITY. Peacock plant needs high humidity. Mist your plant daily with a spray bottle of water on a mist setting, use a handheld mister, or put a humidifier in the room. Put the pot in a saucer or tray of water, making sure the bottom of the pot never sits directly in the water by raising the pot up on pot feet or pebbles.

POTTING MEDIUM. Use any good organic, well-drained, general-purpose potting soil that incorporates organic fertilizer, mycorrhizal fungi, and other beneficial microbes.

FERTILIZER. Use any organic fertilizer, in either a powder or liquid formulation, where the first number (nitrogen) is higher than the other two. Apply once a month year-round.

POTTING. When your plant needs up-potting, shift it to a container with a diameter 4 inches larger than the current pot.

PROPAGATION. Peacock plant is propagated by division, but it can be fussy. Divide only really large, crowded plants and do it in the spring. Expect the plant to sulk after this operation.

COMMON PROBLEMS

Watch for leaves turning brown (page 251), spider mites (page 263), and root rot (page 272).

Peperomia

Peperomias are well worth growing for their attractive evergreen leaves. They are quietly undemanding, not at all flashy or flamboyant,

Peperomia (aka baby rubber plant, radiator plant, watermelon peperomia).

and because they tolerate a wide range of environmental conditions, they are easy to keep as houseplants. The most commonly cultivated species are *Peperomia argyreia*, *P. caperata*, and *P. obtusifolia*. Plants are small and compact, less than 12 inches tall and wide. Flowers are microscopic and tightly packed by the hundreds onto whitish rat-tail-like conical structures—interesting curiosities, perhaps, but not at all showy. It is the foliage that is the reason to grow these plants. Some peperomias have small, heart-shaped leaves; others have longer, oval leaves. Sometimes the veins of the leaves are lined with silver. In other forms the leaf is deeply corrugated or waffled, and in still others the leaves are variegated with creamy yellowish patches. In all, the leaves are thick and waxy, and the stems are fat and slightly succulent, which might lead you to think these are dought-tolerant plants, but you would be wrong. These tropical beauties are not adapted to arid environments.

Read the Introduction for the specifics of each recommendation.

MEDIUM LIGHT. Bright filtered light from an east window or even the low light of a north window suits these plants perfectly. They also do very well under artificial lights.

MODERATE TEMPERATURE. Daytime 70 to 80°F, nighttime 60 to 70°F.

AMPLE WATER. Water whenever the top of the potting medium becomes dry to a depth of 0.5 inch.

HUMIDITY. Mist your plant regularly with a spray bottle of water on a mist setting, or use a hand-held mister. Put the pot in a saucer or tray of water, making sure the bottom of the pot never sits directly in the water by raising the pot up on pot feet or pebbles.

POTTING MEDIUM. Use any good organic, well-drained, general-purpose potting soil that incorporates organic fertilizer, mycorrhizal fungi, and other beneficial microbes.

FERTILIZER. Use any organic fertilizer, in either a powder or liquid formulation, where the first number (nitrogen) is higher than the other two. Apply at half-strength every two weeks through the growing season, once a month in winter.

POTTING. When your plant needs up-potting, shift it to a container with a diameter 2 inches larger than the current pot. These plants are small so keep the pots small as well. Putting them in too large a pot will lead to root rot.

PROPAGATION. *Peperomia obtusifolia* is easy to propagate from stem tip cuttings in spring. Propagate *P. argyreia* and *P. caperata* by leaf cuttings.

COMMON PROBLEMS

Watch for edema (page 247), mealybugs (page 262), and root rot (page 272).

Piggy-back plant

Most good houseplants are tropical, adapted to warm nighttime temperatures and rainforest conditions. Piggy-back plant (*Tolmiea menziesii*) is an exception. The maritime climate from which this native Pacific Northwesterner hails is very different from the typical home environment, and yet piggy-back plant holds its own as a houseplant. Its tiny inconspicuous flowers are reddish brown and carried on 1- to 2-foot-tall stems. The softly hairy foliage is roughly heart-shaped with scalloped and lobed edges. The leaves, 2 to 5 inches long, are borne on hairy leaf

Piggy-back plant (aka hedge nettle, thousand mothers, youth-on-age).

stalks that likewise vary in length. Leaf color is typically bright medium green, but variegated cultivars are available. Piggy-back plant has the distinctive habit of growing new baby plantlets where the leaf stalk joins the leaf blade. As these baby plantlets grow larger, they form little plantlets of their own, and the result is a cascading chain of foliage. These long chains of leaves, with plantlets attached, are especially attractive dangling from a hanging basket.

Some people are sensitive to the hairs on the leaves and stems of piggy-back plant, from which they can acquire a contact dermatitis. If you think you might be sensitive, or just want to be cautious, wear gloves when handling this plant.

OPTIMUM HOUSEHOLD ENVIRONMENT

Read the Introduction for the specifics of each recommendation.

MEDIUM LIGHT. Filtered light with no direct sun suits piggy-back plant best.

LOW TEMPERATURE. Daytime 65 to 75°F, nighttime 55 to 65°F.

MODERATE WATER. Water whenever the top of the potting medium becomes dry to a depth of 1 inch.

HUMIDITY. Mist your plant occasionally with a spray bottle of water on a mist setting, or use a handheld mister. Put the pot in a saucer or tray of water, making sure the bottom of the pot never sits directly in the water by raising the pot up on pot feet or pebbles.

POTTING MEDIUM. Use any good organic, general-purpose potting soil that incorporates organic fertilizer, mycorrhizal fungi, and other beneficial microbes.

FERTILIZER. Use any balanced organic fertilizer. Apply every two weeks through the growing season and monthly in winter.

POTTING. When your plant needs up-potting, shift it to a container with a diameter 2 inches larger than the current pot.

PROPAGATION. Piggy-back plant is easy to propagate from leaf cuttings and by division of the rhizome.

COMMON PROBLEMS

Watch for brown leaf tips (page 246) and spider mites (page 263).

Poinsettia

A major contributor to poinsettia's popularity is the fact that it can be brought into bloom at will by growers simply by manipulating daylength. This, in combination with flaming red "flowers" and deep green leaves, more or less predestined poinsettia (*Euphorbia pulcherrima*) to become wildly popular during the winter holiday season. It is ubiquitous across North America in homes, offices, public buildings, and churches every December. So popular, in fact, that 75 million poinsettias are sold every year. The actual flowers of poinsettia are inconspicuous, grouped into little yellow clusters and hidden in the heart of the plant. But they are surrounded by the large brilliant scarlet bracts (modified leaves) that make the plants irresistible at Christmas time.

Poinsettias are tropical evergreen shrubs with slender woody stems that can bloom when only 12 to 18 inches tall. They get larger over the years, though, if given the chance and a suitably large pot. A 3-foot-wide container can hold a 7-foot-tall specimen. Poinsettia leaves and bracts are 3 to 6.5 inches long and coarsely serrate along the margins with soft, broad teeth. When the plant is in bloom, the bracts in the upper part of the plant, the ones surrounding the tiny flowers, turn bright red, pink, white— any color other than dark green. Recent years

Poinsettia (aka Christmas star, lobsterplant, Mexican flameleaf).

flowering; and the night cannot be interrupted by flashlights, streetlights, or headlights. After ten weeks of these long nights, the plant flowers.

A lot of people are concerned about the poinsettia being poisonous to pets, but the truth is that it's only mildly toxic and not nearly as much of a concern as other seasonal threats, like mistletoe or holly.

OPTIMUM HOUSEHOLD ENVIRONMENT

Read the Introduction for the specifics of each recommendation.

MEDIUM LIGHT. Poinsettia prefers bright filtered light.

MODERATE TEMPERATURE. Daytime 70 to 80°F, nighttime 60 to 70°F.

AMPLE WATER. Water whenever the top of the potting medium becomes dry to a depth of 0.5 inch.

HUMIDITY. Put the pot in a saucer or tray of water, making sure the bottom of the pot never sits directly in the water by raising the pot up on pot feet or pebbles.

POTTING MEDIUM. Use any good organic, well-drained, general-purpose potting soil that incorporates organic fertilizer, mycorrhizal fungi, and other beneficial microbes.

FERTILIZER. Use any organic fertilizer, in either a powder or liquid formulation, where the second number (phosphorus) is higher than the other two to promote flowering. Apply once a month.

POTTING. When your plant needs up-potting, shift it to a container with a diameter 4 inches larger than the current pot.

PROPAGATION. Poinsettia is easy to propagate from stem tip cuttings taken in July and grown in shade.

COMMON PROBLEMS

Watch for leaf drop (page 249), whiteflies (page 265), and root rot (page 272).

have seen the development of varieties with cream, orange, pale green, and marbled/variegated bracts.

For most people, the poinsettia is a temporary houseplant that either ends up on the compost pile after the holidays or is planted out in the garden, if they happen to live in a frost-free area. But many keep poinsettias indoors year-round and bring them into bloom regularly. To initiate bloom at any time through the year, put your poinsettia into a light-free space, like a closet, every night from 5pm to 7am the next morning. Then bring it into light during the daytime. Poinsettias need 14-hour nights to initiate

Polka dot plant

The short-lived polka dot plant (*Hypoestes phyllostachya*) is grown for its unusual and often colorful foliage. The 2-inch-long leaves look almost as though they've been painted with white, red, or (the favorite) pink enamel, shot through with green veins and random green polka dots. As a houseplant, polka dot plant will perform well for you for the first year, growing into a loose-limbed little bush about 2 feet high, but in its second year it may try to flower and, if it does, it will deteriorate rapidly and either go dormant or die. Since tighter, bushier plants have more leaves, pinch out the tips of stems that grow more than 10 inches long to encourage side branching and bushiness. More foliage means a more colorful and dramatic impact. The inconspicuous lavender flowers are borne on 6-inch-long spikes. Pinching off these flower spikes keeps the plant going for a while, but it seems that once flowering has been initiated the plant is pretty much on a downhill slide.

Polka dot plant (aka freckle face, measles plant, pink polka-dot plant).

OPTIMUM HOUSEHOLD ENVIRONMENT

Read the Introduction for the specifics of each recommendation.

HIGH LIGHT. This plant requires bright indirect light or filtered direct sun to develop the most colorful foliage. If it doesn't get enough light the leaves gradually turn green; if it's getting too much light the leaf tips will turn brown.

MODERATE TEMPERATURE. Daytime 70 to 80°F, nighttime 60 to 70°F.

MODERATE WATER. Water whenever the top of the potting medium becomes dry to a depth of 1 inch.

HUMIDITY. Put the pot in a saucer or tray of water, making sure the bottom of the pot never sits directly in the water by raising the pot up on pot feet or pebbles.

POTTING MEDIUM. Use any good organic, general-purpose potting soil that incorporates organic fertilizer, mycorrhizal fungi, and other beneficial microbes.

FERTILIZER. Use any balanced liquid organic fertilizer. Apply at half-strength every two weeks.

POTTING. When your plant needs up-potting, shift it to a container with a diameter 4 inches larger than the current pot.

PROPAGATION. Polka dot plant is easy to propagate from seed. Stem cuttings will eventually take root but are very slow to develop.

COMMON PROBLEMS

Watch for leaves changing color (page 249), whiteflies (page 265), and powdery mildew (page 272).

Prayer plant (aka maranta, herringbone plant, rabbit's foot).

Prayer plant

Prayer plant (*Maranta leuconeura*) is a low-growing, rhizomatous houseplant prized for its beautiful evergreen foliage. Whenever it gets dark, it rolls its striking leaves up into cylinders and holds them erect, as if in evening prayer. In the morning, or when you turn the lights on, the leaves unroll and lie flat again. You can watch prayer plant do its leaf-rolling trick by turning lights on and off, or moving the plant from light to dark and back to light again. This is even more fun than opening and closing the fridge door with your toddler to watch the light go on and off. The 5-inch-long, oval leaves are bizarrely marked with contrasting colors. Some cultivars (var. *kerchoviana*) have splotches of dark green that alternate down the midrib, suggesting rabbit tracks. Others (var. *erythroneura*) have patches of bright yellow green on a dark green background and bright red veins that curve gracefully from the midrib to the margins. Prayer plant grows to 12 inches tall and 16 inches wide and rarely flowers in the house, but this is no great loss. The small, white, and tubular flowers pale into insignificance beside the magnificent foliage. Prayer plant slows its growth in winter and takes a rest. Give it less water and fertilizer during its resting period. It will resume vigorous growth in the spring.

OPTIMUM HOUSEHOLD ENVIRONMENT

Read the Introduction for the specifics of each recommendation.

MEDIUM LIGHT. Filtered light from an east window is best. Prayer plant also does well with low light from a north window and artificial light.

MODERATE TEMPERATURE. Daytime 70 to 80°F, nighttime 60 to 70°F.

MODERATE WATER. Water whenever the top of the potting medium becomes dry to a depth of 1 inch.

HUMIDITY. Mist your plant several times a week with a spray bottle of water on a mist setting, or use a handheld mister. Put the pot in a saucer or tray of water, making sure the bottom of the pot never sits directly in the water by raising the pot up on pot feet or pebbles.

POTTING MEDIUM. Use any good organic, well-drained, general-purpose potting soil that incorporates organic fertilizer, mycorrhizal fungi, and other beneficial microbes.

FERTILIZER. Use any liquid organic fertilizer where the first number (nitrogen) is higher than the other two. Apply at half-strength every two weeks through the growing season, once a month in winter.

POTTING. Re-pot annually in spring. Prayer plant likes a lot of air around its roots so do not pack the potting medium tightly around it. When your plant needs up-potting, shift it to a container with a diameter 2 inches larger than the current pot.

PROPAGATION. Prayer plant is easy to propagate by division; however, it will sulk for a few weeks after this operation.

COMMON PROBLEMS

Watch for brown leaf tips (page 246) and spider mites (page 263).

Purple passion plant

Purple passion plant is a hybrid of two closely related species, *Gynura aurantiaca* and *G. procumbens*. Velvety soft amethyst-purple hairs cover the new growth and the dark green stems, and when the sun lights them up, this houseplant really stands out. It's a fast-growing evergreen to 20 inches tall and wide with weak stems that are woody at the base. As plants age the stems tend to sprawl and then trail. Some forms (often sold as *G. aurantiaca*) are more or less erect, especially in young plants. Others (often sold as *G. procumbens*) are vine-like with stems that hang down or trail, making them suitable for hanging baskets. Both forms are easy to grow. Coarsely toothed leaves to 8 inches long are dark green and somewhat egg-shaped with a broad base and a pointy tip. A white-variegated

Purple passion plant (aka velvet plant, purple velvet plant, royal velvet plant, purple passion vine).

cultivar is available; purple hairs give its white patches and blotches a pinkish purple cast.

Once your purple passion plant begins to bloom, it has reached maturity. Deep orange-yellow flowers perfectly complement the plant's overall psychedelic purple look, but they are small, and they smell so bad that most people cut them off. After the plant blooms it will start to decline. Be sure to start new plants from stem tip cuttings before the onset of flowering. When your new and vigorously growing cuttings are established you can transfer your old plant to the compost heap.

OPTIMUM HOUSEHOLD ENVIRONMENT

Read the Introduction for the specifics of each recommendation.

MEDIUM LIGHT. Bright filtered light through sheer curtains is perfect for this plant. The purple effect tends to fade in too much shade. If this happens, try giving the plant brighter light, but avoid full sun. Hot direct light will scorch the leaves.

LOW TEMPERATURE. Daytime 65 to 75°F, nighttime 55 to 65°F.

MODERATE WATER. Water whenever the top of the potting medium becomes dry to a depth of 1 inch. If the plant ever gets too dry it will wilt rapidly. Fortunately it recovers quickly when adequately rehydrated.

HUMIDITY. Avoid misting this plant. Its hairy leaves stay too wet too long when misted and present an open invitation to disease. Put the pot in a saucer or tray of water, making sure the bottom of the pot never sits directly in the water by raising the pot up on pot feet or pebbles.

POTTING MEDIUM. Use any good organic, well-drained, general-purpose potting soil that incorporates organic fertilizer, mycorrhizal fungi, and other beneficial microbes.

FERTILIZER. Use any organic fertilizer, in either a powder or liquid formulation, where the first number (nitrogen) is higher than the other two. Apply as directed on the package.

POTTING. When this fast-growing plant needs up-potting, shift it to a container with a diameter 4 inches larger than the current pot. Re-pot in spring, but if plants are more than two years old propagate new ones from stem tip cuttings.

PROPAGATION. Purple passion plant is easy to propagate from stem tip cuttings. Take your cuttings when your plant is mature but before it starts to flower.

COMMON PROBLEMS

Watch for sunburn (page 256), mealybugs (page 262), and gray mold (page 268).

Rex begonia

Begonia rex has been used extensively in hybridization with *B. masoniana* and other species and hybrids to give rise to the Rex Cultorum group of complex hybrids, known collectively as rex begonias. Rex begonias, with their showstopping foliage, are the kings of the begonia world. Shimmering colors reminiscent of fine ceramics on spiral-shaped leaves to 6 inches long are the hallmarks of these plants. Stunning patterns, ribbons, and marks of iridescent silver, glittering rose, and dark green and burgundy velvet create infinite variations from one plant to the next. Some have leaves with smooth margins and some have toothed, fringed, or lobed leaves. As with all begonias, leaves are asymmetrical. One side of the leaf is much longer and wider than the other side, which causes them to grow in a spiral or coil. The same phenomenon gives rise to the attractive but more sedate leaf shape of the angel wing begonias. Rex begonias kick it up a notch, however, and many have

Rex begonia (aka fancy-leafed begonia, iron cross, king begonia, painted-leaf begonia).

tightly coiled foliage. No two plants are alike, and most garden centers and nurseries offer a wealth of choices.

Flowers of rex begonias are pretty enough, but they're small, pink, and completely upstaged by the dramatic leaves. These evergreen perennials generally spread to 2 feet but are only half as tall, short enough to do well under artificial lights. Some go dormant in winter and will even drop their leaves. If your plant does this, let it rest. Don't let it dry out completely, but water it much less frequently and don't fertilize it when it's dormant. In the spring it will resume active growth and be drop-dead gorgeous once again.

OPTIMUM HOUSEHOLD ENVIRONMENT

Read the Introduction for the specifics of each recommendation.

MEDIUM LIGHT. Light from an east window filtered by sheer curtains is ideal. Low light from a north window also works well, as does artificial light. Do not put rex begonias in direct hot sun because it will burn the foliage.

MODERATE TEMPERATURE. Daytime 70 to 80°F, nighttime 60 to 70°F.

MODERATE WATER. Water whenever the top of the potting medium becomes dry to a depth of 1 inch. Be careful not to overwater; these plants are susceptible to root rot.

HUMIDITY. Rex begonias want high humidity, but don't mist them because it encourages powdery mildew and gray mold. Put the pot in a saucer or tray of water, making sure the bottom of the pot never sits directly in the water by raising the pot up on pot feet or pebbles.

POTTING MEDIUM. Use any good organic, well-drained, general-purpose potting soil that incorporates organic fertilizer, mycorrhizal fungi, and other beneficial microbes.

FERTILIZER. Use any liquid organic fertilizer where the first number (nitrogen) is higher than the other two. Apply at half-strength every two weeks.

POTTING. When your plant needs up-potting, shift it to a container with a diameter 4 inches larger than the current pot. Use shallow pots for these beauties.

PROPAGATION. Rex begonias are easy to propagate by division of the rhizome and from leaf cuttings.

COMMON PROBLEMS

Watch for brown leaf tips (page 246), mealybugs (page 262), and powdery mildew (page 272).

Selloum

Selloum (*Philodendron bipinnatifidum*), like other *Philodendron* species, is an excellent houseplant, well adapted to the reduced light and warm nights of our homes. You'll also frequently find this plant in shopping malls, hospitals, and lobbies of public buildings, where it creates a tropical jungle ambiance. It's a big, bold plant, 3 to 6 feet tall and wide at maturity, so it commands considerable real estate in private homes and offices. Newer, more dwarf cultivars fit nicely into smaller spaces and are just as handsome as their big brothers.

Over time selloum develops a stout, short trunk, 3 to 4 feet tall and 4 to 5 inches thick. The trunk is crowned by huge leaves at the apex and develops a large number of rope-like aerial roots that sprout from the side of the trunk and snake their way down to the pot. The trunk is marked with an attractive characteristic pattern of "eye-drop" leaf scars, left by leaves that were discarded as the plant grew. The leaves are somewhat arrowhead-shaped, wide at the base and pointed at the tip, but are fringed with finger-like lobes along both sides. The lobing of the edges of the leaves is what gives the plant its airy, lace-like quality. The larger cultivars have leaf blades as much as 3 feet long and 2 feet wide on 18-inch stalks. Smaller cultivars have much smaller leaves with 1-foot-long blades on 8-inch stalks. It is very rare for this plant to flower indoors. The inflorescence is a small, pale green, funnel-shaped spathe surrounding a finger-like spadix covered with minute flowers. Female flowers near the base of the spadix form red berries after fertilization.

🛈 This plant is toxic to people and pets and should be kept in an out-of-the-way place. Its tissues contain calcium oxalate crystals, and if leaves are chewed the crystals penetrate the soft tissues of lips, tongue, and throat, causing painful swelling, drooling, and vomiting. If you suspect a person or pet has ingested parts of this plant, or if a person or pet exhibits serious symptoms such as difficulty breathing, call your local emergency hotline, poison control center, or vet.

Selloum (aka anchor philodendron, lacy-tree philodendron, tree philodendron).

OPTIMUM HOUSEHOLD ENVIRONMENT

Read the Introduction for the specifics of each recommendation.

MEDIUM LIGHT. Selloum tolerates full sun but does best with a half-day of morning sun from an east window. It also does very well with bright filtered light.

MODERATE TEMPERATURE. Daytime 70 to 80°F, nighttime 60 to 70°F.

MODERATE WATER. Water whenever the top of the potting medium becomes dry to a depth of 1 inch.

HUMIDITY. Mist your plant frequently with a spray bottle of water on a mist setting, or use a handheld mister. Put the pot in a saucer or tray of water, making sure the bottom of the pot never sits directly in the water by raising the pot up on pot feet or pebbles.

POTTING MEDIUM. Use any good organic, well-drained, general-purpose potting soil that incorporates organic fertilizer, mycorrhizal fungi, and other beneficial microbes.

FERTILIZER. Use any organic fertilizer, in either a powder or liquid formulation, where the first number (nitrogen) is higher than the other two. Apply once a month year-round.

POTTING. When your plant needs up-potting, shift it to a container with a diameter 4 inches larger than the current pot. Re-pot in spring and place the aerial roots in the potting medium.

PROPAGATION. Selloum can be propagated by potting up the pups that appear at the plant's base. Or decapitate the plant, making sure the leafy top has plenty of aerial roots to support it. The headless base of the plant will sprout new shoots.

COMMON PROBLEMS

Watch for yellowing leaves (page 257), aphids (page 260), and root rot (page 272).

Spider plant

Spider plant (*Chlorophytum comosum*) is a perennial favorite, among the most common, easy-to-grow, and undemanding of all house-plants. You frequently see it in hanging baskets, but it does just as well in pots on a table or desk. Numerous strap-shaped evergreen leaves, to 18 inches long and 1 inch wide, arise from thick, fleshy, tuberous roots, forming a clump to 2 feet tall and wide. Starry 1-inch-wide white flowers are carried on string-like stems that emerge from the center of the crown of grass-like foliage. The slender flowering stems continue to grow out and down, eventually developing little plantlets at their tips. Often the little plantlets produce stems with still more plantlets, so that the mother plant is characteristically surrounded by a cloud of dangling babies on chains as long as 3 feet. Plants less than one year old are too young to flower, but they'll flower in their second year. Flowering is initiated in the autumn, when days are short and nights are long. If your plant is in a room where you have the lights on at night, the plant's flowering response will be delayed or even aborted.

'Vittatum' has a broad white stripe down the middle of each leaf bordered on both sides by dark green ribbons. 'Variegatum' reverses that pattern with a broad green stripe down the middle of the leaf bordered on both sides by white. These white-striped forms are almost the only kinds available these days.

OPTIMUM HOUSEHOLD ENVIRONMENT

Read the Introduction for the specifics of each recommendation.

MEDIUM LIGHT. Spider plant does really well with bright filtered light. It tolerates a couple of hours of full sun from an east window, but

Spider plant (aka airplane plant, hen-and-chickens, ribbon plant).

the leaves will burn if they're exposed to too much sun.

MODERATE TEMPERATURE. Daytime 70 to 80°F, nighttime 60 to 70°F.

MODERATE WATER. Water whenever the top of the potting medium becomes dry to a depth of 1 inch. This plant is sensitive to fluoride so use bottled or distilled water if your tap water is fluoridated. If the leaf tips turn brown and you can rule out sunburn, try switching your water source.

HUMIDITY. Mist your plant occasionally with a spray bottle of water on a mist setting, or use a handheld mister. Put the pot in a saucer or tray of water, making sure the bottom of the pot never sits directly in the water by raising the pot up on pot feet or pebbles. If your plant's pot is inside a hanging basket and there is a saucer inside the basket under the pot, make sure the plant is not sitting in water by, again, raising the pot up on pot feet or pebbles.

POTTING MEDIUM. Use any good organic, well-drained, general-purpose potting soil that incorporates organic fertilizer, mycorrhizal fungi, and other beneficial microbes.

FERTILIZER. Use any organic fertilizer, in either a powder or liquid formulation, where the first number (nitrogen) is higher than the other two. Apply at half-strength every two weeks through the growing season, once a month in winter.

POTTING. When your young plant needs up-potting, shift it in spring to a container with a diameter 4 inches larger than the current pot. Handle the roots carefully; they are easily broken. Mature plants need re-potting only every two years.

PROPAGATION. Spider plant is easy to propagate by division or by layering the flowering stems.

COMMON PROBLEMS

Watch for leaves turning brown (page 251), spider mites (page 263), and root rot (page 272).

Streptocarpus

Gorgeous large flowers hover on wiry stems above a flat rosette of hairy, wrinkled leaves in these unusual plants. Many of these tropical evergreens are in cultivation, but the primary ones grown as houseplants are *Streptocarpus* ×*hybridus*. These complex hybrids derive from *S. dunnii*, *S. johannis*, and the miniature *S. cyanandrus*, among others. Plants are generally 12 to 18 inches tall and wide, including flower stalks, but some are tiny little miniatures, 3 to 6 inches tall and wide. Flower size and leaf size varies enormously, too, depending on which species occur in the plant's background. Rarely

Streptocarpus (aka Cape primrose).

More typical are flowers in blue, purple, red, pink, and white. Most have contrasting darker lines, stripes, and spots on the lower three lobes. Some are basically white with intense color on the edges of the lobes—a picotee effect. The flowers are held horizontally, facing away from the center of the plant. Flower stems originate from the base of the leaves. Another strange habit: many streptocarpus shed the upper half of a leaf in winter. The basal half of the leaf begins new growth in the spring. Most commonly available streps will have several hairy tongue-shaped leaves that grow close to the ground in a rosette; however, some kinds have only one leaf that grows continuously.

OPTIMUM HOUSEHOLD ENVIRONMENT

Read the Introduction for the specifics of each recommendation.

MEDIUM LIGHT. Bright light filtered by sheer curtains is best. Streptocarpus also does very well under artificial lights. The plants will tolerate a couple of hours of direct sun from an east window in the cool of the morning. But they suffer if they get too hot, and the leaves will burn if they're exposed to more than a couple of hours of full sunlight.

LOW TEMPERATURE. Daytime 65 to 75°F, nighttime 55 to 65°F. This plant likes cooler temperatures than other gesneriads.

LOW WATER. Water whenever the top of the potting medium becomes dry to a depth of 2 inches. Try to water just before the plant wilts but don't let it completely dry out. If you misjudge and the plant wilts it will rehydrate quickly and won't skip a beat once you have watered it. These plants do not tolerate soil that is too wet so keep them on the dry side.

HUMIDITY. Mist your plant twice a week with a spray bottle of water on a mist setting, or use a handheld mister. Put the pot in a saucer or

are streptocarpus offered in big box stores and supermarkets. You'll sometimes see them in local, independent garden centers, but if you look for them on the Internet you'll find a lot of reliable suppliers.

The velvety flowers of most modern hybrids are 3 inches long, and 2 inches wide at the mouth. Five petals fuse together into a trumpet-like tube that flares out into five lobes at the tip. The two upper lobes are a little smaller than the three lower lobes. The newest and harder to find colors are orange and yellow.

String of pearls (aka string of beads).

tray of water, making sure the bottom of the pot never sits directly in the water by raising the pot up on pot feet or pebbles.

POTTING MEDIUM. Use any good organic, well-drained, general-purpose potting soil that incorporates organic fertilizer, mycorrhizal fungi, and other beneficial microbes. Good drainage is key for streptocarpus. You can always add extra perlite to your potting medium to improve drainage if you have any doubts about it. Adding 1 part perlite to 3 parts general-purpose organic potting soil makes a good mix for this plant.

FERTILIZER. Use any liquid organic fertilizer where the second number (phosphorus) is higher than the other two to promote flowering. Apply at half-strength every two weeks through the growing season, once a month in winter.

POTTING. When your plant needs up-potting, shift it to a container with a diameter 2 inches larger than the current pot. Avoid deep pots for this shallow-rooted plant.

PROPAGATION. Streptocarpus is easy to propagate from leaf cuttings.

COMMON PROBLEMS

Watch for yellowing leaves (page 257), mealybugs (page 262), and gray mold (page 268).

String of pearls

String of pearls (*Senecio rowleyanus*) is a strange little desert succulent, a botanical oddity that looks exactly like its common name, except that the pearls are green—like a string of peas. Long, trailing, string-like stems hang down around all sides of the pot and it's the leaves, swollen, fleshy, and pea-like, that form the beads. Because of its trailing habit this plant is often grown in hanging baskets. String of pearl flowers are pale yellowish white, really not much to look at. But they have a surprisingly strong and delightful fragrance of cinnamon and allspice, with a little clove mixed in. The spaghetti-like stems lie flat on the ground and grow roots from the nodes so the plant eventually forms a mat to 3 feet wide. These same stems can get 3 feet long when allowed to cascade down all around the edges of the plant's container.

Internet rumor has it that the fleshy, bead-like leaves are poisonous to people and pets, but no authoritative scientific study to support this idea is ever cited. Both the ASPCA and the Humane Society now consider this plant non-toxic.

OPTIMUM HOUSEHOLD ENVIRONMENT

Read the Introduction for the specifics of each recommendation.

HIGH LIGHT. Full sun is ideal for this succulent, but it also tolerates bright filtered light.

MODERATE TEMPERATURE. Daytime 70 to 80°F, nighttime 60 to 70°F, during the growing season. In winter give it a cool rest at 55 to 65°F.

LOW WATER. Water whenever the top of the potting medium becomes dry to a depth of 2 inches.

HUMIDITY. This plant tolerates dry air very well.

POTTING MEDIUM. Use any good organic, well-drained, cactus potting medium that incorporates organic fertilizer, mycorrhizal fungi, and other beneficial microbes. You can make your own cactus mix by adding 1 part sand to 3 parts general-purpose organic potting soil.

FERTILIZER. Use any balanced organic fertilizer. Apply at half-strength once a month through the growing season. You probably don't need to fertilize in winter when the plant is not actively growing.

POTTING. When your plant needs up-potting, shift it to a container with a diameter 2 inches larger than the current pot. This plant is shallow-rooted so use a shallow pot.

PROPAGATION. String of pearls is easy to propagate from stem tip cuttings.

COMMON PROBLEMS

Watch for mealybugs (page 262) and root rot (page 272).

Zanzibar gem

In many ways Zanzibar gem (*Zamioculcas zamiifolia*) is the ideal houseplant. It's very slow growing, tough, easy to grow, low maintenance, and resistant to insect attack. In addition to all its maintenance merits, the plant is really pretty. This is an evergreen foliage plant, not grown for its flowers. Plants grow to 2 feet tall and wide from a thick, fleshy, underground, somewhat potato-like rhizome that stores water. A crown of glossy, thick, leathery, fern-like leaves arches gracefully out of the pot from the soil level. Each 2-foot-long leaf is pinnately compound (feather-like), with six or eight pairs of smooth, shiny, dark green leaflets. The leaves look and feel almost artificial they're so sturdy. But they give the plant an artistic, sculptural quality that enhances any decor. It is very rare for Zanzibar gem to flower indoors. If it does you'll see a small, yellow-green, funnel-shaped spathe surrounding a finger-like spadix covered with minute flowers. The inflorescence seems to sprout directly out of the soil at the base of the plant. Female flowers near the base of the spadix form berries after fertilization.

❶ This plant is toxic to people and pets and should be kept in an out-of-the-way place. Its tissues contain calcium oxalate crystals, and if leaves are chewed the crystals penetrate the

Zanzibar gem (aka aroid palm, eternity plant, fat boy, zz plant).

soft tissues of lips, tongue, and throat, causing painful swelling, drooling, and vomiting. If you suspect a person or pet has ingested parts of this plant, or if a person or pet exhibits serious symptoms such as difficulty breathing, call your local emergency hotline, poison control center, or vet.

OPTIMUM HOUSEHOLD ENVIRONMENT

Read the Introduction for the specifics of each recommendation.

MEDIUM LIGHT. Zanzibar gem performs best in bright filtered light. It tolerates low light from a north window, but it is more lush in brighter light. It will not tolerate direct sun, which will burn the foliage.

MODERATE TEMPERATURE. Daytime 70 to 80°F, nighttime 60 to 70°F.

LOW WATER. Water whenever the top of the potting medium becomes dry to a depth of 2 inches.

HUMIDITY. This plant tolerates dry air very well.

POTTING MEDIUM. Use any good organic, well-drained, cactus potting medium that incorporates organic fertilizer, mycorrhizal fungi, and other beneficial microbes. You can make your own cactus mix by adding 1 part sand to 3 parts general-purpose organic potting soil.

FERTILIZER. Use any organic fertilizer, in either a powder or liquid formulation, where the first number (nitrogen) is higher than the other two. Apply at half-strength every three months.

POTTING. When your plant needs up-potting, shift it to a container with a diameter 2 inches larger than the current pot.

PROPAGATION. Zanzibar gem is easy to propagate by division and from leaf cuttings.

COMMON PROBLEMS

Watch for yellowing leaves (page 257) and root rot (page 272).

Vines and
Vine-like Plants

Arrowhead plant

One of the easiest, lowest maintenance house-plants of all, arrowhead plant (*Syngonium podophyllum*) has been cultivated indoors for a long time. It is especially nice in hanging baskets, which show its gracefully draping vining stems to best advantage. Alternatively, it can be attached to upright moss-covered stakes and allowed to clamber all the way to the ceiling and back. Modern cultivars, however, have been selected for shorter, less rambunctious habits and are much more compact and less vine-like. Its leaves, which change shape and size as plants mature, are the primary reason for growing arrowhead plant. The plants most often seen for sale are youngsters with juvenile foliage to 6 inches long and 3 inches wide; these baby leaves are shaped like arrowheads and are simple, not compound. Mature leaves are palmately compound with five to 11 leaflets and grow to 15 inches long and 12 inches wide. The three largest leaflets point down and the two smaller leaflets point up. Most of the commonly available cultivars have foliage with varying degrees of white variegation. Some offer bright green leaves with crisp white veins; others have white patches covering most of the leaf. Newer cultivars add pinkish or bronze tones to the color range. It is very rare for arrowhead plant to flower indoors. The inflorescence is a scoop-shaped, greenish white spathe surrounding a finger-like spadix covered with very tiny flowers that look like little greenish white bumps. Female flowers near the base of the spadix form brown-black berries after fertilization.

❶ This plant is toxic to people and pets and should be kept in an out-of-the-way place. Its tissues contain calcium oxalate crystals, and if leaves are chewed the crystals penetrate the soft tissues of lips, tongue, and throat, causing painful swelling, drooling, and vomiting. If you

Arrowhead plant (aka African evergreen, American evergreen, arrowhead philodendron, arrowhead vine, goosefoot plant, nephthytis, syngonium).

suspect a person or pet has ingested parts of this plant, or if a person or pet exhibits serious symptoms such as difficulty breathing, call your local emergency hotline, poison control center, or vet.

OPTIMUM HOUSEHOLD ENVIRONMENT

Read the Introduction for the specifics of each recommendation.

MEDIUM LIGHT. Bright filtered light is best for arrowhead plant. It does not like full sun and too much light causes the leaves to lose color, becoming pale and limp.

MODERATE TEMPERATURE. Daytime 70 to 80°F, nighttime 60 to 70°F.

MODERATE WATER. Water whenever the top of the potting medium becomes dry to a depth of 1 inch. Strive to keep the soil slightly moist at all times but don't overwater. Water less often in winter.

HUMIDITY. This plant needs regular misting to raise humidity. Use a spray bottle of water on a mist setting, or use a handheld mister. Put the pot in a saucer or tray of water, making sure the bottom of the pot never sits directly in the water by raising the pot up on pot feet or pebbles.

POTTING MEDIUM. Use any good organic, well-drained, general-purpose potting soil that incorporates organic fertilizer, mycorrhizal fungi, and other beneficial microbes.

FERTILIZER. Use any organic fertilizer, in either a powder or liquid formulation, where the first number (nitrogen) is higher than the other two. Apply at half-strength every two weeks through the growing season, once a month in winter.

POTTING. When your plant needs up-potting, shift it to a container with a diameter 4 inches larger than the current pot. Re-pot in spring, but only every two years or so.

PROPAGATION. Arrowhead plant is easy to propagate from stem tip cuttings or by layering.

COMMON PROBLEMS

Watch for leaves changing color (page 249) and scale insects (page 262).

....

Blushing and heartleaf philodendrons

Philodendrons are superstars of the houseplant world. They've been popular for many decades, and deservedly so, because they're perfectly comfortable living in the same environments as humans. Not only are they lovely to look at,

Blushing philodendron (aka climbing philodendron).

they tolerate being moved with aplomb. You can relocate them from room to room or take them outside for a summer vacation without fearing they'll have a hissy fit and throw all their leaves on the ground. Two basic kinds of philodendrons, mounding and vining, are commonly grown as houseplants. The two discussed here have a vining habit.

Blushing philodendron (*Philodendron erubescens*) is a robust vine with waxy arrowhead-shaped leaves, up to 16 inches long and 8 inches wide, on bright red stems. In some cultivars, leaves are burgundy or red when young, turning greener as they mature. Blushing philodendron doesn't have tendrils, and it doesn't twine, so the stems need to be fastened to a sturdy stake or moss-covered pole for support. Once you have tied it to the pole, it will slowly wrap its aerial roots around the support. After several years of growth, it forms a mound or column 6 feet tall and 3 to 4 feet wide.

Heartleaf philodendron.

Heartleaf philodendron (*Philodendron hederaceum* var. *oxycardium*) is more finely textured and smaller than blushing philodendron. The 2- to 4-inch, rounded, heart-shaped leaves are borne on slender green stems that are lax and trailing. Cultivars with variegated leaves are available. Heartleaf philodendron does very well in a hanging basket or on a high shelf where its flexible stems can dangle down all around the container. The stems can also be fastened to a trellis or pole, easily climbing to 8 feet or more. Like blushing philodendron, heartleaf does not have tendrils and does not twine, so you have to tie it to the support. Once fastened, it will slowly attach itself to the support via its aerial rootlets.

It is very rare for these plants to flower indoors. The inflorescence is a small, scoop-shaped spathe surrounding a finger-like spadix covered with tiny flowers. Female flowers near the base of the spadix form berries after fertilization. In blushing philodendron the spathe is deep red and the flowers are fragrant. Heartleaf philodendron has white spathes.

🛈 These plants are toxic to people and pets and should be kept in an out-of-the-way place. Plant tissues contain calcium oxalate crystals, and if leaves are chewed the crystals penetrate the soft tissues of lips, tongue, and throat, causing painful swelling, drooling, and vomiting. If you suspect a person or pet has ingested parts of these plants, or if a person or pet exhibits serious symptoms such as difficulty breathing, call your local emergency hotline, poison control center, or vet.

OPTIMUM HOUSEHOLD ENVIRONMENT

Read the Introduction for the specifics of each recommendation.

MEDIUM LIGHT. Bright filtered light, artificial light, or low light works well for these very forgiving plants.

MODERATE TEMPERATURE. Daytime 70 to 80°F, nighttime 60 to 70°F.

MODERATE WATER. Water whenever the top of the potting medium becomes dry to a depth of 1 inch.

HUMIDITY. Mist your plant frequently with a spray bottle of water on a mist setting, or use a handheld mister. Not only will misting raise the humidity, it will also moisten the pole and stimulate the aerial roots. Put the pot in a saucer or tray of water, making sure the bottom of the pot never sits directly in the water by raising the pot up on pot feet or pebbles.

POTTING MEDIUM. Use any good organic, well-drained, general-purpose potting soil that incorporates organic fertilizer, mycorrhizal fungi, and other beneficial microbes.

FERTILIZER. Use any organic fertilizer, in either

a powder or liquid formulation, where the first number (nitrogen) is higher than the other two. Apply once a month through the growing season, every other month in winter.

POTTING. When your plant needs up-potting, shift it to a container with a diameter 4 inches larger than the current pot. Re-pot in spring or early summer every two years.

PROPAGATION. These philodendrons are easy to propagate from stem tip cuttings or by layering.

COMMON PROBLEMS

Watch for yellowing leaves (page 257), aphids (page 260), and root rot (page 272).

Creeping fig

Creeping fig (*Ficus pumila*) is a modest little woody evergreen vine that forms tiny roots all along its stems. Vigorous and fast-growing, it is perfectly capable of engulfing stone walls and covering houses in mild-winter regions (zones 9 through 11). As a houseplant, it will cover the pot's surface, crawl over the rim, and climb down its sides. Although it sounds like the blob that ate Chicago, this pretty tiny-leaved thing really is worthy of a place in any home. And besides, it's very easy to grow. It's a true fig, but the extremely inconspicuous flowers require pollination by an equally small wasp in order to make fruit. So don't expect any figs when it's grown indoors. The reason to grow this vine is for its beautiful little leaves. New leaves are only 1 inch long, heart-shaped, and reddish bronze at first, maturing to a longer and more leathery glossy, bright green. Cultivars offer white-variegated leaves, oak-leaf-shaped leaves, and ivy-shaped leaves. You'll need to prune this vigorous plant, whether its grown in a hanging basket, on a topiary form, or in an ordinary pot, to keep its size manageable. Happily, creeping fig tolerates pruning with aplomb. Prune it in spring and be aware that the stems have milky white sap, like all figs, which dries to rubber and sticks to your tools. Wipe your tools, and hands, with a damp cloth before the sap dries.

OPTIMUM HOUSEHOLD ENVIRONMENT

Read the Introduction for the specifics of each recommendation.

MEDIUM LIGHT. This plant does well with bright filtered light. It does not like full sun.

MODERATE TEMPERATURE. Daytime 70 to 80°F, nighttime 60 to 70°F.

MODERATE WATER. Water whenever the top of the potting medium becomes dry to a depth of 1 inch.

HUMIDITY. Creeping fig does well with average room humidity.

Creeping fig (aka climbing fig, creeping ficus, creeping rubber plant).

POTTING MEDIUM. Use any good organic, well-drained, general-purpose potting soil that incorporates organic fertilizer, mycorrhizal fungi, and other beneficial microbes.

FERTILIZER. Use any organic fertilizer, in either a powder or liquid formulation, where the first number (nitrogen) is higher than the other two. Apply once a month.

POTTING. When your plant needs up-potting, shift it to a container with a diameter 4 inches larger than the current pot.

PROPAGATION. Creeping fig is easy to propagate from stem tip cuttings.

COMMON PROBLEMS

Watch for leaves turning brown (page 251) and aphids (page 260).

Grape ivy (aka Venezuela treebine).

Grape ivy

Grape ivy (*Cissus alata*) is a tropical evergreen vine that climbs by means of tendrils. Indoors, in a pot, it can be kept to a manageable 2 feet tall with annual pruning in spring. Two other species, begonia vine (*C. discolor*) and kangaroo vine (*C. antarctica*), are also frequently seen as houseplants. All three are in the same family as the cultivated grape, genus *Vitis*. Flowers are tiny, inconspicuous, greenish, and borne in clusters like the flowers of grapes. They are so underwhelming you'd probably never notice them if your plant ever did flower, something it rarely does indoors. Because they are vines their stems are long and flexible, and they don't stand erect on their own. In order to grow tall they need something to climb on like trellises or bamboo stakes. Their tendrils coil around and hold tight to these supports and allow them to gain height to 10 feet or more. Otherwise, without a support of some kind, the stems hang gracefully down around the sides of the pot and are particularly attractive in hanging baskets. When young the stems of grape ivy and kangaroo vine are clothed in reddish brown fuzz that gradually disappears as the stems mature. The stems of begonia vine are smooth, not fuzzy.

Grape ivy and kangaroo vine have glossy, dark green, compound leaves with three leaflets. The individual leaflets are diamond-shaped and have coarse teeth around the edges. The upper surface of the mature leaflet is glossy and dark green while the undersurface has silky brown hair. Young leaves, like the stems, are clothed in brownish fuzz that disappears from the upper surface as the leaves age.

In begonia vine, the leaves are simple (not compound) and velvety (not glossy), and the leaf shape is a long, drawn-out, pointed heart. But it's the color that's the most dramatic difference. These leaves are painted burgundy over green with a herringbone pattern of shiny silver splashes between the veins. The colors are brightest and most dramatic in new, young leaves, tending to fade somewhat as the leaves mature. Underneath, the leaves are bright purple-red. The stems and tendrils are red too, adding another color note to the plant. Begonia vine is, however, much more fussy to grow than either grape ivy or kangaroo vine. It demands higher humidity and warmer, more tropical temperatures than its cousins.

You can keep all these vines smaller and bushier by pinching out the growing tips and forcing side branches to grow out. Another way to accomplish the same thing is to take stem tip cuttings and propagate more plants yourself.

OPTIMUM HOUSEHOLD ENVIRONMENT

Read the Introduction for the specifics of each recommendation.

MEDIUM LIGHT. Grape ivy, kangaroo vine, and begonia vine grow well with bright filtered light from an east window, or under artificial lights.

MODERATE TEMPERATURE. Daytime 70 to 80°F, nighttime 60 to 70°F. In winter grow grape ivy and kangaroo vine five degrees cooler, day and night. Begonia vine appreciates temperatures five degrees warmer in all seasons.

AMPLE WATER. During the growing season, water whenever the top of the potting medium becomes dry to a depth of 0.5 inch. Water less often in winter by waiting till the potting medium is dry to a depth of 1 inch.

HUMIDITY. All three vines really like high humidity. Mist your plant daily with a spray bottle of water on a mist setting, or use a handheld mister. Group other houseplants under and around your hanging baskets to raise the humidity. If your plant is not in a hanging basket, put the pot in a saucer or tray of water, making sure the bottom of the pot never sits directly in the water by raising the pot up on pot feet or pebbles.

POTTING MEDIUM. Use any good organic, well-drained, general-purpose potting soil that incorporates organic fertilizer, mycorrhizal fungi, and other beneficial microbes.

FERTILIZER. Use any organic fertilizer, in either a powder or liquid formulation, where the first number (nitrogen) is higher than the other two. Apply once a month.

POTTING. When your plant needs up-potting, shift it to a container with a diameter 4 inches larger than the current pot. Up-pot or re-pot in early summer and provide a trellis or other support for the plant to climb. Younger, smaller plants always look good in hanging baskets, but older, larger specimens do very well in large pots set on the floor.

PROPAGATION. All three vines are easy to propagate from stem tip cuttings.

COMMON PROBLEMS

Watch for brown leaf tips (page 246), aphids (page 260), and powdery mildew (page 272).

Ivy

Ivy (*Hedera helix*) can find a safe haven in any home, whether potted or rooted in a vase of water. It will grow happily in semi-darkness for months with zero attention or care. Many nurseries and garden centers also carry other super easy and equally low maintenance species, such as Algerian ivy (*H. algeriensis*), Irish ivy (*H. hibernica*), Japanese ivy (*H. rhombea*), Persian ivy (*H. colchica*), Nepal ivy (*H. nepalensis*), or Russian ivy (*H. pastuchovii*). Ivy starts life as a broadleaf evergreen vine. However, like a teenager, it alters its appearance and behavior dramatically when it reaches sexual maturity, turning itself into a bush and changing its leaf

Algerian ivy.

size and shape. Cuttings taken from the bushy adult remain shrubby; they're not capable of becoming vine-like again. Cuttings of the juvenile vines will remain juvenile for many years, probably indefinitely as houseplants indoors. Ivy should remain indoors, because it is highly invasive. It is illegal to even sell the wild species in Oregon, for example. But the more than 500 cultivars of *H. helix* are much more mannerly and well behaved. So long as they are maintained indoors, in their juvenile state, they are unable to flower. Thus, they are unable to form black berries (beloved by birds—and rats!) and escape cultivation through dissemination of their seeds. All can, of course, escape by rooting into the soil wherever a stem touches the ground, so watch your pots on summer vacations out of doors.

People treasure ivy as a houseplant for its attractive juvenile leaves. The leaves are glossy, dark green, leathery, and palmately lobed like a maple leaf. Leaf size varies between cultivars, with the normal size being 2 to 4 inches across. Small-leaf and miniature-leaf cultivars ('Needlepoint' and 'Needlepoint Miniature', for example) have leaves 1 to 2 inches across. Leaf shape varies from deeply lobed, to ruffled, arrow-shaped, or divided into leaflets. And leaf color varies from the standard glossy dark green to variegated with crisp white blotches or yellow patches.

❶ Ivy foliage is poisonous to people and pets if it is eaten in large quantities. It can also cause severe skin irritation (contact dermatitis) if the sap gets on the skin, so keep it in an out-of-the-way place. If you think a victim is in serious trouble, call your local emergency hotline, poison control center, or vet.

OPTIMUM HOUSEHOLD ENVIRONMENT

Read the Introduction for the specifics of each recommendation.

MEDIUM LIGHT. Bright filtered light serves these plants best. Avoid full sun.

LOW TEMPERATURE. Daytime 65 to 75°F, nighttime 55 to 65°F.

MODERATE WATER. Water whenever the top of the potting medium becomes dry to a depth of 1 inch.

HUMIDITY. Mist your plant occasionally, especially in hot weather, with a spray bottle of water on a mist setting, or use a handheld mister. Put the pot in a saucer or tray of water, making sure the bottom of the pot never sits directly in the water by raising the pot up on pot feet or pebbles.

POTTING MEDIUM. Use any good organic, well-drained, general-purpose potting soil that incorporates organic fertilizer, mycorrhizal fungi, and other beneficial microbes.

FERTILIZER. Use any organic fertilizer, in either a powder or liquid formulation, where the first number (nitrogen) is higher than the other two. Apply once a month.

POTTING. When your plant needs up-potting, shift it to a container with a diameter 2 inches larger than the current pot. Re-pot in spring or fall every two years.

PROPAGATION. Ivy is easy to propagate from stem tip cuttings.

COMMON PROBLEMS
Watch for leaves changing color (page 249), spider mites (page 263), and leaf spot fungus (page 269).

Jasmine

The attractive evergreen leaves of jasmine (*Jasminum polyanthum*) are pinnately compound (feather-like) with five to seven leaflets that are bright green on the upper surface and lighter green on the undersurface. Indoors, this robust

Jasmine (aka Chinese jasmine, pink jasmine, white jasmine, winter jasmine).

Because it tends toward rampant growth you'll likely want to prune it to keep it under control. Do your pruning in spring after flowering is finished. You can also pinch the stem tips during the growing season to encourage bushiness. But don't do any more pruning after late summer because it will be forming flower buds at that time, and you don't want to accidentally cut them off. The blossoming of jasmine is a delightful gift to brighten winter's gloom and remind us that spring is on the way. Dark red to bright pink buds give way to clusters of 1-inch-wide, trumpet-shaped, pure white, starry flowers in February. The flowers are scented, especially at night. The fragrance is not as powerful as Arabian jasmine (*J. sambac*), the one used to flavor tea, but is nevertheless strong and very pleasant. Arabian jasmine is also sometimes seen as a houseplant but is more finicky than jasmine and needs extra warmth and humidity.

Jasmine needs a cold treatment in order to set flower buds. Put your plant outdoors in the autumn for six weeks prior to your first killing frost. It will easily tolerate temperatures down to 40°F but don't let it get much colder than that. Jasmine also needs long nights. Make sure it is not exposed to any artificial light after sundown during the autumn cold treatment as that will also disrupt the initiation of flowering. Before your first frost, bring it back indoors; give it cool temperatures and indirect light until it flowers again in late winter.

OPTIMUM HOUSEHOLD ENVIRONMENT

Read the Introduction for the specifics of each recommendation.

HIGH LIGHT. Jasmine wants direct sun through the growing season in order to grow well and set abundant flower buds. It will tolerate a half-day of direct sun from an east window.

LOW TEMPERATURE. Daytime 65 to 75°F,

twining vine accommodates itself very well to a container, wrapping its stems around a support such as a trellis or bamboo stakes inserted into its pot. It will also grow in a hanging basket, latching onto the ropes or chains supporting the basket and climbing up to the ceiling. In addition, it lolls gracefully down all around the pot.

nighttime 55 to 65°F. Cool nighttime temperatures are critical in autumn in order to stimulate flowering.

AMPLE WATER. Water whenever the top of the potting medium becomes dry to a depth of 0.5 inch. Never let the soil dry out completely, but avoid soggy, waterlogged soil.

HUMIDITY. Mist jasmine frequently with a spray bottle of water on a mist setting, or use a handheld mister. Put the pot in a saucer or tray of water, making sure the bottom of the pot never sits directly in the water by raising the pot up on pot feet or pebbles. Consider putting a humidifier in the room.

POTTING MEDIUM. Use any good organic, well-drained, general-purpose potting soil that incorporates organic fertilizer, mycorrhizal fungi, and other beneficial microbes.

FERTILIZER. Use any organic fertilizer, in either a powder or liquid formulation, where the second number (phosphorus) is higher than the other two to promote flowering. Apply at half-strength every two weeks through the growing season to help set flower buds. Don't fertilize in winter.

POTTING. Re-pot annually in spring when it's finished flowering and after you've pruned it. Make sure jasmine has a trellis or bamboo stakes to climb. When it needs up-potting, shift it to a container with a diameter 4 inches larger than the current pot.

PROPAGATION. Jasmine is easy to propagate from stem tip cuttings.

COMMON PROBLEMS
Watch for failure to flower (page 247), mealybugs (page 262), and root rot (page 272).

Pothos

Pothos (*Epipremnum aureum*) is often considered the easiest and most foolproof of all houseplants. It has shiny, gold-flecked, heart-shaped leaves on trailing stems that get 8 feet long and dangle from a hanging basket or a container on a high shelf. Most are very sedate, graceful vines with leaves 2 to 4 inches across. Fastened to a support, pothos can easily cover a lot of territory. One office specimen in a 12-inch pot had stems more than 20 feet long! If your pothos gets too rambunctious and outgrows its allotted space, cut the stem tips back by removing up to a third of the stem's length. This will cause the remaining stem to branch and make it bushier. Use the severed stem tips as cuttings and root them to make new plants. Pothos is one of those intriguing aroids that changes leaf size and shape dramatically when it's given a chance

Pothos (aka Australian native monstera, centipede Tonga vine, devil's ivy, golden pothos, hunter's robe, ivy arum, money plant, silver vine, Solomon Islands ivy, taro vine).

to climb up a support. It is very rare for pothos to flower indoors. If yours flowers you will see a small, scoop-shaped spathe surrounding a finger-like spadix covered with minute flowers. Female flowers near the base of the spadix form berries after fertilization.

❶ This plant is toxic to people and pets and should be kept in an out-of-the-way place. Its tissues contain calcium oxalate crystals, and if leaves are chewed the crystals penetrate the soft tissues of lips, tongue, and throat, causing painful swelling, drooling, and vomiting. If you suspect a person or pet has ingested parts of this plant, or if a person or pet exhibits serious symptoms such as difficulty breathing, call your local emergency hotline, poison control center, or vet.

OPTIMUM HOUSEHOLD ENVIRONMENT

Read the Introduction for the specifics of each recommendation.

MEDIUM LIGHT. Bright filtered or artificial light is best for pothos. It will tolerate an hour or two of direct sun but too much sun will burn the leaves.

MODERATE TEMPERATURE. Daytime 70 to 80°F, nighttime 60 to 70°F.

MODERATE WATER. Water whenever the top of the potting medium becomes dry to a depth of 1 inch.

HUMIDITY. Mist pothos occasionally with a spray bottle of water on a mist setting, or use a hand-held mister. Put the pot in a saucer or tray of water, making sure the bottom of the pot never sits directly in the water by raising the pot up on pot feet or pebbles.

POTTING MEDIUM. Use any good organic, well-drained, general-purpose potting soil that incorporates organic fertilizer, mycorrhizal fungi, and other beneficial microbes.

FERTILIZER. Use any organic fertilizer, in either a powder or liquid formulation, where the first number (nitrogen) is higher than the other two. Apply every two weeks through the growing season, once a month in winter.

POTTING. Re-pot annually in spring. When pothos needs up-potting, shift it to a container with a diameter 2 inches larger than the current pot.

PROPAGATION. Pothos is easy to propagate from stem tip cuttings or by layering.

COMMON PROBLEMS

Watch for leaves changing color (page 249), mealybugs (page 262), and root rot (page 272).

Split-leaf philodendron

Split-leaf philodendron (*Monstera deliciosa*) is actually a monstera, a cousin of philodendrons. The genus name is a reference to the monstrous holes and slits in its foliage. Few houseplants evoke tropical jungles as effectively as this one. When you first acquire one it will likely be about 2 feet tall with lustrous green leaves 6 to 8 inches long. However, it does not stay small. After several years it will reach 6 to 8 feet tall with foot-long leaves. As your split-leaf philodendron grows, and you move it up to larger pots, the stems will get thicker and heavier, and it will need a sturdy support to climb. Small specimens are happy with a bamboo stake or a moss-covered pole. Like philodendrons and pothos, split-leaf philodendron grows aerial roots from its stems, and it will attach itself to the support with those roots. If it gets too rambunctious and outgrows its allotted space, cut the stem tips back by removing up to a third of the stem's length. This will cause the remaining stem to branch and make it bushier. Use the

Split-leaf philodendron (aka ceriman, cheese plant, fruit salad plant, Mexican breadfruit, monster fruit, monstera, Swiss cheese plant, windowleaf).

severed stem tips as cuttings and root them to make new plants. It is very rare for this plant to flower indoors, but in the wild, the inflorescence is a small, creamy white, scoop-shaped spathe surrounding a finger-like spadix covered with minute flowers. When fully ripe, the banana-like spadix is indeed "deliciosa"—it is edible and tastes like pineapple.

❶ This plant is toxic to people and pets and should be kept in an out-of-the-way place. Its tissues contain calcium oxalate crystals, and if leaves are chewed the crystals penetrate the soft tissues of lips, tongue, and throat, causing painful swelling, drooling, and vomiting. If you suspect a person or pet has ingested parts of this plant, or if a person or pet exhibits serious symptoms such as difficulty breathing, call your local emergency hotline, poison control center, or vet. The crystals are also present in the green, unripe fruit and it is not safe to eat until it is ripe. Wait until the fruit is fully ripe, aromatic, soft, and custardy before you attempt to eat it.

OPTIMUM HOUSEHOLD ENVIRONMENT

Read the Introduction for the specifics of each recommendation.

MEDIUM LIGHT. Bright filtered light with no direct sun suits split-leaf philodendron well.

MODERATE TEMPERATURE. Daytime 70 to 80°F, nighttime 60 to 70°F.

MODERATE WATER. Water whenever the top of the potting medium becomes dry to a depth of 1 inch.

HUMIDITY. Mist your split-leaf philodendron occasionally with a spray bottle of water on a mist setting, or use a handheld mister. Put the pot in a saucer or tray of water, making sure the bottom of the pot never sits directly in the water by raising the pot up on pot feet or pebbles.

POTTING MEDIUM. Use any good organic, well-drained, general-purpose potting soil that incorporates organic fertilizer, mycorrhizal fungi, and other beneficial microbes.

FERTILIZER. Use any organic fertilizer, in either a powder or liquid formulation, where the first number (nitrogen) is higher than the other two. Apply every two weeks during the growing season, once a month in winter.

POTTING. When your split-leaf philodendron

needs up-potting, shift it to a container with a diameter 4 inches larger than the current pot. As it grows it will need a very heavy pot to keep it from toppling over.

PROPAGATION. Split-leaf philodendron is easy to propagate from stem tip cuttings or by air layering.

COMMON PROBLEMS

Watch for brown leaf tips (page 246), mealybugs (page 262), and root rot (page 272).

Swedish ivy

Swedish ivy (*Plectranthus verticillatus*) is neither Swedish nor an ivy. It comes to us from southern Africa and is a lovely, fast-growing evergreen perennial that is very easy to grow as a houseplant. The plant is only 8 to 12 inches high, but its somewhat fleshy and semi-succulent stems spread 4 to 6 feet wide and trail as they mature. In a hanging basket its long, flexible stems dangle around its planter and are very attractive. They are clothed with lush, thick, glossy green leaves, 1.5 inches long and wide, with deep purple undersides. Some cultivars have all green leaves and some have leaves variegated in white. Flowers are whitish to pale lavender or pink with deep lavender freckles and have the typical two-lipped shape of most of their mint family relatives. Individual flowers are small, but they're borne in 8-inch-long upright clusters of many flowers. Flowers can appear any time of year but show up most frequently in spring or summer. Swedish ivy doesn't climb. It doesn't have tendrils, it doesn't twine, and it doesn't have aerial rootlets to grab onto a support. Basically, if you grew it outside in the garden it would be a groundcover.

OPTIMUM HOUSEHOLD ENVIRONMENT

Read the Introduction for the specifics of each recommendation.

MEDIUM LIGHT. Bright filtered light year-round with very little direct sun suits Swedish ivy best. It will tolerate a couple of hours of cool morning sun, but if leaves look dull and the plant seems to droop it's getting too much light. It will perk up in the shade.

(top) Swedish ivy (aka creeping Charlie, money plant, Swedish begonia, whorled plectranthus).

(above) Swedish ivy, flowers.

MODERATE TEMPERATURE. Daytime 70 to 80°F, nighttime 60 to 70°F.

MODERATE WATER. Water whenever the top of the potting medium becomes dry to a depth of 1 inch.

HUMIDITY. Mist Swedish ivy several times a week with a spray bottle of water on a mist setting, or use a handheld mister. If you have it in a pot rather than a hanging basket, put the pot in a saucer or tray of water, making sure the bottom of the pot never sits directly in the water by raising the pot up on pot feet or pebbles.

POTTING MEDIUM. Use any good organic, well-drained, general-purpose potting soil that incorporates organic fertilizer, mycorrhizal fungi, and other beneficial microbes.

FERTILIZER. Use any organic fertilizer, in either a powder or liquid formulation, where the first number (nitrogen) is higher than the other two. Apply every two weeks during the growing season, once a month in winter.

POTTING. Re-pot annually in spring. When your Swedish ivy needs up-potting, shift it to a container with a diameter 4 inches larger than the current pot.

PROPAGATION. Swedish ivy is easy to propagate from stem tip cuttings.

COMMON PROBLEMS

Watch for leaves changing color (page 249), spider mites (page 263), and root rot (page 272).

Wandering Jew (aka inch plant, purple heart, purple queen, river spiderwort, small-leaf spiderwort, wandering gypsy, wandering sailor, wandering tradescantia, wandering Willie), variegated form.

Wandering Jew

Three different wandering Jews are commonly seen as fast-growing, easy, excellent houseplants, valued for their ability to clean indoor air. All three are in the genus *Tradescantia* (spiderworts), characterized by three-petaled flowers, and all three need the same cultural conditions. Like the Israelites who wandered the desert for 40 years after their exodus from Egypt, these plants do, in fact, wander. They are so good at wandering that they are ranked as invasive noxious weeds in the U.S. South and in Australia.

Tradescantia fluminensis has 1-inch-wide white flowers. Its 1.5- to 2.5-inch-long leaves are egg-shaped, flat, green, shiny, smooth, and slightly succulent. The soft, hairless, fleshy stems are indefinite in length and wander across the ground, rooting at the nodes. In a hanging basket the green stems and leaves dangle gracefully all around the pot. Variegated cultivars are available.

Tradescantia pallida 'Purpurea' has 1.5-inch-wide bright pink flowers. Its 4- to 6-inch-long leaves are V-shaped, pointed, and violet-purple. The thick, somewhat succulent stems are also violet-purple and grow 6 to 9 inches tall. Stems are floppy, spreading to 18 inches, and trail across the ground, rooting as they go. In a hanging basket the plant forms a bright purple cascade.

Tradescantia zebrina has 1-inch-wide purple flowers. Its 2.5-inch-long leaves are flat, egg-shaped, and blue-green with two broad silvery stripes. The leaves are solid purple on the undersides. Plants typically grow about 6 inches tall and 2 feet wide and, just like the others, they plant themselves as they crawl across the ground. In hanging baskets they form a colorful display of green, purple, and silver.

OPTIMUM HOUSEHOLD ENVIRONMENT

Read the Introduction for the specifics of each recommendation.

MEDIUM LIGHT. Bright filtered light is best for *Tradescantia fluminensis* and *T. zebrina*. *Tradescantia pallida* 'Purpurea' does better and will be more brightly colored with a few hours of full sun.

MODERATE TEMPERATURE. Daytime 70 to 80°F, nighttime 60 to 70°F.

MODERATE WATER. Water whenever the top of the potting medium becomes dry to a depth of 1 inch.

HUMIDITY. These plants are somewhat drought tolerant and do not need to be misted.

POTTING MEDIUM. Use any good organic, well-drained, general-purpose potting soil that incorporates organic fertilizer, mycorrhizal fungi, and other beneficial microbes.

FERTILIZER. Use any organic fertilizer, in either a powder or liquid formulation, where the first number (nitrogen) is higher than the other two. Apply every two weeks through the growing season, once a month in winter.

POTTING. When wandering Jew needs up-potting, shift it to a container with a diameter 4 inches larger than the current pot. After two to three years it tends to shed its lower leaves and become unsightly. Cut it back heavily to rejuvenate it, or start new plants from stem tip cuttings and discard the old one.

PROPAGATION. Wandering Jew is easy to propagate from stem tip cuttings and by division.

COMMON PROBLEMS

Watch for brown leaf tips (page 246), aphids (page 260), and root rot (page 272).

Wax plant

People have cultivated wax plant (*Hoya carnosa*) for 200 years. That this semi-succulent subtropical vine so often survives neglect in doctor's offices and dim parlor corners is testament to its durability. You will be astonished when it transforms itself by bursting into fragrant bloom, even under adverse conditions. Wax plant twines up a trellis or other support, reaching 10 feet in height and 1 to 2 feet in width. Its stems twist around in a counterclockwise circle until they bump into something. When they touch an object they'll wrap themselves around it and corkscrew their way up to the top. Stems are clothed in pairs of handsome, dark green leaves up to 4 inches long. Leaves are so thick, firm, and waxy, they feel almost like plastic. Some cultivars have leaves variegated in creamy white or cream with a pink tinge.

The intricate jewel-like flowers seem not to belong to the sturdy vine that supports them. Each satiny flower, only 0.5 inch in diameter, is borne in a tight, crown-like cluster (umbel) of ten to 30 flowers. These clusters look like little nosegays. Flowers are white to very pale pink or dark pink, with a star-shaped red-orange corona in the center. Their sweet scent is heavenly. The

Wax plant (aka Hindu rope plant, honey plant, hoya, porcelain flower).

flower clusters are held on spurs (specialized short stems). Each spur is long-lived and flowers year after year, so don't remove them when you're deadheading your plant after flowering is finished. The flowers produce a lot of sugary sweet nectar to attract pollinators, and excess nectar sometimes drips out of the flowers and onto the floor. While your plant is developing flower buds or is actively blooming don't move it to a new location or try to re-pot it. It will freak out and drop all its flower buds.

OPTIMUM HOUSEHOLD ENVIRONMENT
Read the Introduction for the specifics of each recommendation.

MEDIUM LIGHT. Bright light filtered by sheer curtains or a half-day of morning sun from an east window provides enough light for wax plant to flower well. It will tolerate low light, meaning it won't die, but it won't flower for you either. Avoid hot afternoon summer sun, which will scorch the foliage.

MODERATE TEMPERATURE. Daytime 70 to 80°F, nighttime 60 to 70°F.

MODERATE WATER. Water whenever the top of the potting medium becomes dry to a depth of 1 inch.

HUMIDITY. Wax plant's thick, semi-succulent leaves tolerate dry air very well, so average home humidity is adequate.

POTTING MEDIUM. Use any good organic, well-drained, general-purpose potting soil that incorporates organic fertilizer, mycorrhizal fungi, and other beneficial microbes.

FERTILIZER. Use any organic fertilizer, in either a powder or liquid formulation, where the second number (phosphorus) is higher than the other two to promote flowering. Apply every two weeks through the growing season, once a month in winter.

POTTING. When wax plant needs up-potting, shift it to a container with a diameter 2 inches larger than the current pot. Hoyas have a reputation of blooming more reliably when they are slightly rootbound.

PROPAGATION. Wax plant is easy to propagate from stem tip cuttings or by layering. This plant has milky white sap that dries to rubber and will stain clothing and furniture. Use a damp cloth to wipe up the sap when you prune wax plant or take cuttings.

COMMON PROBLEMS
Watch for failure to flower (page 247), mealybugs (page 262), and root rot (page 272).

Ferns and
Fern-like Plants

Asparagus fern

Two very different looking houseplants share the common name asparagus fern. Neither is actually a fern, but both *Asparagus aethiopicus* and *A. densiflorus* really are asparagus, closely related to the popular vegetable. Both are low-maintenance, drought-tolerant evergreen perennials, with a cascading habit that makes them attractive subjects for hanging baskets. Their cut stems are often used as long-lasting greens in floral arrangements. The stems of *A. aethiopicus* tend to be more loose and floppy, cascading out of a hanging basket with the branchlets spreading wide. The 1-inch-long and 0.1-inch-wide needle-like "leaves" (technically, modified stems) also spread wide. The stems of *A. densiflorus* are more upright, very tightly columnar, like the tail of a fox. The stems have very short branchlets with small "leaves" all held close together like a bottlebrush. In a hanging basket this species is more stiffly erect, its stems arching gracefully out and away from the center. Its cultivar 'Myersii' has earned the Royal Horticultural Society's Award of Garden Merit.

Asparagus ferns have small greenish white flowers. The sexes are borne on separate plants, and only female plants make red berries. Plants are easily rejuvenated by pruning off old, decrepit stems at ground level; then they make brand new stems from the root system in the spring.

❶ Both ferns are toxic to people and pets and should be kept in an out-of-the-way place. If someone should eat the berries or foliage, gastrointestinal symptoms (diarrhea, vomiting, abdominal pain) can result. If you suspect a person or pet has ingested parts of these plants, call your local emergency hotline, poison control center, or vet.

Asparagus fern (aka emerald fern, lace fern, Sprenger's asparagus fern).

OPTIMUM HOUSEHOLD ENVIRONMENT

Read the Introduction for the specifics of each recommendation.

MEDIUM LIGHT. Bright filtered light is best for this plant. Avoid hot afternoon sun because it causes the leaves to turn yellow.

MODERATE TEMPERATURE. Daytime 70 to 80°F, nighttime 60 to 70°F.

MODERATE WATER. Asparagus ferns have thick, fleshy, tuberous roots that store water, so during the growing season, water whenever the top of the potting medium becomes dry to a depth of 1 inch. In winter, cut back on watering and wait till the top of the potting medium becomes dry to a depth of 2 inches, but don't let it dry out completely.

HUMIDITY. Asparagus fern prefers high humidity.

Foxtail fern (aka plume asparagus).

Mist your plant daily with a spray bottle of water on a mist setting, or use a handheld mister. Put the pot in a saucer or tray of water, making sure the bottom of the pot never sits directly in the water by raising the pot up on pot feet or pebbles.

POTTING MEDIUM. Use any good organic, well-drained, general-purpose potting soil that incorporates organic fertilizer, mycorrhizal fungi, and other beneficial microbes.

FERTILIZER. Use any liquid organic fertilizer where the first number (nitrogen) is higher than the other two. Apply at half-strength once a month through the growing season.

POTTING. When your fern needs up-potting, shift it to a container with a diameter 2 inches larger than the current pot. This plant prefers being slightly rootbound. Re-pot in spring after pruning off old stems to make way for new growth.

PROPAGATION. Asparagus fern is easy to propagate by division. Be sure that each division has several of the tuber-like roots.

COMMON PROBLEMS

Watch for yellowing leaves (page 257), spider mites (page 263), and leaf spot fungus (page 269).

Bird's nest fern

Bird's nest fern (*Asplenium nidus*) is a gorgeous true fern, though it doesn't look like one. Its long, strap-shaped leaves sprout directly from a very short, mostly underground rhizome. Leaves aren't divided or compound or even ferny. They are bright chartreuse-green, like a Granny Smith apple, and have a black midrib. Indoors in a pot, they'll easily get 2 feet tall. A dozen or more of these big beautiful leaves grow in a rosette from the crown at the soil line, arching out and away from the center like the spokes of a wheel. The overall shape of the plant is like a large basket, or a bird's nest, thus the common name. Leaf edges are smooth and, in some cultivars, rippled or undulating. Brown spots (sori) on the undersides of the leaves contain the spores by which this and all ferns reproduce. Those leaves that sporulate gradually turn brown and eventually die. The old, dead leaves curl up at the base of the plant, and you can just cut them off to keep your plant tidy and fresh-looking. Shiny new green leaves quickly replace old brown decrepit ones.

If you like to give your plants a summer vacation outdoors, watch this one carefully for snail and slug damage. Those creatures love to feast on ferns, and one snail can easily and quickly disfigure the gorgeous leaves. This fern is also

Bird's nest fern (aka Hawaii birdnest fern, nest fern).

sensitive to chemical sprays—insecticides, fungicides, leaf-polishing agents. Any chemical other than insecticidal soap, in fact, causes a phytotoxic reaction that burns the foliage and turns the leaves brown.

OPTIMUM HOUSEHOLD ENVIRONMENT

Read the Introduction for the specifics of each recommendation.

MEDIUM LIGHT. This plant prefers moderately bright filtered light and will even tolerate quite a bit of shade in low light conditions. However, it will not tolerate full sun.

MODERATE TEMPERATURE. Daytime 70 to 80°F, nighttime 60 to 70°F.

AMPLE WATER. Water whenever the top of the potting medium becomes dry to a depth of 0.5 inch. This fern needs a lot of water but fares poorly if the soil is soggy.

HUMIDITY. This plant needs high humidity. Mist it daily with a spray bottle of water on a mist setting, or use a handheld mister. Put the pot in a saucer or tray of water, making sure the bottom of the pot never sits directly in the water by raising the pot up on pot feet or pebbles. Consider putting a humidifier in the room and growing this fern with orchids and bromeliads.

POTTING MEDIUM. Use any potting medium designed for semi-terrestrial orchids, one that incorporates organic fertilizer, mycorrhizal fungi, and other beneficial microbes. Be sure it is rich in organic matter yet very well drained.

FERTILIZER. Use any liquid organic fertilizer

where the first number (nitrogen) is higher than the other two. Apply at half-strength every two weeks through the growing season.

POTTING. When your plant needs up-potting, shift it to a container with a diameter 2 inches larger than the current pot. Even though you're using smallish pots, choose heavy ones to prevent these top-heavy plants from toppling over.

PROPAGATION. Bird's nest fern can't be divided and has to be raised from spores, a difficult task for the average houseplant grower.

COMMON PROBLEMS

Watch for leaves turning brown (page 251) and scale insects (page 262).

Boston fern (aka Boston swordfern, fishbone fern, tuber ladder fern, wild Boston fern).

Boston fern

Boston fern (*Nephrolepis exaltata*) is the classic parlor fern: its long, bright green leaves curve gracefully out of a container or hanging basket, adding simple homespun charm to any room. All plants in cultivation are natural mutations of the species. The original mutant, 'Bostoniensis', was discovered in 1894 in a shipment of ferns sent to Boston by a Philadelphia grower. In contrast to the species, which has upright fronds, its fronds dangled down and away from the central crown. Since then other mutations with curly, twisted, drooping, or doubly-pinnate fronds have appeared (e.g., 'Florida Ruffle', 'Fluffy Duffy', 'Compacta'). Plants generally grow to 3 feet tall and wide, but the leaves can be 2 to 7 feet long depending on the cultivar. Leaves are pinnately compound (feather-like) with 1- to 3-inch-long wedge-shaped pinnae (leaflets) alternating on each side of the midrib. This evergreen perennial is a true fern, reproducing by means of spores, so it does not make flowers, fruits, or seeds.

OPTIMUM HOUSEHOLD ENVIRONMENT

Read the Introduction for the specifics of each recommendation.

HIGH LIGHT. Bright but indirect light from a south window and no direct sun fulfills this plant's needs.

MODERATE TEMPERATURE. Daytime 70 to 80°F, nighttime 60 to 70°F.

MODERATE WATER. Water whenever the top of the potting medium becomes dry to a depth of 1 inch. This plant needs constant moisture but you don't want to drown it. Just make sure it never dries out or it will drop all its leaves.

HUMIDITY. Mist your plant twice a week with a spray bottle of water on a mist setting, or use a handheld mister. Put the pot in a saucer or tray of water, making sure the bottom of the pot never sits directly in the water by raising the pot up on pot feet or pebbles. Or put a humidifier in the room.

POTTING MEDIUM. Use any good organic, well-drained, general-purpose potting soil that incorporates organic fertilizer, mycorrhizal fungi, and other beneficial microbes.

FERTILIZER. Use any organic fertilizer, in either a powder or liquid formulation, where the first number (nitrogen) is higher than the other two. Apply at half-strength once a month through the growing season.

POTTING. Re-pot annually in early summer. When your plant needs up-potting, shift it to a container with a diameter 2 inches larger than the current pot.

PROPAGATION. Boston fern is easy to propagate by division in spring.

COMMON PROBLEMS
Watch for yellowing leaves (page 257) and spider mites (page 263).

Davallia fern

What's not to love about a furry-footed fern? Three davallias are commonly grown as houseplants: deer's foot fern (*Davallia canariensis*), rabbit's foot fern (*D. fejeensis*), and squirrel's foot fern (*D. trichomanoides*). Their softly furry rhizomes really do look like little animal feet. The color of the fuzz, light brown or silvery, adds to the illusion. Davallia ferns produce broadly triangular, glossy, dark green, semi-evergreen fronds 12 to 18 inches tall at regular intervals along the rhizomes. The fronds are finely divided three or four times and are pinnate (feather-like). They look very delicate and airy, but they're actually pretty tough. The plants shed some of their leaves in winter but replace

Davallia fern.

them in spring. All three species are at their very best in hanging baskets. If plants are kept consistently moist, the furry rhizomes crawl across the surface of the plant's container and then out and over the sides, covering the pot or dangling in mid-air—a delightful feature of these pretty houseplants. The rhizomes absorb moisture and nutrients from damp surfaces, and in big old plants can grow as long as 2 feet or more. Plants eventually form large clumps, 2 to 4 feet wide and 2 feet tall. Ferns that big are daunting and heavy to handle in hanging baskets, so it's probably best to divide them into smaller plants when you re-pot. Cut the rhizome into pieces, with each piece having a good supply of roots and several leaves. When re-potting be careful not to bury the furry rhizomes because they'll rot. Get the roots down into the potting medium but keep the rhizomes on the surface.

Davallia ferns are sensitive to chemical sprays—insecticides, fungicides, leaf-polishing agents. Any chemical other than insecticidal soap, in fact, causes a phytotoxic reaction that burns the foliage and turns the leaves brown.

OPTIMUM HOUSEHOLD ENVIRONMENT

Read the Introduction for the specifics of each recommendation.

LOW LIGHT. These plants do well in ambient light from a north window. They can be placed in cool morning light from an east window as long as the light is filtered by sheer curtains. Artificial light also works well. Avoid full sun.

MODERATE TEMPERATURE. Daytime 70 to 80°F, nighttime 60 to 70°F.

MODERATE WATER. Water whenever the top of the potting medium becomes dry to a depth of 1 inch. Strive to keep the soil consistently moist but not soggy and waterlogged.

HUMIDITY. Mist your plant every day with a spray bottle of water on a mist setting, or use a handheld mister. Put the pot in a saucer or tray of water, making sure the bottom of the pot never sits directly in the water by raising the pot up on pot feet or pebbles. Put a humidifier in the room.

POTTING MEDIUM. Choose a good organic, well-drained, general-purpose potting soil that incorporates organic fertilizer, mycorrhizal fungi, and other beneficial microbes, and mix it 50/50 with peat moss to increase the water-holding capacity.

FERTILIZER. Use any liquid organic fertilizer where the first number (nitrogen) is higher than the other two. Apply at half-strength every two weeks.

POTTING. When your plant needs up-potting, shift it to a container with a diameter 2 inches larger than the current pot. Choose a shallow pot, one wider than it is deep, or use a hanging basket. Re-pot in spring, every two years. Despite davallia's toughness when it comes to its growing conditions, handle the fuzzy rhizomes carefully—they're brittle and can break. Be careful not to bury them when re-potting.

PROPAGATION. Davallia ferns are easy to propagate by division of the rhizome.

COMMON PROBLEMS

Watch for leaves turning brown (page 251), spider mites (page 263), and root rot (page 272).

Hare's foot fern

Hare's foot fern (*Phlebodium aureum*) is so called for its creeping rhizome, 0.5 to 1 inch thick and densely clothed in golden brown, fur-like scales, very much resembling the tiny paw of a hare. This really is a classic fern in looks and habit: large, robust, 2 to 4 feet tall and spreading to 2 feet wide. It hails from tropical rainforests, so as a houseplant it may decide to shed its leaves if it gets too dry. Keep it watered and it will remain leafy. Should it drop its leaves, it will grow a new set fairly quickly. Fronds are pinnatifid (deeply lobed) with large, wavy-edged pinnae (leaflets). The pinnae are widely spaced on the fronds, which gives the plant a rather coarse texture. Brown spots (sori) on the undersides of the leaves contain the spores by which this and all ferns reproduce. Leaf color varies from bright green to blue-green. Most clones in cultivation have blue-green foliage and wavy undulating edges.

Hare's foot fern (aka bear's paw fern, cabbage palm fern, gold-foot fern, golden polypody, golden serpent fern).

POTTING MEDIUM. Add extra perlite to improve drainage of a good organic, general-purpose potting soil that incorporates organic fertilizer, mycorrhizal fungi, and other beneficial microbes. This fern wants a potting medium that drains rapidly.

FERTILIZER. Use any liquid organic fertilizer where the first number (nitrogen) is higher than the other two. Apply at half-strength once a month.

POTTING. When this fast-growing plant needs up-potting, shift it to a container with a diameter 4 inches larger than the current pot. Use a shallow pot, wider than deep.

PROPAGATION. Hare's foot fern is easy to propagate by division of the rhizome.

COMMON PROBLEMS

Watch for leaf drop (page 249) and mealybugs (page 262).

Holly fern

Holly fern (*Cytomium falcatum*) is quite beautiful, with long leaves that resemble mahonias (Oregon grape) or a less prickly holly tree. And it's easy to grow. It is unusual for such a cold tolerant plant (zones 6 through 10) to succeed as a houseplant. Most houseplants are tropical; that's why they do well inside our homes. Holly fern succeeds as a houseplant for one reason: its leathery leaves tolerate dry air quite well. This evergreen perennial grows 1 to 2 feet tall and spreads 2 to 3 feet wide. The pinnately compound (feather-like) leaves are borne in a vase-shaped cluster. Leaves are 1.5 feet long and have six to ten glossy, dark green leaflets. Each thick, leathery leaflet is slightly toothed along the edges and either flat or wavy, with a net-like pattern of veins.

OPTIMUM HOUSEHOLD ENVIRONMENT

Read the Introduction for the specifics of each recommendation.

MEDIUM LIGHT. This fern wants brighter light than many ferns but not direct sun. Filtered light from east windows is perfect.

LOW TEMPERATURE. Daytime 65 to 75°F, nighttime 55 to 65°F.

AMPLE WATER. Water whenever the top of the potting medium becomes dry to a depth of 0.5 inch.

HUMIDITY. Mist your plant daily with a spray bottle of water on a mist setting, or use a handheld mister. Put the pot in a saucer or tray of water, making sure the bottom of the pot never sits directly in the water by raising the pot up on pot feet or pebbles. Or put a humidifier in the room.

Holly fern (aka Japanese holly fern, Japanese net-vein holly fern).

OPTIMUM HOUSEHOLD ENVIRONMENT

Read the Introduction for the specifics of each recommendation.

MEDIUM LIGHT. Holly fern succeeds in bright filtered light from an east window. It tolerates brighter light than most ferns, even a little bit of direct sun; however, the leaves burn in too much sun, so it's better to err on the side of shade.

LOW TEMPERATURE. Daytime 65 to 75°F, nighttime 55 to 65°F.

MODERATE WATER. Water whenever the top of the potting medium becomes dry to a depth of 1 inch. This fern tolerates occasional dry spells quite well.

HUMIDITY. Holly fern's thick, leathery leaves tolerate low humidity so you probably don't need to mist your plant to keep it happy.

POTTING MEDIUM. Use any good organic, general-purpose potting soil that incorporates organic fertilizer, mycorrhizal fungi, and other beneficial microbes.

FERTILIZER. Use any liquid organic fertilizer where the first number (nitrogen) is higher than the other two. Apply at half-strength once a month.

POTTING. When your plant needs up-potting, shift it to a container with a diameter 4 inches larger than the current pot.

PROPAGATION. Holly fern is propagated by division of the rhizome in spring.

COMMON PROBLEMS

Watch for scale insects (page 262) and leaf spot fungus (page 269).

Maidenhair fern

Maidenhair ferns (*Adiantum* spp.) have a well-deserved reputation for being persnickety, but boy do they deliver in the houseplant categories of "distinctive character" and "strong sculptural quality." Their demands are simple, but they are also uncompromising. Give them what they want or they'll die. And what they want is high humidity, warmth, and shade. Give them less than that and they go belly-up fairly quickly. The ones that succeed best as houseplants are Venus maidenhair (*A. capillus-veneris*), delta maidenhair (*A. raddianum*), and rosy maidenhair (*A. hispidulum*). The fronds of these evergreen perennials arise from creeping rhizomes at the soil level. Fronds are delicate, lacy, and gorgeous, with wiry, glossy black stems that contrast beautifully with the bright green leaflets. In most of these ferns the leafstalks arch gracefully so that the leaflets dangle in a layered, downward cascade. The small, 0.5-inch-wide leaflets are fan-shaped, with wedge-shaped bases and lobed tips.

Venus maidenhair fern grows only 6 to 12 inches high and 12 to 36 inches wide and its glossy black stem is not forked. Nor is it in delta maidenhair fern; its fronds are three- or four-times pinnate (feather-like), 12 to 24 inches long and 6 inches wide. Rosy maidenhair fern grows 12 to 18 inches tall and wide. Its fronds are two- or three-times pinnate and 14 inches long, with a forked leafstalk. New growth is pink, maturing to green or bronze-green.

OPTIMUM HOUSEHOLD ENVIRONMENT

Read the Introduction for the specifics of each recommendation.

LOW LIGHT. Maidenhair ferns cannot tolerate direct sun. They'll do well in ambient light from a north window or in the stronger light of an east window so long as the cool morning sun is filtered by sheer curtains.

HIGH TEMPERATURE. Daytime 75 to 85°F, nighttime 65 to 75°F.

AMPLE WATER. Water whenever the top of the potting medium becomes dry to a depth of 0.5 inch. These ferns need lots of water but they also need good drainage. They don't want soggy soil.

HUMIDITY. Maidenhair ferns require high humidity and so do well in bathrooms and kitchens. Mist your plant daily with a spray bottle of water on a mist setting, or use a handheld mister. Put the pot in a saucer or tray of water, making sure the bottom of the pot never sits directly in the water by raising the pot up on pot feet or pebbles, or use a humidifier in the room.

POTTING MEDIUM. Use any good organic, general-purpose potting soil that incorporates organic fertilizer, mycorrhizal fungi, and other beneficial microbes.

FERTILIZER. Use any liquid organic fertilizer where the first number (nitrogen) is higher than the other two. Apply at half-strength once a month through the growing season.

POTTING. Re-pot every year or two. Divide your plant at re-potting time. When your plant needs up-potting, shift it to a container with a diameter 2 inches larger than the current pot.

PROPAGATION. Maidenhair fern is easy to propagate by division.

COMMON PROBLEMS

Watch for leaves turning brown (page 251), scale insects (page 262), and root rot (page 272).

Staghorn fern

Staghorn fern (*Platycerium bifurcatum*) is an interesting, bizarre-looking plant guaranteed to attract attention and start conversations. And though it is a true fern, it's not lacy, or delicate, or ferny in any way. In its native

Maidenhair fern.

tropical rainforests, it is an epiphyte (a plant that grows on another plant for support), perching on the branches or trunks of trees. Staghorn fern has two distinctly different kinds of leaves: basal and aerial. Its basal leaves are flat and kidney-shaped. In nature, they tightly clasp the tree on which the fern grows, and the rhizome grows underneath them. Aerial leaves are divided into large, strap-shaped lobes that resemble deer antlers, thus the common name. These leaves arch out horizontally into mid-air and can grow to 3 feet long and wide. Young staghorn ferns are sometimes grown in pots, but because they are epiphytes, they do best when mounted on plaques of wood or bark hung on walls or suspended in air. Hanging baskets, in which leaves emerge through the sides of the baskets, are another alternative. The plant eventually encloses the basket with its fronds.

OPTIMUM HOUSEHOLD ENVIRONMENT

Read the Introduction for the specifics of each recommendation.

MEDIUM LIGHT. Bright filtered light, but no direct sun, suits these ferns best.

MODERATE TEMPERATURE. Daytime 70 to 80°F, nighttime 60 to 70°F.

AMPLE WATER. Plants mounted on plaques or in hanging baskets should be watered when the potting medium is dry to a depth of 0.5 inch. Provide more water as temperatures rise in summer. Make sure drainage is perfect; the water should drain away quickly.

HUMIDITY. Staghorn ferns require high humidity. Mist your plant frequently with a spray bottle of water on a mist setting, or use a handheld mister. Put a humidifier in the room and group other houseplants nearby to raise the humidity.

POTTING MEDIUM. In a hanging basket, use any good organic, well-drained, general-purpose potting soil that incorporates organic fertilizer, mycorrhizal fungi, and other beneficial microbes.

FERTILIZER. Use any liquid organic fertilizer where the first number (nitrogen) is higher than the other two. Apply at half-strength every two weeks.

POTTING. When your fern needs up-potting, shift it to a hanging basket with a diameter 2 inches larger than the current one. To mount the fern on a plaque, wrap the roots in a ball of moss and tie the plant to the plaque with some old pantyhose.

PROPAGATION. Staghorn fern is easy to propagate by division.

COMMON PROBLEMS

Watch for sunburn (page 256), scale insects (page 262), and bacterial leaf spot (page 267).

Staghorn fern (aka elkhorn fern).

Temporary Houseplants

Amaryllis

Huge, red, and incredible don't begin to describe the amazing amaryllis (*Hippeastrum* spp.), a beloved winter holiday gift. The first thing to emerge from your potted bulb will be bright green, strap-shaped leaves. As they elongate, a thick flower stalk begins to grow straight up from the center of the foliage. Maybe a week later, enormous flower buds develop on top of the stalk and slowly begin to open. In a couple of days, flowers will be fully open, with petals spread wide. The sight will knock your socks off! Every year during the winter holiday season, millions of amaryllis bulbs find their way into garden centers, supermarkets, and big box stores. They come in attractive, full-color boxes displaying photos of their stunningly gorgeous flowers. Each box contains a complete kit with the bulb, a pot, and a bag of potting medium. All one has to do is plant the bulb in the pot and, in a few short weeks, just in time for Christmas it will flower gloriously. Modern hybrids have been developed from six different species, *H. aulicum, H. leopoldii, H. pardinum, H. puniceum, H. reginae,* and *H. vittatum.* The huge flowers come in various shades of red, pink, salmon, near-orange, creamy yellow, or white. Some are striped, or have colored petal edges (picotee), or are variously streaked and spotted. The plant has two or three flowers, each 8 to 9 inches across, borne in a cluster atop a hollow 2-foot-tall stem.

When it's finished flowering, cut the flower stalk off 3 to 5 inches above the bulb. Do not cut off any of the leaves, and be careful not to damage them. Since amaryllis is a perennial bulb, the leaves must make enough food to store in the bulb to flower again next year, and the plant can best accomplish that task by being outdoors in dappled shade through the growing season. So, in spring, after all danger of frost has passed, put your amaryllis outdoors. Then, before any expected frost, bring it back inside and put it in a dark place at 50 to 55°F. Amaryllis needs this cold treatment for eight to ten weeks in order to flower. During this cold-dark treatment the foliage turns brown and dies back. Just cut the dead leaves off. Don't water it during this time. While it's dormant take it out of the pot; remove the used potting medium and replace it with fresh potting medium. After your cold treatment, bring the dormant bulb in its pot out into light and warmth and start watering it. Soon this temporary houseplant will flower again—just in time for another holiday season, if you've timed it right.

OPTIMUM HOUSEHOLD ENVIRONMENT

Read the Introduction for the specifics of each recommendation.

Amaryllis (aka hippeastrum).

MEDIUM LIGHT. Bright filtered light but no direct sun is best for amaryllis.

MODERATE TEMPERATURE. Daytime 70 to 80°F, nighttime 60 to 70°F.

MODERATE WATER. Water whenever the top of the potting medium becomes dry to a depth of 1 inch.

HUMIDITY. Put the pot in a saucer or tray of water, making sure the bottom of the pot never sits directly in the water by raising the pot up on pot feet or pebbles.

POTTING MEDIUM. Use any good organic, general-purpose potting soil that incorporates organic fertilizer, mycorrhizal fungi, and other beneficial microbes.

FERTILIZER. Use any organic fertilizer where the second number (phosphorus) is higher than the other two to promote flowering. While the plant is in flower, use a liquid fertilizer. During the summer, use dry fertilizer.

POTTING. Re-pot annually when dormant, and be sure the top third of the bulb is not buried in the potting medium. If the bulb appears to be root-bound, up-pot to a container with a diameter 2 inches larger than the current pot.

PROPAGATION. Like all hybrids, amaryllis hybrids don't come true from seed. They're propagated asexually. Slice the bulb from top to bottom into 12 pieces. Be sure each piece has a chunk of the basal plate and a few bulb scales. Plant each piece in damp vermiculite and keep them in the dark. The pieces will grow tiny little bulbs called bulbils that can then be planted and grown on into mature plants.

COMMON PROBLEMS

Watch for failure to flower (page 247), mealy-bugs (page 262), and leaf spot fungus (page 269).

Caladium

People grow and love caladium (*Caladium bicolor*) for its fantastic foliage. The leaves are large and shaped like an arrowhead, very thin and delicate. The more than a thousand available cultivars offer every imaginable combination of color: flaming red, bright pink, white, and green. The leaves are often spotted and mottled with veins in contrasting colors. Unfortunately this tropical perennial has those incredibly showy leaves only from spring to autumn; it is dormant and leafless all winter long, which is why we've labeled it a temporary houseplant. Caladium develops a cluster of leaves, 12 to 30 inches tall and wide, from underground tubers. The very colorful leaf blades are up to 18 inches long and put on a very dramatic show during the growing season. It is very rare for caladium to flower indoors. The inflorescence is a small, pale greenish white, scoop-shaped spathe surrounding a finger-like spadix covered with minute flowers.

Caladium (aka angel wings, elephant ears, heart of Jesus).

Caladium.

Female flowers near the base of the spadix form berries after fertilization. Many of caladium's close aroid relatives are valued air-filtering plants. It is possible that further research may prove caladium too to be valuable in this regard.

❶ This plant is toxic to people and pets and should be kept in an out-of-the-way place. Its tissues contain calcium oxalate crystals, and if leaves are chewed the crystals penetrate the soft tissues of lips, tongue, and throat, causing painful swelling, drooling, and vomiting. If you suspect a person or pet has ingested parts of this plant, or if a person or pet exhibits serious symptoms such as difficulty breathing, call your local emergency hotline, poison control center, or vet.

OPTIMUM HOUSEHOLD ENVIRONMENT

Read the Introduction for the specifics of each recommendation.

LOW LIGHT. Caladium does well in ambient light from a north window where it does not get any direct sun. Medium filtered light from an east window also works well. In general, the wider the foliage, the more shade the plant needs.

HIGH TEMPERATURE. Daytime 75 to 85°F, nighttime 65 to 75°F.

AMPLE WATER. Water whenever the top of the potting medium becomes dry to a depth of 0.5 inch.

HUMIDITY. Caladium requires high humidity. Mist your plant daily with a spray bottle of water on a mist setting, or use a handheld mister. Put the pot in a saucer or tray of water, making sure the bottom of the pot never sits directly in the water by raising the pot up on pot feet or pebbles. Consider putting a humidifier in the room.

POTTING MEDIUM. Use any good organic, general-purpose potting soil that incorporates organic fertilizer, mycorrhizal fungi, and other beneficial microbes.

FERTILIZER. Use any liquid organic fertilizer where the first number (nitrogen) is higher than the other two. Apply every two weeks during the growing season.

POTTING. Each autumn, when the leaves die back, move your plant to a dry, cool (55°F) location. Re-pot before active growth begins again in spring: take the dormant tubers out of the pot, remove the old soil, and plant them in fresh potting medium. If you up-pot, choose a container with a diameter 4 inches larger than the current pot.

PROPAGATION. Caladium is easy to propagate by dividing the dormant tubers.

COMMON PROBLEMS

Watch for leaves turning brown (page 251), aphids (page 260), and leaf spot fungus (page 269).

Cupid's bow

Achimenes erecta with bright red flowers and *A. longiflora* with big blue flowers are two of the main species used to create the Cupid's bow hybrids. This is another large group of houseplants with a pronounced dormant period. In winter the whole plant goes away. It doesn't die, it just goes to sleep. Its underground rhizomes resprout in the spring. In summer, tubular flowers 3 inches wide and 2 inches long—in every color of the rainbow—adorn the lax stems. The softly furry, deep green leaves are borne in pairs, are up to 3 inches long, and have serrated edges. Some cultivars have stems that droop and trail, cascading down as much as 2 feet; these are perfect in hanging baskets. Others are more erect and do well in ordinary pots. Flowers flare out at the tip, like the bell of a trumpet, and have five petals. They're borne on short stems in the axils of the leaves and, although each flower lasts only a few days, Cupid's bow blooms continuously through the growing season. Flower color varies by cultivar and includes red and blue through pink, white, purple, violet-blue, and yellow. Some varieties are striped.

At the end of summer your Cupid's bow starts to turn yellow and begins to die back to the ground. When this happens, stop watering it until it has gone completely dormant. When dormancy is complete, cut it to the ground and knock it out of the pot. Shake off the old potting medium and put the rhizomes in a paper bag with some fresh but dry potting medium. Keep the rhizomes dry, dark, and cool (but above 50°F) through the winter. In late winter or very early spring, replant the little rhizomes (they look like tiny pine cones) in 4- or 6-inch pots in fresh potting soil and bring them into the light and warmth. Discard any shriveled or rotted rhizomes and plant only the healthy ones. Begin watering and feeding them, and they'll soon be growing and flowering again.

Cupid's bow (aka achimenes, Cupid's bower, hot water plant, magic flower, orchid pansy).

OPTIMUM HOUSEHOLD ENVIRONMENT

Read the Introduction for the specifics of each recommendation.

MEDIUM LIGHT. Cupid's bow does best in very bright filtered light with no direct sun. An east or west window with sheer curtains is perfect. If its leaves start to turn brown, it's probably getting too much light.

MODERATE TEMPERATURE. Daytime 70 to 80°F, nighttime 60 to 70°F. This tropical species dislikes temperatures below 50°F and hates cold drafts.

AMPLE WATER. Water whenever the top of the potting medium becomes dry to a depth of 0.5 inch. However, be certain your potting medium is well drained because Cupid's bow hates waterlogged soil. On the other hand, if it ever dries out it'll go dormant.

HUMIDITY. Put the pot in a saucer or tray of water, making sure the bottom of the pot never sits directly in the water by raising the pot up on pot feet or pebbles.

POTTING MEDIUM. Use any good organic, African violet potting soil that incorporates organic fertilizer, mycorrhizal fungi, and other beneficial microbes.

FERTILIZER. Use any liquid organic fertilizer where the second number (phosphorus) is higher than the other two to promote flowering. Apply at half-strength every two weeks during the growing season.

POTTING. When Cupid's bow needs re-potting in the spring, plant the little rhizomes in 4- or 6-inch pots.

PROPAGATION. Cupid's bow is easy to propagate by division of the rhizome.

COMMON PROBLEMS

Watch for leaves turning brown (page 251), aphids (page 260), and root rot (page 272).

Florist azalea

A classic Mother's Day gift, the florist azalea is a hybrid evergreen shrub derived from various *Rhododendron* species. Unlike deciduous azaleas, these evergreen types are not hardy and cannot tolerate freezing temperatures. They are grown in greenhouses and forced into bloom as spring holiday gifts. In that season, a florist azalea literally covers itself with pink, white, peach, lavender, red, or bicolored blossoms, making a gorgeous living bouquet for three to four weeks when kept in a cool room. But it's tricky to get it to repeat the show the following year. It really

needs to be outdoors during the spring and summer growing season. After it's finished blooming indoors and all danger of frost has passed, take your plant outdoors and grow it in the shade through autumn. Just sink the pot into the garden soil up to the rim. Azaleas need the cool fall weather (or even mild winter weather) to set the flower buds that will open next spring. Be sure to exhume the plant, pot and all, and bring it back indoors in the fall before the first frost. Indoors in winter, it will remain evergreen but won't bloom until spring. That's why it's a temporary houseplant. Florist azaleas are typically dwarf shrubs, up to 1.5 feet tall and wide, with dark green oval leaves. Flowers are 1 to 2 inches across and are borne in clusters at the tips of thin, woody branches.

❶ All parts of the azalea—foliage, flowers, and nectar—contain grayanotoxins, chemicals that are toxic to people and pets. Plants should be kept in an out-of-the-way place. The physiological effects on gastrointestinal, cardiovascular, and central nervous systems are mild to severe, depending on how much of the toxin was consumed. If you suspect a person or pet has ingested parts of this plant, call your local emergency hotline, poison control center, or vet.

OPTIMUM HOUSEHOLD ENVIRONMENT

Read the Introduction for the specifics of each recommendation.

MEDIUM LIGHT. Florist azaleas do well with bright filtered light, no direct sun, during their time indoors. Outdoors, in summer, keep them in filtered shade.

LOW TEMPERATURE. Daytime 65 to 75°F, nighttime 55 to 65°F. Outdoors, temperatures need to be between 40 and 55°F for six weeks in autumn in order for your plant to set flower buds for next spring. Bring this tender shrub back indoors if temperatures threaten to go below 40°F.

Florist azalea.

MODERATE WATER. Water whenever the top of the potting medium becomes dry to a depth of 1 inch and try to maintain even moisture. If your tap water is hard and has a lot of calcium (lime) in it, water your azalea with distilled water. Since the potting medium is half peat moss, it can be difficult to re-wet if it dries out too much between waterings. If that happens, submerge the entire pot in tepid water for at least 15 minutes until all the bubbles stop rising to the surface. Then pull the pot out of the water and let it drain.

HUMIDITY. These plants benefit from medium to high humidity. Put the pot in a saucer or tray of water, making sure the bottom of the pot never sits directly in the water by raising the pot up on pot feet or pebbles. Consider putting a humidifier in the room.

POTTING MEDIUM. Use any good organic, general-purpose potting soil, one that incorporates organic fertilizer, mycorrhizal fungi, and other beneficial microbes, and mix it 50/50 with peat moss.

FERTILIZER. The plant requires an acidic organic fertilizer, in either a powder or liquid formulation. Choose one that supplies iron and whose second number (phosphorus) is higher than the other two to promote flowering. Feed your azalea once a year, as soon as it's finished blooming.

POTTING. When your plant needs up-potting, every three years or so, shift it to a container with a diameter 4 inches larger than the current pot. Up-pot or re-pot in spring after the last blooms have withered.

PROPAGATION. Florist azalea can be propagated from stem tip cuttings, but it is slow to root. It is easy to grow from seed, but like all hybrids, it doesn't come true from seed.

COMMON PROBLEMS

Watch for flower bud drop (page 248), whiteflies (page 265), and root rot (page 272).

Freesia

Freesias are herbaceous perennials from bulb-like corms that have the same growth habit as spring bulbs; they're in active growth during cool, wet winter/spring weather, and they go dormant in hot, dry summers. The ones treasured as temporary houseplants are all hybrids derived from *Freesia corymbosa, F. laxa, F. refracta*, and other species. Appreciation for freesia's lovely flowers is nearly universal, but people wax most eloquent over their fragrance, which can perfume an entire room. Flowers come in a wide array of beautiful colors, including lavender, pink, orange, red, yellow, white, and multicolor blends. They are 2 inches wide, trumpet-shaped, and borne appealingly on one side of the flowering spike, which is 12 to 18 inches tall. The flowering stems emerge from a tuft of narrow, grass-like foliage 4 to 12 inches tall.

When your potted freesia finishes flowering, take it outdoors for the summer and put it in full sun to finish its growth cycle. It needs to cycle from a cool, wet winter to a hot and dry heat treatment in summer to flower. Keep it watered

Freesia.

until the foliage turns yellow and dies back. In late spring or early summer, all the foliage dies down and the plant goes dormant. At this time stop watering the plant and let it dry out and cook in high summer heat. In late summer or early fall, dump the contents of the pot out and sort out the corms, discarding the old soft and wrinkled ones (which are not going to flower again) and the used potting medium. There should be a lot of new, young corms that are firm and smooth. Keep these in a paper bag until planting time in autumn. The corms are about 1 inch in diameter and have a pointy side and a flat side. When you plant them, be sure the pointy side is up. Freesias flower best after six months of dormancy at high temperatures.

OPTIMUM HOUSEHOLD ENVIRONMENT

Read the Introduction for the specifics of each recommendation.

HIGH LIGHT. Full sun or very bright indirect light is best for freesias. Cool morning sun makes the flowers last longer.

LOW TEMPERATURE. Daytime 65 to 75°F, nighttime 55 to 65°F, while the plants are flowering. After corms have been planted, give them 80°F until they start to sprout. Once they're actively growing, cool them down.

MODERATE WATER. Water whenever the top of the potting medium becomes dry to a depth of 1 inch.

HUMIDITY. Freesias enjoy moderate humidity. Put the pot in a saucer or tray of water, making sure the bottom of the pot never sits directly in the water by raising the pot up on pot feet or pebbles.

POTTING MEDIUM. Use any good organic, general-purpose potting soil that incorporates organic fertilizer, mycorrhizal fungi, and other beneficial microbes.

FERTILIZER. Use any liquid organic fertilizer where the second number (phosphorus) is higher than the other two to promote flowering. Apply at half-strength twice a month during the growing season.

POTTING. Re-pot corms in autumn, like tulip bulbs. They'll bloom in late winter to early spring.

PROPAGATION. Freesia is easy to propagate from corms.

COMMON PROBLEMS

Watch for flower bud drop (page 248), spider mites (page 263), and root rot (page 272).

Persian violet

When in full bloom Persian violet (*Exacum affine*) is a knockout. And it is very easy to grow—for a while. But if you acquire one as an impulse purchase, don't be disappointed when it gives up the ghost despite your best efforts to keep it alive. This irresistible plant is an annual with a death wish, determined to bloom itself into oblivion, so it is only a temporary houseplant. The plant makes a perfect little mound to 12 inches high. Despite its common name, it is not a violet but a gentian, a family renowned for tubular flowers in intense shades of blue. Lightly scented 0.5-inch-wide Persian violet flowers look flat because their five lobes flare out wide. In the center of each is a small button of stamens in brilliant yellow, the perfect complement to the violet petals. The flowers are further set off by the glossy bright green leaves. If you were determined to snip off every flower as it fades, you might keep Persian violet alive for a few months. But in the usual course of events, you see it in full bloom at the garden center so you have to have it, you take it home—and it starts to fail shortly after. A few weeks later it's dead. Nonetheless, Persian violet is well worth having as a living bouquet. If you're looking to buy one, look for one that has lots of buds that have not yet opened. If it has not yet reached peak bloom, it will last longer in your home.

OPTIMUM HOUSEHOLD ENVIRONMENT

Read the Introduction for the specifics of each recommendation.

HIGH OR MEDIUM LIGHT. Light from a south, east, or west window serves this plant well.

MODERATE TEMPERATURE. Daytime 70 to 80°F, nighttime 60 to 70°F.

Persian violet (aka German violet, Arabian violet, tiddly-winks).

MODERATE WATER. Water whenever the top of the potting medium becomes dry to a depth of 1 inch.

HUMIDITY. Mist your plant regularly with a spray bottle of water on a mist setting, or use a hand-held mister. Put the pot in a saucer or tray of water, making sure the bottom of the pot never sits directly in the water by raising the pot up on pot feet or pebbles.

POTTING MEDIUM. Use any good organic, general-purpose potting soil that incorporates organic fertilizer, mycorrhizal fungi, and other beneficial microbes.

FERTILIZER. Use any balanced liquid organic fertilizer. Apply at half-strength every two weeks until death do you part.

POTTING. If your plant is rootbound and needs up-potting, shift it to a container with a diameter 4 inches larger than the current pot. Disturb the roots as little as possible when up-potting.

PROPAGATION. Persian violet is easy to propagate from the very tiny seeds.

COMMON PROBLEMS

Watch for flower bud drop (page 248), aphids (page 260), and root rot (page 272).

Rieger begonia

Riegers (*Begonia* ×*hiemalis*) are a hybrid begonia strain created in 1955 by German plant breeder Otto Rieger, who crossed tuberous begonias (*B. ×tuberhybrida*) and wax begonias (*B. cucullata*). The 2-inch-wide flowers are often perfect replicas, in miniature, of their fabulous parent the tuberous begonia, and they have a slightly translucent quality that makes them seem to glow. Plants generally grow 12 to 18 inches tall and wide with reddish, fleshy, succulent stems that are somewhat jointed. The thick stems are brittle and easily broken. As with most begonias,

Rieger begonia (aka elatior hybrid, Rieger hybrid begonia, winter-blooming begonia).

Rieger begonia.

leaves are asymmetrical, larger on one side of the midrib, like an angel wing. They are glossy, rather frilly, and have serrated edges. This hybrid begonia is usually grown for a single season and discarded when it disappears for its dormant period. But it is a perennial, and it will come back to life after it rests for about six weeks. Because it blooms in winter, it does very well on a windowsill with amaryllis, Christmas cactus, or other winter holiday plants, brightening short days with its flowers, which come in mouthwatering, candy-colored shades of red, pink, salmon, orange, or yellow.

When your Rieger begonia flags and begins to go out of bloom, cut the stems back to 3-inch stubs and move the plant to a cool location outdoors in shade for six weeks in summer. Keep it on the dry side. When it starts back into active growth, move it to bright indirect light and start watering and fertilizing. The short days and cool nights of fall and winter stimulate it to bloom again.

OPTIMUM HOUSEHOLD ENVIRONMENT

Read the Introduction for the specifics of each recommendation.

MEDIUM LIGHT. Rieger begonias do best with a half-day of filtered sunlight, especially cool morning light from an east window with sheer curtains. Because these are short-day (long-night) plants that flower in winter, try to avoid locations that provide supplemental light at night, such as streetlights and indoor lighting, because the extra light can cause them to stop flowering.

LOW TEMPERATURE. Daytime 65 to 75°F, nighttime 55 to 65°F.

MODERATE WATER. Water whenever the top of the potting medium becomes dry to a depth of 1 inch. Avoid getting water on the foliage because the moisture promotes fungus diseases.

HUMIDITY. Put the pot in a saucer or tray of water, making sure the bottom of the pot never sits directly in the water by raising the pot up on pot feet or pebbles.

POTTING MEDIUM. Use any good organic, African violet potting soil that incorporates organic fertilizer, mycorrhizal fungi, and other beneficial microbes.

FERTILIZER. Use any liquid organic fertilizer where the second number (phosphorus) is higher than the other two to promote flowering. Apply once a month through the winter growing season. Stop fertilizing when the plant stops flowering in spring.

POTTING. When your Rieger begonia begins to grow again after its resting period, it may need up-potting. Shift it to a container with a diameter 2 inches larger than the current pot.

PROPAGATION. Rieger begonias are easy to propagate from leaf cuttings.

COMMON PROBLEMS

Watch for leaves turning brown (page 251), mealybugs (page 262), and gray mold (page 268).

Spring bulbs

Crocus, daffodils, grape hyacinths, hyacinths, and tulips will grace your home at a time when winter has a firm grip on the garden. Their riotous, happy colors in full bloom—red, pink, orange, yellow, blue, deep purple, lavender, and white—are a great tonic for chasing away winter's gloom. These bulbs are temporary houseplants because they decorate your home only briefly, as living bouquets, before and during their flowering time. The rest of the year they have to be outdoors because they require a three-month cold treatment to flower. Paperwhites (*Narcissus papyraceus*) are a bit of an exception. This type of daffodil is tender to cold. They are usually started indoors in water in autumn, brought into bloom for the winter holidays, and then discarded.

To force spring bulbs into early indoor bloom plant them in pots outdoors in autumn. Keeping them outside in cold weather stimulates the root system to grow. Bringing them indoors in mid-winter, into light and warmth, stimulates the tops and flowers to grow. When the flowering is done, they go back outside into the sunshine where the foliage dies and the bulbs go dormant. Then the cold wet weather of autumn stimulates them to start the cycle all over again. If you live in a warm climate, where winters aren't cold enough, you'll have to put your bulbs in the refrigerator, or buy pre-chilled bulbs from a reliable supplier.

To rebloom spring bulbs, let the pots dry out during their summer dormancy. In the autumn, dump them out of their pots, remove the old potting medium, and re-pot the bulbs in fresh medium. The bulbs will probably have made a number of small new bulbs or bulblets during their last growing season. Segregate the smaller from the larger bulbs and pot them up separately. The smallest bulbs take a couple years to

Daffodils.

get big enough to flower. The larger bulbs will probably flower, but don't be surprised if the flowers are smaller than they were in their first season. Water the pots after planting so that root growth can begin when cold weather arrives.

OPTIMUM HOUSEHOLD ENVIRONMENT

Read the Introduction for the specifics of each recommendation.

HIGH LIGHT. Spring bulbs need full sun.

LOW TEMPERATURE. Daytime 65 to 75°F, night-time 55 to 65°F.

MODERATE WATER. Water whenever the top of the potting medium becomes dry to a depth of 1 inch.

HUMIDITY. Put the pot in a saucer or tray of water, making sure the bottom of the pot never sits directly in the water by raising the pot up on pot feet or pebbles.

POTTING MEDIUM. Use any good organic, general-purpose potting soil that incorporates organic fertilizer, mycorrhizal fungi, and other beneficial microbes.

FERTILIZER. Use any organic fertilizer, in either a powder or liquid formulation, where the second number (phosphorus) is higher than the other two to promote flowering. Apply once a month, indoors and out, until the plants go dormant.

POTTING. Bulbs are usually crowded into shallow 6-inch pots.

PROPAGATION. Spring bulbs are easy to propagate by planting the little new bulblets that are produced each growing season.

COMMON PROBLEMS

Watch for flower bud drop (page 248), spider mites (page 263), and root rot (page 272).

Orchids and Bromeliads

Beallara and Aliceara

The huge and utterly fascinating orchid world contains thousands of fully fertile complex hybrids made between species in different genera. Beallaras and aliceareas are in the Odontoglossum/Oncidium alliance. Many of these hybrid genera in this alliance were named after the first orchid breeder to register the cross with the Royal Horticultural Society in England. For example, many years ago, Mr. Beall of the old Beall's Orchid Nursery on Vashon Island in Puget Sound created *Beallara* Tahoma Glacier, and the genus name honors him. Most Tahoma Glaciers have large off-white flowers with purple-red blotches in the middle of the petals; they're pretty easy to recognize and commonly available, often seen in full bloom in big box and grocery stores. Another gorgeous hybrid orchid that's fairly common in supermarket floral departments is *Aliceara* Marfitch, whose flowers look like a Tahoma Glacier dipped in raspberry juice.

Aliceara.

Beallara.

All the species in the background of these hybrids are epiphytes in nature, clinging to tree branches high in the tropical rainforest canopy. They never grow in soil. They are similar in growth habit and in flower structure because both have pansy orchids and spider orchids in their makeup. Both have 2-foot-long, 1-inch-wide, strap-shaped, flexible foliage growing from the tops of pseudobulbs. The smooth, bright yellow-green pseudobulbs, which function as water storage devices, are usually teardrop-shaped, 4 inches tall, 2 inches wide, and about 0.5 inch thick. They are clustered together at the soil line and produced at regular intervals from a creeping rhizome. Flowers are 3.5 inches wide and are borne on 5-foot-long wiry stems that arise from the base of the pseudobulbs. Each flowering stem carries as many as 14 to 16 flowers, and each flower lasts from 20 to 30 days, so plants are in bloom for a long time.

OPTIMUM HOUSEHOLD ENVIRONMENT

Read the Introduction for the specifics of each recommendation.

MEDIUM LIGHT. Bright filtered light from an east window is best for orchids in the Odontoglossum/Oncidium alliance. No direct sun. And avoid the heat load of a south or west window.

MODERATE TEMPERATURE. Daytime 70 to 80°F, nighttime 60 to 70°F.

LOW WATER. Give these orchids a good long drink once a week. Orchids are sensitive to water quality and should be irrigated with filtered, rain-, or distilled water, rather than tap water. Let tepid water flow through the entire root zone until all the potting medium is soaked. Let the pot drain and air out, then put it back in its place. Mark the pot so that your plant is returned to its original position every time. Turning your orchid causes the flowers to twist and bend to face the light, which destroys their elegant arrangement.

HUMIDITY. Mist your plant several times a week with a spray bottle of water on a mist setting, or use a handheld mister. Put the pot in a saucer or tray of water, but make absolutely sure the bottom of the pot never sits directly in the water by raising the pot up on pot feet or pebbles. Consider putting a humidifier in the room.

POTTING MEDIUM. Use any good organic, orchid potting medium such as medium orchid bark. Do not use garden soil or ordinary potting soil because it will kill this epiphytic orchid.

FERTILIZER. Use any organic fertilizer, in either a water soluble or liquid formulation, one where the second number (phosphorus) is higher than the other two to promote flowering. Apply at one-quarter-strength once a week, right after watering the plant.

POTTING. Your orchid needs to be up-potted every two years or so. Choose a pot with a diameter 2 inches larger than the current pot. Orchids generally prefer being rootbound in smallish pots.

PROPAGATION. Beallaras and alicedaras are easy to propagate by division of the rhizome. Next time you need to up-pot your plant, cut the rhizome into two pieces so that each piece has a decent number of roots, pseudobulbs, and leaves.

COMMON PROBLEMS

Watch for sunburn (page 256), scale insects (page 262), and root rot (page 272).

Corsage orchid

Corsage orchids acquired their common name during the 1940s and '50s when *Cattleya* corsages were all the rage among fashionable women of high society. First Lady Mamie Eisenhower popularized them; she was rarely seen in

Corsage orchid (aka cattleya).

Corsage orchid.

public without a corsage of one or two of these orchids during her husband's two terms as President of the United States. The flowers are huge, 6 inches across or more, strongly fragrant, and come in every color except true blue. The lower petal, or lip, of the flower is usually very large, frilly, and rolled into a tube at the base. The two upper petals are flat, often as wide as the lip, and may or may not be the same color as the lip. The three sepals are more narrow and pointy than the three petals.

Corsage orchids are in the Cattleya alliance. Each natural genus in the alliance has several species, and some have many. *Cattleya*, for example, has 113 species and *Broughtonia*, only six. Hybridizers have been busy making every conceivable intergeneric cross in this group, and hybrids with as many as seven different

genera in their backgrounds are known. Many of the plants in this group are fairly large. A standard-sized Cattleya alliance orchid has tall, slender pseudobulbs that look a bit like jointed stems. They're very hard (almost woody), rather club-shaped (thick at the top, thin at the bottom), furrowed, and green. They range in size from 1 to 4.5 feet, depending on the species or hybrids involved in the plant's background. Each pseudobulb has a single leaf (unifoliate) or two leaves (bifoliate) at its top. The leaves are extremely stiff, leathery, and firm—so hard, they feel more like plastic. The plants have a creeping rhizome that sprouts new pseudobulbs until your pot becomes crowded with them. Some growers like to up-pot their plants into wider and wider pots as the years go by until they have produced a magnificent specimen that, in bloom with dozens of flowers all at once, is a spectacular sight. But it's a challenge to get a plant that large and avoid root rot. Most growers opt to divide their cattleya orchids periodically, keeping them smaller and more manageable. Modern breeders have created a whole world of delightful and easy-to-grow miniature cattleyas (mini-catts, for short) that often stay under 6 inches tall in a 4-inch pot, the perfect size for many situations, including a windowsill in your home.

The flower stalks of corsage orchids emerge from the top of the pseudobulbs. In some species, such as *Broughtonia sanguinea*, the flower stalks are 2 feet long, slender, and carry several 2-inch-wide flowers. In others, like *Cattleya coccinea*, the flower stalk is short, stout, and carries few 3-inch-wide flowers. A large species like *C. labiata* has a short, stocky inflorescence with three huge 6- to 8-inch-wide flowers. Intergeneric hybrids, of course, vary enormously in the size, number, and disposition of their flowers.

Usually, when you buy a corsage orchid, it's in full flower. Then when the flowers fade you hope the plant blooms again for you next year. However, many people have trouble getting their orchids to rebloom. The trick with corsage orchids, as with any houseplant orchid, is to pay attention to the plant's growth patterns. After the last flowers fade on your corsage orchid look for new roots and new growing points emerging from the rhizomes. When you see these new bright green roots with their white tips, be diligent about keeping your plant well watered and fertilized. Do not let it get desiccated and make sure it's getting enough light, warmth, and constant weak fertilizer. That new growth you spotted slowly matures into a new pseudobulb, which will flower for you next year.

OPTIMUM HOUSEHOLD ENVIRONMENT

Read the Introduction for the specifics of each recommendation.

HIGH LIGHT. Cattleya alliance orchids need very bright light, but they can't take direct sun because their thick leaves cook and burn. A south window with sheer curtains to filter the light is best, but an east or west window also works well.

MODERATE TEMPERATURE. Daytime 70 to 80°F, nighttime 60 to 70°F. Corsage orchids are not nearly as sensitive to heat as some orchids, but the temperature should not exceed 85°F.

LOW WATER. Give these orchids a good long drink once a week. Orchids are sensitive to water quality and should be irrigated with filtered, rain-, or distilled water, rather than tap water. Let tepid water flow through the entire root zone until all the potting medium is soaked. Let the pot drain and air out, then put it back in its place. Mark the pot so that your plant is returned to its original position every time. Turning your orchid causes the flowers to twist and bend to face the light, which destroys their elegant arrangement.

HUMIDITY. Mist your plant several times a week with a spray bottle of water on a mist setting, or use a handheld mister. Put the pot in a saucer or tray of water, making sure the bottom of the pot never sits directly in the water by raising the pot up on pot feet or pebbles. Consider putting a humidifier in the room.

POTTING MEDIUM. Use any good organic, orchid potting medium like medium orchid bark. Do not use garden soil or ordinary potting soil because it will kill this epiphytic orchid.

FERTILIZER. Use any balanced organic fertilizer, in either a water soluble or liquid formulation, to promote good growth and flowering. Apply at one-quarter-strength at least once a week right after you water your orchid.

POTTING. Your corsage orchid needs to be

up-potted every two years or so. Choose a pot with a diameter 2 inches larger than the current pot. Orchids generally prefer being rootbound in smallish pots. Re-pot after flowering is complete and when new growth and new roots start to emerge. Corsage orchid roots are thick and tough, and they adhere to their pots, especially clay pots, like glue. They are easily damaged when you rip them off the surface of the pot so treat them gently. Be attentive to watering after up-potting or re-potting these plants and do not allow them to dry out.

PROPAGATION. Corsage orchids are easy to propagate by division of the rhizome.

COMMON PROBLEMS

Watch for sunburn (page 256), mealybugs (page 262), and root rot (page 272).

Cymbidium.

Cymbidium

Cymbidiums are attractive even when not in flower—something that cannot be said of many orchids. The trouble is, their huge size and need for low temperatures make standard cymbidiums (*Cymbidium* spp.) challenging as houseplants, and Asian miniature cymbidiums, although tiny, require high temperatures to thrive. Fortunately, a third kind of cymbidium, modern cymbidium hybrids, are intermediate in their size and temperature needs. These modern hybrids result from hybridization between the big standard cymbidiums and the Asian miniatures, making them much more easy to grow as houseplants than either of their parents. Before purchasing a cymbidium for your home, look at the label or tag, or ask the grower or store personnel what kind of cymbidium it is. If you cannot get an answer to this question, don't buy the plant from that source. Go instead to one of the many reliable mail order orchid houses. You need to know what kind of cymbidium you have to know its temperature requirements. Given that basic information, you'll be able to grow it successfully.

Cymbidium orchids have large, rounded pseudobulbs that look a bit like pointy green baseballs encased by the bases of the plant's numerous leaves. The leaves, 2 to 3 feet long, narrow, flexible, and grass-like, arch gracefully out and away from the center of the plant. The plant's very short creeping rhizome sprouts new pseudobulbs that are closely crowded together. Older pseudobulbs shed all their leaves, but they still have a vital function, to feed and support the new growth. Whenever you divide your cymbidium, make sure each division has two or three of these old pseudobulbs in addition to the new growth.

There is a simple trick to get your cymbidiums to bloom again. Give them a cold treatment

Cymbidium.

in the autumn so they can set flower buds. Grow them outdoors in summer, or just put them outdoors at night for a week or two in autumn. Don't let them freeze. But let them have 55°F nights, and they will flower again in late winter or early spring.

OPTIMUM HOUSEHOLD ENVIRONMENT

Read the Introduction for the specifics of each recommendation.

HIGH LIGHT. Cymbidiums need a lot of light and tolerate a half-day of full sun from an east window quite well. Too much sun causes leaves to turn yellow or even burn, however, so filter the light with sheers if that happens.

TEMPERATURE. For standard cymbidiums, provide daytime temperatures of 65 to 75°F. For Asian miniatures, provide daytime temperatures of 75 to 85°F. For modern hybrid cymbidiums, provide daytime temperatures of 70 to 80°F. All three kinds of cymbidiums need nighttime temperatures of at least 50 to 55°F in autumn to set flower buds, so put your plants outside at night for a couple weeks in the fall. Bring them indoors in the daytime and whenever frost is threatening. You could also leave them outdoors in partial shade in the daytime so long as there's no danger of frost.

LOW WATER. Give these orchids a good long drink once a week. Orchids are sensitive to water quality and should be irrigated with filtered, rain-, or distilled water, rather than tap water. Let tepid water flow through the entire root zone until all the potting medium is soaked. Let the pot drain and air out, then put it back in its place. Mark the pot so that your plant is returned to its original position every time. Turning your orchid causes the flowers to twist and bend to face the light, which destroys their elegant arrangement.

HUMIDITY. Mist your plant often with a spray bottle of water on a mist setting, or use a handheld mister. Put the pot in a saucer or tray of water, making sure the bottom of the pot never sits directly in the water by raising the pot up on pot feet or pebbles. Consider putting a humidifier in the room.

POTTING MEDIUM. Use any good organic potting medium designed for semi-terrestrial orchids, one that incorporates organic fertilizer, mycorrhizal fungi, and other beneficial microbes.

FERTILIZER. Use any balanced organic fertilizer, in either a water soluble or liquid formulation, to promote good growth and flowering. Apply at one-quarter-strength at least once a week right after you water your orchid.

POTTING. When your orchid needs up-potting, shift it to a container with a diameter 4 inches larger than the current pot.

PROPAGATION. Cymbidiums are easy to propagate by division of the rhizome.

COMMON PROBLEMS

Watch for sunburn (page 256), spider mites (page 263), and root rot (page 272).

Dancing lady

Dancing ladies (*Oncidium* spp.) are among the easiest orchids to grow successfully as houseplants. The plants are as beautiful as the flowers, and they can be relied on to repeat bloom so long as you provide them with the conditions they need. The flowers are small, about 1 inch long and half as wide. But they're borne by the dozens on every flowering stem, and a well-grown dancing lady orchid can have many flowering stems all blooming at once. What's more, dancing ladies are in the Odontoglossum/Oncidium alliance, and the crossing of these complex intergenerics is one of the hottest fields in orchid breeding today. The result is that large

Dancing lady (aka oncidium).

numbers of these gorgeous orchids find their way to your local supermarkets, big box stores, and independent garden centers, at very reasonable prices. Though flowers occur in red, pink, magenta, and white, most dancing lady orchids you'll regularly encounter have flowers that are yellow with small brown freckles (e.g., Gower Ramsey). Their large, frilly, yellow lip does indeed look like a can-can or flamenco skirt, and the brown and yellow petals look like the arms and head of a tiny dancer. Another commonly available dancing lady, Sharry Baby, has brick red markings on a cream background and smells just like chocolate.

The genus *Oncidium* actually includes 330 natural species, which are epiphytes in nature, and many thousands of hybrids that range in size from tiny little guys barely 6 inches tall to giants 5 feet tall and wide. Oncidiums have glossy, bright yellow-green pseudobulbs, 3 to 5 inches tall, 2 to 3 inches wide, and up to 1 inch thick. Usually shaped like flattened teardrops, they function as water storage devices and are really quite pretty. The pseudobulbs are clustered together and produced at regular intervals from a creeping rhizome. Grassy, flexible, 2-foot-long, 1-inch-wide foliage grows from the top of each pseudobulb. Flower stalks, 2 to 3 feet long, bearing clouds of small flowers, generally erupt from the pseudobulb's base.

OPTIMUM HOUSEHOLD ENVIRONMENT

Read the Introduction for the specifics of each recommendation.

MEDIUM LIGHT. Bright filtered light from an east window is best for the kinds of dancing ladies prevalent in your local stores, and is the key to getting them to rebloom. No direct sun. And avoid the heat load of a south or west window. Some oncidiums do like full sun and high heat, but these are usually available only from specialty orchid houses, not your local garden center.

MODERATE TEMPERATURE. Daytime 70 to 80°F, nighttime 60 to 70°F.

LOW WATER. Give dancing ladies a good long

drink once a week. Orchids are sensitive to water quality and should be irrigated with filtered, rain-, or distilled water, rather than tap water. Let tepid water flow through the entire root zone until all the potting medium is soaked. Let the pot drain and air out, then put it back in its place. Mark the pot so that your plant is returned to its original position every time. Turning your orchid causes the flowers to twist and bend to face the light, which destroys their elegant arrangement.

HUMIDITY. Mist your plant several times a week with a spray bottle of water on a mist setting, or use a handheld mister. Put the pot in a saucer or tray of water, but make absolutely sure the bottom of the pot never sits directly in the water by raising the pot up on pot feet or pebbles. Consider putting a humidifier in the room.

POTTING MEDIUM. Use any good organic, orchid potting medium such as medium orchid bark. Do not use garden soil or ordinary potting soil because it will kill this epiphytic orchid.

FERTILIZER. Use any balanced organic fertilizer, in either a water soluble or liquid formulation, to promote good growth and flowering. Apply at one-quarter-strength at least once a week right after you water your orchid.

POTTING. Your dancing lady orchid needs to be up-potted every two years or so. Choose a pot with a diameter 2 inches larger than the current pot. Orchids generally prefer being rootbound in smallish pots.

PROPAGATION. Dancing lady orchids are easy to propagate by division of the rhizome. Next time you need to up-pot your plant cut the rhizome into two pieces so that each piece has a decent number of roots, pseudobulbs, and leaves.

COMMON PROBLEMS

Watch for sunburn (page 256), scale insects (page 262), and root rot (page 272).

Dendrobium

Dendrobium is one of the largest genera of orchids, with more than 1,600 species and many, many hybrids, offering flowers in every color (except true blue). The growing requirements for so many different orchids are just as various. The specifications given here for growing dendrobiums successfully in your home are for the Jaquelyn Thomas hybrids. These hybrids are readily available in big box stores, supermarkets, and independent garden centers. Jaquelyn Thomas hybrids grow tall, 2 to 4 feet, with long, slender, furrowed pseudobulbs called canes. The canes stand erect but sometimes need to be staked to keep them from flopping over. These orchids have a creeping rhizome that generates new canes regularly. The canes are leafy,

Dendrobium.

Dendrobium.

especially in the top third, and flower stalks appear in the upper leaf axils of the cane and out of the very top of the cane. The flower stalks are 12 inches long and carry a dozen or more flowers in white, pink, and combinations of white and pink. Each cane produces several inflorescences at a time. The flowers are 2 to 3 inches across and long-lived. Plants are epiphytic and evergreen, with leaves to 4 inches long, glossy, narrow, and pointed at the tip. Canes keep their leaves for a couple of years but gradually shed

them as they age, so that really old canes are leafless. If you forget to water your plant and allow it to dry out completely, it sheds its leaves.

OPTIMUM HOUSEHOLD ENVIRONMENT

Read the Introduction for the specifics of each recommendation.

HIGH LIGHT. Dendrobiums need very bright light but they can't take direct sun because their leaves cook and burn. A south window with sheer curtains to filter the light is best, but an east or west window also works well. If your dendrobium is reluctant to bloom for you, try giving it more light.

MODERATE TEMPERATURE. Daytime 70 to 80°F, nighttime 60 to 70°F. Dendrobiums are not nearly as sensitive to heat as some orchids, but the temperature should not exceed 85°F.

MODERATE WATER. When your dendrobium is actively growing new roots and canes, or is flowering, give it water twice a week; the rest of the year give it a good long drink once a week. Orchids are sensitive to water quality and should be irrigated with filtered, rain-, or distilled water, rather than tap water. Let tepid water flow through the entire root zone until all the potting medium is soaked. Let the pot drain and air out, then put it back in its place. Mark the pot so that your plant is returned to its original position every time. Turning your orchid causes the flowers to twist and bend to face the light, which destroys their elegant arrangement.

HUMIDITY. Mist your plant several times a week with a spray bottle of water on a mist setting, or use a handheld mister. Put the pot in a saucer or tray of water, making sure the bottom of the pot never sits directly in the water by raising the pot up on pot feet or pebbles. Consider putting a humidifier in the room.

POTTING MEDIUM. Use any good organic, orchid potting medium like medium bark or plain ordinary 0.5-inch gravel. Believe it or not, dendrobiums actually like to grow in gravel. This helps to keep the plant upright. Many dendrobiums grow tall and get quite top-heavy for their ridiculously tiny pots. Do not use garden soil or ordinary potting soil because it will kill this epiphytic orchid, and if you choose gravel, be sure to follow the fertilizer guidelines.

FERTILIZER. Use any balanced organic fertilizer, in either a water soluble or liquid formulation, to promote good growth and flowering. Apply at one-quarter-strength at least once a week right after you water your orchid.

POTTING. Your dendrobium needs to be up-potted every two years or so. Choose a pot with a diameter 2 inches larger than the current pot. Orchids generally prefer being rootbound in smallish pots, and dendrobiums are the extreme in that regard. Heavy, 2-foot-tall dendrobiums in tiny 4-inch pots are commonplace. Re-pot after flowering is complete and when new growth and new roots start to emerge. Dendrobium roots are thin and delicate. They can be easily damaged when you dump the plant out of the pot so treat them gently. Be attentive to watering after up-potting or re-potting these plants, and do not allow them to dry out completely.

PROPAGATION. Dendrobiums are easy to propagate by division of the rhizome.

COMMON PROBLEMS
Watch for failure to flower (page 247), mealybugs (page 262), and root rot (page 272).

Earthstar

The commonly cultivated earthstars *Cryptanthus acaulis* and *C. zonatus* are bromeliads grown strictly for their foliage. Their starry, wavy-edged and sharply spiny leaves come in shades of red, rose, pink, green, and brown—even nearly black with silver. The stiff leaves are longitudinally striped like ribbons in contrasting colors (*C. acaulis*) or are zebra-striped (*C. zonatus*). The flowers, borne in the center of the plant, are insignificant (hence *Cryptanthus*, "hidden flower"). Plants flower when they are three to five years old and then, like all bromeliads, they die. But as they die, earthstars make pups, new little plants that are clones (identical copies) of the mother plant, in the nodes of the outermost leaves.

Earthstars are terrestrial bromeliads, that is, they grow on the ground like ordinary plants, unlike their mostly epiphytic cousins. All bromeliad leaves absorb moisture from the air through specialized scales. Most bromeliads have leaves that form a "vase" that holds water. In earthstar, this cup is very shallow because its leaves spread flat and wide. In nature, the leaves absorb nutrients from anything that falls into the tank of water, a feature that makes bromeliads very easy to fertilize as houseplants by just spraying the foliage. Some nutrients are absorbed immediately by the leaves and some accumulate in the tank to be taken up later. Any fertilizer that reaches the potting medium is taken up by the roots.

OPTIMUM HOUSEHOLD ENVIRONMENT

Read the Introduction for the specifics of each recommendation.

MEDIUM LIGHT. Earthstar does well with a half-day of full sun from an east or west window or really bright filtered light. It loses color and goes green if it's not getting enough light. Too much sun, however, burns the foliage. Earthstar also does very well under artificial lights.

HIGH TEMPERATURE. Daytime 75 to 85°F, nighttime 65 to 75°F.

MODERATE WATER. Water your earthstar by pouring a little distilled water or rainwater into the plant's shallow tank. Try to maintain a constant supply of water in the tank and don't let

Earthstar (aka chameleon plant, starfish plant, air plant).

your plant dry out. At the same time, however, do not water so heavily that the potting medium becomes saturated and soggy. A little water frequently is the ticket, and too much water can easily lead to root rot. Don't use tap water for these plants; they are sensitive to the chemicals it contains.

HUMIDITY. Earthstars really like high humidity. Mist your plant daily with a spray bottle of water on a mist setting, or use a handheld mister. Put the pot in a saucer or tray of water, making sure the bottom of the pot never sits directly in the water by raising the pot up on pot feet or pebbles. Consider putting a humidifier in the room or growing your plants in a terrarium.

POTTING MEDIUM. Use any good organic potting medium designed for semi-terrestrial orchids, one that incorporates organic fertilizer, mycorrhizal fungi, and other beneficial microbes.

FERTILIZER. Use any balanced liquid organic fertilizer mixed at half-strength and spray it on the leaves once a month through the growing season. In winter, apply fertilizer every other month.

POTTING. When your plant needs up-potting, shift it in the spring to a container with a diameter 2 inches larger than the current pot. Use a shallow pot, wider than deep, and be gentle; this plant has only a few shallow roots. A 5- or 6-inch pot is plenty big enough for a mature earthstar.

PROPAGATION. Earthstars are easy to propagate by separating the pups from the parent plant. When these pups are about one-third the size of the parent plant, cut them off and pot them up in the same kind of medium as the parent plant. Keep them in a clear plastic bag to maintain high humidity, and put them in a warm place for a month or so until they're established.

COMMON PROBLEMS

Watch for brown leaf tips (page 246), scale insects (page 262), and root rot (page 272).

Flaming sword

Flaming sword (*Vriesea splendens*) is a bromeliad common in garden centers, supermarkets, and big box stores. It's a popular houseplant both for its impressive, bright red inflorescence and for its colorful leaves, whose alternating cross-wise bands of maroon and silvery green look rather like Pippi's long stockings. Like all bromeliads, the leaves of the flaming sword absorb moisture from the air through specialized scales. Most bromeliads have leaves that form a "vase" that holds water, and in the flaming sword this cup (or tank) is substantial because the leaves arch up and out from the center of the plant. In nature, the leaves

Flaming sword (aka painted feather, zebra bromeliad, vriesea).

absorb nutrients from anything that falls into the water tank, a feature that makes bromeliads very easy to fertilize by just spraying the foliage. Some nutrients are absorbed immediately by the leaves and some accumulate in the tank to be taken up later. Any fertilizer that reaches the potting medium is taken up by the roots.

Flaming sword grows about 20 inches tall and 24 inches wide with a dozen stiff, strap-like, 15-inch-long and 2-inch-wide leaves that overlap at their bases, forming the water-holding cup. The plant flowers when it's three to four years old, sending a 2-foot-tall spike from the center of the water tank. The top half of the spike has brilliant scarlet, tightly overlapping bracts that make the spike 2 to 3 inches wide. This quill-like inflorescence with its colorful bracts lasts for months. Small bright yellow flowers peek out from between the bright red bracts on the spike. Each individual flower is short-lived. The plant blooms for months and then it slowly dies a long, graceful death over the course of a year. As it dies, however, it clones itself by producing one or more pups off to one side of the mother plant. If your plant is in flower when you purchase it, don't fret when it begins its decline. It will produce at least one pup, and in another three to four years the pup will flower. Most flaming swords are sold potted, since that's the easiest way for growers to produce these plants. However, you could grow this epiphyte on a slab of bark, an untreated board, or some other wooden perch if you want to.

OPTIMUM HOUSEHOLD ENVIRONMENT

Read the Introduction for the specifics of each recommendation.

MEDIUM LIGHT. Bright filtered light is perfect for flaming sword. The plant appreciates a daily dose of a couple of hours of direct morning sun in winter.

MODERATE TEMPERATURE. Daytime 70 to 80°F, nighttime 60 to 70°F.

MODERATE WATER. Flaming sword bromeliad has a fairly capacious tank, from which it obtains most of its water. Empty the tank and refill it with fresh distilled water or rainwater every two weeks or so. Moisten the potting medium at the same time but not so much that it becomes saturated and soggy. A little water frequently is the ticket, and too much water can easily lead to root rot. Don't use tap water for these plants; they are sensitive to the chemicals it contains.

HUMIDITY. Flaming swords like high humidity. Mist your plant at least once a week with a spray bottle of water on a mist setting, or use a handheld mister. Put the pot in a saucer or tray of water, making sure the bottom of the pot never sits directly in the water by raising the pot up on pot feet or pebbles. Consider putting a humidifier in the room.

POTTING MEDIUM. Use any good organic potting medium designed for semi-terrestrial orchids, one that incorporates organic fertilizer, mycorrhizal fungi, and other beneficial microbes.

FERTILIZER. Use any balanced liquid organic fertilizer mixed at half-strength and spray it on the leaves once a month through the growing season. In winter, apply fertilizer every other month.

POTTING. If you are growing flaming sword in a pot, up-pot young plants to a container with a diameter 2 inches larger than the current pot. Up-pot them in the spring. Use a shallow pot, wider than deep, and be gentle; this plant has only a few shallow roots. A 6-inch pot is plenty big enough for a mature flaming sword. Once it matures it does not need up-potting; and, of course, once it flowers it's going to die.

To grow it on a slab of bark or piece of driftwood, gently knock the plant out of its pot and shake off most but not all of the potting medium. Handle the roots gently and position your plant on its side on the slab of bark. Cover the roots with a little bit of moist sphagnum moss. Tack three or four small nails into the slab all around the base of your plant. Wrap plastic-coated wire around the head of one of the nails, then wrap the wire across the base of your plant over to another nail and wrap the wire around that nail's head. Continue wrapping from nail to nail until your plant is securely bound to the slab with a crisscrossed network of wire. Tuck moistened sphagnum moss all around the roots and the wire to hide the wire. Hang the plant in a warm, humid, shaded location until it's established on its new perch.

PROPAGATION. Flaming swords are easy to propagate by separating the pup from the parent plant when the pup is half grown. Pot up the pup in the same kind of medium as the parent plant or on its own slab. Keep it in a clear plastic bag in warm temperatures for a month until it's established.

COMMON PROBLEMS
Watch for sunburn (page 256), scale insects (page 262), and root rot (page 272).

Guzmania

Floral bracts in a wide array of colors—flaming scarlet, red, pink, orange, lavender, or yellow—form a globular inflorescence that stands above the handsome, glossy leaves of this popular bromeliad. Guzmania plants (*Guzmania lingulata*, *G. sanguinea*, and numerous hybrids) are about 10 inches tall and 12 inches wide, with narrow, strap-shaped leaves to 18 inches in length that arch up and out from the funnel-shaped rosette at the plant's center. Like all bromeliads, the leaves of guzmania absorb moisture from the air through specialized scales. Most bromeliads have leaves that form a "vase" that holds water,

Guzmania (aka scarlet star, vase plant).

and in guzmania the overlapping bases of the leaves form this watertight cup in its heart. In nature, the leaves absorb nutrients from anything that falls into the water tank, a feature that makes bromeliads very easy to fertilize by just spraying the foliage. Some nutrients are absorbed immediately by the leaves and some accumulate in the tank to be taken up later. Any fertilizer that reaches the potting medium is taken up by the roots.

Guzmania blooms when it's three to four years old. The flower spike is taller than the foliage and emerges from the center of the water tank. The spike has brilliantly colored, pointed bracts that flare out wide from the spike's stalk.

Guzmania.

This inflorescence with its colorful bracts lasts for a couple of months. Small white flowers peek out from between the bracts on the spike. Each individual flower is short-lived, but the plant blooms for six to eight weeks. After it blooms it dies a long, slow, graceful death over the course of a year, but like all bromeliads, it clones itself as it dies, producing one or two pups around its base. If your plant is in flower when you purchase it, don't fret when it begins its decline. It produces at least one pup, and in another three to four years the new pup should flower. Most guzmanias are sold potted, since that's the easiest way for growers to produce these plants. However, you could grow this epiphyte on a slab of bark, an untreated board, or some other wooden perch if you want to.

OPTIMUM HOUSEHOLD ENVIRONMENT

Read the Introduction for the specifics of each recommendation.

MEDIUM LIGHT. Moderately bright, filtered light with no direct sun suits this plant perfectly. It also does very well under bright artificial lights.

MODERATE TEMPERATURE. Daytime 70 to 80°F, nighttime 60 to 70°F.

MODERATE WATER. Guzmania has a fairly capacious tank, from which it obtains most of its water. Keep about 1 inch of water in the tank. Empty the tank and refill it with fresh distilled water or rainwater every two to three weeks or so. Moisten the potting medium at the same time but not so much that it becomes saturated and soggy. A little water frequently is the ticket, and too much water can easily lead to root rot. Don't use tap water for these plants; they are sensitive to the chemicals it contains.

HUMIDITY. Guzmania likes high humidity. Mist your plant at least once a week with a spray bottle of water on a mist setting, or use a handheld mister. Put the pot in a saucer or tray of water,

making sure the bottom of the pot never sits directly in the water by raising the pot up on pot feet or pebbles. Consider putting a humidifier in the room.

POTTING MEDIUM. Use any good organic potting medium designed for semi-terrestrial orchids, one that incorporates organic fertilizer, mycorrhizal fungi, and other beneficial microbes.

FERTILIZER. Use any balanced liquid organic fertilizer mixed at half-strength and spray it on the leaves once a month through the growing season. In winter, apply fertilizer every other month.

POTTING. If you grow guzmania in a pot, young plants need up-potting to a container with a diameter 2 inches larger than the current pot. Up-pot them in the spring. Use a shallow pot, wider than deep, and be gentle; this plant has only a few shallow roots. A 6-inch pot is plenty big enough for a mature guzmania. These plants are top-heavy and tend to tip over, so choose a heavy pot for your plant. Once it matures it does not need up-potting; and, of course, once it flowers it's going to die.

To grow it on a slab of bark or piece of driftwood, gently knock the plant out of its pot and shake off most but not all of the potting medium. Handle the roots gently and position your plant on its side on the slab of bark. Cover the roots with a little bit of moist sphagnum moss. Tack three or four small nails into the slab all around the base of your plant. Wrap plastic-coated wire around the head of one of the nails, then wrap the wire across the base of your plant over to another nail and wrap the wire around that nail's head. Continue wrapping from nail to nail until your plant is securely bound to the slab with a crisscrossed network of wire. Tuck moistened sphagnum moss all around the roots and the wire to hide the wire. Hang the plant in a warm, humid, shaded location until it's established on its new perch.

PROPAGATION. Guzmania is easy to propagate by separating the pup from the parent plant when the pup is 3 inches tall. Pot up the pup in the same kind of medium as the parent plant but keep it in a loose clear plastic bag in warm temperatures for a month until it's established.

COMMON PROBLEMS

Watch for brown leaf tips (page 246), mealybugs (page 262), and root rot (page 272).

Lady's slipper

Although this common name is applied to three different genera of orchids, the genus we'll discuss here is *Paphiopedilum*. Paphiopedilums are the best of all the lady's slippers and the ones you'll readily find in your local stores. They are among the easiest of all orchids to grow and to rebloom in your home. These tropical semi-terrestrial rhizomatous orchids are adapted to low light and warm temperatures, which makes them very good household companions.

When you see a lady's slipper in flower, it's impossible not to do a double take. You have to, to take in all the fascinating detail of the blossoms. The often somber flower colors include mahogany, honey, yellow, white, pink, and green, usually with stripes, spots, and warts. The petals are smooth, stiff, waxy, and sometimes wavy-edged. The pouchy lip has a glossy lacquered look and is surprisingly firm. But none of these words conveys the distinctive character of these flowers. Almost as if they have individual personalities, the flowers are commanding, charismatic presences that lure you in for a closer look. They are borne on tall stalks well above the leaves, each stalk usually carrying only one flower, although some hybrids have more than one flower per stalk. Each individual flower can easily last in good condition for

Lady's slipper (aka Venus' slipper, paphiopedilum).

two months on the plant, which makes paphs among the longest-lived blooms of any houseplant. The leaves of all forms, whether species or hybrid, are rather soft for an orchid and are carried in a basal rosette near ground level. Some hybrids have narrow, long, strap-like leaves that arch gracefully, while others have shorter, wider leaves. Foliage is either solid green or mottled like a delicate checkerboard with pale greenish white patches.

OPTIMUM HOUSEHOLD ENVIRONMENT

Read the Introduction for the specifics of each recommendation.

LOW LIGHT. Paphiopedilums do not like direct sun and do best in bright ambient light from a north window or medium filtered light from an east or west window. If you're having trouble getting your paph to rebloom, give it a little more light and cooler temperatures for a couple of weeks.

MODERATE TEMPERATURE. Daytime 70 to 80°F, nighttime 60 to 70°F.

AMPLE WATER. Water whenever the top of the potting medium becomes dry to a depth of 0.5 inch. These orchids are among the few that do not have pseudobulbs as water storage structures and need to be kept moist all the time. Orchids are sensitive to water quality and should be irrigated with filtered, rain-, or distilled water, rather than tap water. Let tepid water flow through the entire root zone until all the potting medium is soaked. Tip the plant back and forth to drain all the water out of the crown of the plant. Let the pot drain and air out, then put it back in its place. Mark the pot so that your plant is returned to its original position every time. Turning your orchid causes the flowers to twist and bend to face the light, which destroys their elegant arrangement.

HUMIDITY. Mist your plant several times a week with a spray bottle of water on a mist setting, or use a handheld mister. Put the pot in a saucer or tray of water, making sure the bottom of the pot never sits directly in the water by raising the pot up on pot feet or pebbles. Consider putting a humidifier in the room.

POTTING MEDIUM. Use any good organic potting medium designed for semi-terrestrial orchids, one that incorporates organic fertilizer, mycorrhizal fungi, and other beneficial microbes.

FERTILIZER. Use any balanced organic fertilizer, in either a water soluble or liquid formulation, to promote good growth and flowering. Apply at one-quarter-strength at least once a week right after you water your orchid.

POTTING. When your plant needs up-potting, shift it to a container with a diameter 2 inches larger than the current pot.

PROPAGATION. Lady's slippers are easy to propagate by division of the rhizome.

COMMON PROBLEMS

Watch for sunburn (page 256), mealybugs (page 262), and bacterial leaf spot (page 267).

Lady's slipper.

Moth orchid

Moth orchids are species and hybrids in the genera *Phalaenopsis* and *Doritis*, and their intergeneric cross, ×*Doritaenopsis*. All are epiphytes in nature (they never grow in soil), and any one of the many available kinds would be a sophisticated addition to your home. The flowers are gorgeous with each of the two huge upper petals making half of a nearly complete circle. The little lower lip is brightly colored and very intricately shaped with various horns, teeth, and lumps. Flower color varies from virginal white or white with a red lip to pink, deep pink, dark purple-pink, yellow, orange, or green. Plants are compact, with three to five, thick, leathery, paddle-shaped green leaves at their base. Long, thin, erect flower stalks arise from below the leaves, each bearing from six to 20 or more flowers, which last in good condition for many weeks. Some plants offer continuous bloom for more than six months.

The plants commonly available at big box stores or supermarket floral departments are the big-flowered standard-sized phals. These are big plants with a leaf spread 24 inches wide and flower stalks 36 inches tall. Flower size on these big boys is an impressive 5 inches across. But it's the elegant disposition of the flowers that is so captivating. Each flower stalk grows straight up, then arches over toward the light, then angles down toward the floor. Each bears a dozen or so of the big flowers, but they are arranged one above the other like a sophisticated double staircase. Each flower presents its flat face to the viewer unimpeded by the flower in front of it. The large-flowered moth orchids increasingly seen at supermarkets offer new and interesting color combinations, such as large deep purple blotches on white petals or pink stripes on a white or pink background.

Aside from the big standard-sized moth orchids, there are many other species of much smaller stature, with smaller, heavier, and waxier flowers in a broader range of colors. *Phalaenopsis lueddemanniana* and others contributed golden yellow colors and stripes and spots to moth orchid hybrids. We have *P. violacea* to thank for adding violet and intriguing patterns to petals and sepals. Tiny *P. equestris* has intensely dark pink flowers only 1 inch across borne in great abundance. The result of all this hybridizing activity is that when you see moth orchids for sale in your local stores, you'll find small-flowered miniatures with a leaf spread of 6 inches or less and a flower stalk from 6 to 12 inches tall. You'll also find the large-flowered

Moth orchid (aka moon orchid).

Moth orchid.

standard size, and everything in between. Modern hybrids have flowers in every color except true blue, with or without stripes, spots, or blotches in contrasting colors.

OPTIMUM HOUSEHOLD ENVIRONMENT

Read the Introduction for the specifics of each recommendation.

LOW LIGHT. Put moth orchids in a warm north window, or put them on a coffee table, a bookshelf, or a table where the light is nice and bright but not sunny. Never expose them to the full sun of a south window because the sun burns their thick leaves very quickly. Sunburned leaves develop large, black, dead patches that are permanent. In the right amount of light, leaves are a medium olive-green. If your plants are getting too much light the foliage turns yellow-green. Insufficient light turns the leaves dark green.

HIGH TEMPERATURE. Daytime 75 to 85°F year-round, nighttime about 65°F except when initiating flowering. In autumn, when outdoor temperatures drop, stimulate flower production by giving your moth orchids a nighttime temperature of 58°F for 30 days. Plants flower in spring.

AMPLE WATER. Water whenever the top of the potting medium becomes dry to a depth of 0.5 inch. Orchids are sensitive to water quality and should be irrigated with filtered, rain-, or distilled water, rather than tap water. Flood the root zone with tepid water. Avoid getting the crown of the foliage wet if you can. Let the pot drain and air out, then put it back in its place.

Mark the pot so that your plant is returned to its original position every time. Turning your orchid causes the flowers to twist and bend to face the light, which destroys their elegant arrangement. Another method of watering your moth orchid is to place two or three ice cubes (not of tap water) on top of the potting medium once a week and let them melt.

HUMIDITY. Kitchens and baths generate a lot of humidity in most homes, and moth orchids appreciate the added moisture in the air. Another method of increasing humidity is to set the pot on top of a tray filled with gravel and water. Just be sure the pot is raised up above the surface level of the water. Sitting in water will kill your plant. Misting your plants midweek between waterings with a spray bottle of water also helps.

POTTING MEDIUM. Moth orchids grow very well in orchid bark and nothing else. Some people add a little coarse peat and some perlite to the mix, but the plants generally perform well in straight Douglas fir bark. Orchid bark comes in three grades: coarse, medium, and fine. Use the fine bark for small plants like minis and seedlings. Use the medium bark for mature full-size plants. Do not use garden soil or ordinary potting soil because it will kill this epiphytic orchid.

FERTILIZER. Use any balanced organic fertilizer, in either a water soluble or liquid formulation, to promote good growth and flowering. Apply at one-quarter-strength at least once a week right after you water your orchid.

POTTING. Your moth orchid needs to be up-potted every two years or so. Choose a pot with a diameter 2 inches larger than the current pot. Orchids generally prefer being rootbound in smallish pots. The largest plants would grow very well in a 6-inch pot and the smallest in a 4-inch pot.

PROPAGATION. Moth orchids have no rhizomes and so cannot be divided. But they do often produce a keiki on the old flower stalk. When the small keiki has two or three leaves and several roots, cut it off the mother plant and pot it up.

COMMON PROBLEMS
Watch for sunburn (page 256), scale insects (page 262), and root rot (page 272).

Neoregelia

These bromeliads are grown primarily for their very showy and colorful foliage. *Neoregelia carolinae* is the most commonly cultivated species. Plants are 2 feet wide and half as tall, flat-topped, with a rosette of 1.5-inch-wide, 12-inch-long, strap-shaped leaves striped like ribbon candy with creamy white. Like all bromeliads, neoregelia leaves absorb moisture from the air through specialized scales. Most bromeliads have leaves that form a "vase" that holds water, and in neoregelias, a shallow water tank is formed by the overlapping bases of the leaves. In nature, the leaves absorb nutrients from anything that falls into the water tank, a feature that makes bromeliads very easy to fertilize by just spraying the foliage. Some nutrients are absorbed immediately by the leaves and some accumulate in the tank to be taken up later. Any fertilizer that reaches the potting medium is taken up by the roots.

Neoregelias bloom when they're three to four years old. The leaves around the center of the plant's tank turn bright red as flowering begins (that's why they're sometimes called blushing bromeliads), and the brilliant colors remain for the rest of the plant's life. The flower spike itself is very short, and you'd probably never know the plant was in bloom if it didn't colorize the foliage so prettily. The violet flowers are not at all showy and are tucked down inside the water tank. After it flowers, your neoregelia slowly dies. It can take a year for this process, during which time the plant clones itself. The mother plant produces several pups around its base. Most neoregelias are sold potted, since that's the easiest way for growers to produce these plants. However, you could grow this epiphyte on a slab of bark, an untreated board, or some other wooden perch if you want to.

OPTIMUM HOUSEHOLD ENVIRONMENT

Read the Introduction for the specifics of each recommendation.

MEDIUM LIGHT. Neoregelias prosper with a half-day of direct sun from an east or west window.

MODERATE TEMPERATURE. Daytime 70 to 80°F, nighttime 60 to 70°F.

MODERATE WATER. Neoregelia obtains most of its water from its shallow tank. Keep about 1 inch of water in the tank. Empty the tank and refill it with fresh distilled water or rainwater every two to three weeks or so. Moisten the potting medium at the same time but not so much that it becomes saturated and soggy. A little water frequently is the ticket, and too much water can easily lead to root rot. Don't use tap water for

Neoregelia (aka blushing bromeliad, cartwheel plant).

these plants; they are sensitive to the chemicals it contains.

HUMIDITY. Neoregelia prefers humidity above 50%, which can be tricky to provide with a half-day of full sun. Mist your plant frequently with a spray bottle of water on a mist setting, or use a handheld mister. Put the pot in a saucer or tray of water, making sure the bottom of the pot never sits directly in the water by raising the pot up on pot feet or pebbles. Consider putting a humidifier in the room.

POTTING MEDIUM. Use any good organic potting medium designed for semi-terrestrial orchids, one that incorporates organic fertilizer, mycorrhizal fungi, and other beneficial microbes.

FERTILIZER. Use any balanced liquid organic fertilizer mixed at half-strength and spray it on the leaves once a month through the growing season. In winter, apply fertilizer every other month.

POTTING. If you grow neoregelia in a pot, young plants need up-potting to a container with a diameter 2 inches larger than the current pot. Up-pot them in the spring. Use a shallow pot, wider than deep, and be gentle; this plant has only a few shallow roots. A 6-inch pot is plenty big enough for a mature neoregelia. Once it matures it does not need up-potting; and, of course, once it flowers it's going to die.

To grow it on a slab of bark or piece of driftwood, gently knock the plant out of its pot and shake off most but not all of the potting medium. Handle the roots gently and position your plant on its side on the slab of bark. Cover the roots with a little bit of moist sphagnum moss. Tack three or four small nails into the slab all around the base of your plant. Wrap plastic-coated wire around the head of one of the nails, then wrap the wire across the base of your plant over to another nail and wrap the wire around that

Neoregelia.

nail's head. Continue wrapping from nail to nail until your plant is securely bound to the slab with a crisscrossed network of wire. Tuck moistened sphagnum moss all around the roots and the wire to hide the wire. Hang the plant in a warm, humid, shaded location until it's established on its new perch.

PROPAGATION. Neoregelia is easy to propagate by separating the pups after the mother plant has died. Pot up the pups in the same kind of medium as the parent plant but keep them in a loose clear plastic bag in warm temperatures for a month until they're established.

COMMON PROBLEMS

Watch for brown leaf tips (page 246), mealybugs (page 262), and root rot (page 272).

Pansy orchid

Gorgeous, elegant, and sophisticated are the adjectives that spring to mind when describing these lovely orchids, whose popularity has exploded in recent years. Well-grown pansy orchids (*Miltoniopsis* hybrids) have long, wiry flower stalks that arch up, out, and down from the center of the plant and carry as many as a dozen 4-inch-long, fragrant flowers perfectly arranged one above the other with their flat faces presented to the viewer. Flower colors vary from red, pink, and lavender to white and yellow. The very large lip of these flowers has a large dark blotch at the base with dark lines bordered in pure white that radiate down the veins of the lip in a waterfall pattern. Really stunning! Easy-to-grow modern hybrids are commonly available in local garden centers, grocery stores, and big box stores everywhere.

Pansy orchids have several 12-inch-long, 1-inch-wide, V-shaped, rather strap-like and flexible leaf-like bracts attached to the base of

Pansy orchid (aka miltoniopsis).

their pseudobulbs. A single leaf is attached to the top of the pseudobulb. The overall effect is full and somewhat grass-like, meaning plants are attractive even when not in flower. The smooth, glossy, light green pseudobulbs, usually small flattened teardrops in shape, are about 2 inches long and partly hidden inside the sheathing bases of the bracts. As in other orchids, the pseudobulbs function as water storage devices and are clustered together at the soil line. Pansy orchids have a creeping rhizome that produces new pseudobulbs at regular intervals. Flower stalks generally erupt from the base of the pseudobulbs.

To get your pansy orchid to bloom again next year, examine the plant frequently after the current crop of flowers fades. About two to four weeks after the last flowers fade look for new growth emerging from the base of the pseudobulb that just flowered. When you see new green roots with white growing tips, be diligent about keeping your plant well watered and fertilized. A pointy, green, new growth emerges along with these new roots and it's going to mature into a new pseudobulb that flowers the next year. Do not let it dry out and make sure it's getting bright but indirect light and cool temperatures. Under adverse conditions where the plant does not get what it needs in terms of light, temperature, water, and fertilizer, that new growth develops but does not flower. A new pseudobulb that fails to flower is called a blind growth.

OPTIMUM HOUSEHOLD ENVIRONMENT

Read the Introduction for the specifics of each recommendation.

MEDIUM LIGHT. Very bright filtered light from an east window is ideal. No direct sun. And avoid the heat load of a south or west window.

LOW TEMPERATURE. Daytime 65 to 75°F, nighttime 55 to 65°F.

MODERATE WATER. Give these orchids a good long drink twice a week. Orchids are sensitive to water quality and should be irrigated with filtered, rain-, or distilled water, rather than tap water. Let tepid water flow through the entire root zone until all the potting medium is soaked. Let the pot drain and air out, then put it back

in its place. Mark the pot so that your plant is returned to its original position every time. Turning your orchid causes the flowers to twist and bend to face the light, which destroys their elegant arrangement.

HUMIDITY. Mist your plant several times a week with a spray bottle of water on a mist setting, or use a handheld mister. Put the pot in a saucer or tray of water, but make absolutely sure the bottom of the pot never sits directly in the water by raising the pot up on pot feet or pebbles. Consider putting a humidifier in the room.

POTTING MEDIUM. Use any good organic, orchid potting medium such as medium orchid bark. Do not use garden soil or ordinary potting soil because it would kill this epiphytic orchid.

FERTILIZER. Use any balanced organic fertilizer, in either a water soluble or liquid formulation, to promote good growth and flowering. Apply at one-quarter-strength at least once a week right after you water your orchid.

POTTING. Your pansy orchid needs to be up-potted every two years or so. Choose a pot with a diameter 2 inches larger than the current pot. Orchids generally prefer being root-bound in smallish pots. Re-pot after flowering is complete and when new growth and new roots start to emerge. *Miltoniopsis* roots are slender, small, and easily damaged, so treat them gently. Be attentive to watering after up-potting or re-potting these plants and do not allow them to dry out.

PROPAGATION. Pansy orchids are easy to propagate by division of the rhizome. Next time you need to up-pot your plant cut the rhizome into two pieces so that each piece has a decent number of roots, pseudobulbs, and leaves.

COMMON PROBLEMS

Watch for accordion-folded leaves (page 246), scale insects (page 262), and root rot (page 272).

Queen's tears

Queen's tears (*Billbergia nutans*) is so beautiful and so easy to grow, it is no wonder it is such a popular houseplant. Plants grow 16 to 18 inches tall and 30 inches wide and are particularly attractive in a hanging pot or basket, where the cascading flowers can be enjoyed at eye level. Leaves arch up and out from a narrow, funnel-shaped rosette at the plant's center; they are 1 inch wide and 18 inches long, somewhat grass-like but wide and flat with saw-toothed edges. Like all bromeliads, the leaves of queen's tears absorb moisture from the air through specialized scales. Most bromeliads have leaves that form a "vase" that holds water, and in queen's tears the densely overlapping bases of the numerous leaves form this watertight cup in its heart. In nature, the leaves absorb nutrients from anything that falls into the water tank, a feature that makes bromeliads very easy to fertilize by just spraying the foliage. Some nutrients are absorbed immediately by the leaves and some accumulate in the tank to be taken up later. Any fertilizer that reaches the potting medium is taken up by the roots.

Queen's tears blooms when it's three to four years old. The first time you see it in bloom, prepare to be taken aback by the artistic combination of soft colors in its long and pendulous flower spike. The teardrop-shaped flower buds are frosty pink and minty green, edged in deep blue-violet. Blue-tipped green petals flare out as the flower opens, revealing bright yellow stamens. The flowers drip little droplets of nectar (hence the common name). Once it flowers your queen's tears slowly dies. It's a graceful process, this dying, and it takes a year to complete. While it dies, however, your queen's tears clones itself by producing several pups around its base. If your plant is in flower when you purchase it, don't fret when it begins its decline. It will produce pups, and then in another three to four years the pups flower for you (or the friends you've shared them with). Most queen's tears are sold potted, since that's the easiest way for growers to produce them. However, you could grow this epiphyte on a slab of bark, an untreated board, or some other wooden perch if you want to.

Queen's tears (aka friendship plant).

OPTIMUM HOUSEHOLD ENVIRONMENT

Read the Introduction for the specifics of each recommendation.

MEDIUM LIGHT. Give queen's tears a half-day of bright filtered light from an east or west window. If you give it a summer vacation outdoors, keep it in partial shade.

MODERATE TEMPERATURE. Daytime 70 to 80°F, nighttime 60 to 70°F, during the summer growing season. In fall, winter, and early spring keep it cool: daytime 60 to 75°F, nighttime 55 to 65°F.

MODERATE WATER. Queen's tears obtains most of its water from its tank. Keep about 1 inch of water in the tank. Empty the tank and refill it with fresh distilled water or rainwater every two to three weeks or so. Moisten the potting medium at the same time but not so much that it becomes saturated and soggy. A little water frequently is the ticket, and too much water can easily lead to root rot. Don't use tap water for these plants; they are sensitive to the chemicals it contains.

HUMIDITY. Queen's tears tolerates dry air better than most bromeliads but nevertheless appreciates misting to increase humidity. Mist your plant often with a spray bottle of water on a mist setting, or use a handheld mister. Put the pot in a saucer or tray of water, making sure the bottom of the pot never sits directly in the water by raising the pot up on pot feet or pebbles. Consider putting a humidifier in the room.

POTTING MEDIUM. Use any good organic potting medium designed for semi-terrestrial orchids, one that incorporates organic fertilizer, mycorrhizal fungi, and other beneficial microbes.

FERTILIZER. Use any balanced liquid organic fertilizer mixed at half-strength and spray it on the leaves once a month through the growing season. In winter, apply fertilizer every other month.

POTTING. If you grow queen's tears in a pot, young plants need up-potting to a container with a diameter 2 inches larger than the current pot. Up-pot them in the spring. Use a shallow pot, wider than deep, and be gentle; this plant has only a few shallow roots. A 6-inch pot is plenty big enough for a mature queen's tears. Once it matures it does not need up-potting; and, of course, once it flowers it's going to die.

To grow it on a slab of bark or piece of driftwood, gently knock the plant out of its pot and shake off most but not all of the potting medium. Handle the roots gently and position your plant on its side on the slab of bark. Cover the roots with a little bit of moist sphagnum moss. Tack three or four small nails into the slab all around the base of your plant. Wrap plastic-coated wire around the head of one of the nails, then wrap the wire across the base of your plant over to another nail and wrap the wire around that nail's head. Continue wrapping from nail to nail until your plant is securely bound to the slab with a crisscrossed network of wire. Tuck moistened sphagnum moss all around the roots and the wire to hide the wire. Hang the plant in a warm, humid, shaded location until it's established on its new perch.

PROPAGATION. Queen's tears is easy to propagate by separating the pups from the parent plant. When the mother plant has died back, cut it off at the soil line leaving the pups to continue to grow. Pot up the pups when they are 6 inches tall in the same kind of medium as the parent plant but keep them in a loose clear plastic bag in warm temperatures for a month until they're established.

COMMON PROBLEMS

Watch for brown leaf tips (page 246), mealybugs (page 262), and root rot (page 272).

Spider orchid.

Spider orchid

A well-grown spider orchid (*Brassia gireoudiana*) in full flower is an astonishing sight. The plant looks like it comes from outer space. The flowers are amazing, bizarre, fascinating. They're huge, as much as 1 foot from top to bottom, with extremely skinny and spidery petals and sepals. They stand stiffly upright on each side of the flower stalk, lined up one behind the other in close formation, like a troupe of Cossack dancers with their arms and legs spread wide. The long-lasting, fragrant flowers are mostly green with large dark brown blotches and spots. Spider orchids are closely related to some other orchids frequently grown as houseplants such as dancing ladies, pansy orchids, and complex intergeneric hybrids like beallaras and aliceáras. Hybridizers have been busy crossing them all, in every possible combination, to create new hybrid genera. Local supermarkets, big box stores, and independent garden centers all carry large numbers of these gorgeous orchids at very reasonable prices, and it is usually very easy to spot the influence of *Brassia* in the hybrids. The genes for large, spotted, spidery flowers are often transmitted to their offspring.

Spider orchids have one to three, 12- to 24-inch-long, 2.5-inch-wide, rather strap-like, leathery leaves borne atop smooth, glossy green pseudobulbs. The large, 6-inch-long pseudobulbs are really quite pretty, usually shaped like flattened teardrops, and function as water storage devices. They are clustered together at the soil line and produced at regular intervals from a creeping rhizome. Flower stalks generally erupt from their base. A new pseudobulb begins to grow about two to four weeks after the last flowers have faded.

Many people find that their spider orchid grows well vegetatively, but fails to flower.

Growers call this a blind growth. You can avoid blind growths in your spider orchids by paying close attention to their needs for light, water, fertilizer, and temperature when the rhizome begins to make a new pseudobulb. Look for new green roots with white tips emerging from the base of the pseudobulb that has just finished flowering. The pointed end of a new growing point begins to show at the same time as the new roots. When you see this new growth of roots and foliage be diligent about meeting your plant's cultural needs. That new growth you spotted slowly matures into a new pseudobulb, which eventually flowers.

OPTIMUM HOUSEHOLD ENVIRONMENT

Read the Introduction for the specifics of each recommendation.

MEDIUM LIGHT. Bright filtered light from an east window is ideal for spider orchids. No direct sun. And avoid the heat load of a south or west window.

LOW TEMPERATURE. Daytime 65 to 75°F, nighttime 60 to 65°F.

LOW WATER. Give these orchids a good long drink once a week. Orchids are sensitive to water quality and should be irrigated with filtered, rain-, or distilled water, rather than tap water. Let tepid water flow through the entire root zone until all the potting medium is soaked. Let the pot drain and air out, then put it back in its place. Mark the pot so that your plant is returned to its original position every time. Turning your orchid causes the flowers to twist and bend to face the light, which destroys their elegant arrangement.

HUMIDITY. Mist your plant several times a week with a spray bottle of water on a mist setting, or use a handheld mister. Put the pot in a saucer or tray of water, but make absolutely sure the bottom of the pot never sits directly in the water by raising the pot up on pot feet or pebbles.

Consider putting a humidifier in the room.

POTTING MEDIUM. Use any good organic, orchid potting medium such as medium orchid bark. Do not use garden soil or ordinary potting soil because it will kill this epiphytic orchid.

FERTILIZER. Use any balanced organic fertilizer, in either a water soluble or liquid formulation, to promote good growth and flowering. Apply at one-quarter-strength at least once a week right after you water your orchid.

POTTING. Your spider orchid needs to be up-potted every two years or so. Choose a pot with a diameter 2 inches larger than the current pot. Orchids generally prefer being rootbound in smallish pots. Re-pot after flowering is complete and when new growth and new roots start to emerge. Spider orchid roots are small, slender, and easily damaged, so treat them gently. Be attentive to watering after up-potting or re-potting these plants and do not allow them to dry out.

PROPAGATION. Spider orchids are easy to propagate by division of the rhizome. Next time you need to up-pot your plant cut the rhizome into two pieces so that each piece has a decent number of roots, pseudobulbs, and leaves.

COMMON PROBLEMS

Watch for sunburn (page 256), mealybugs (page 262), and root rot (page 272).

Tillandsia

Tillandsia is a large genus of small, primarily rootless wonders that are grown as houseplants pinned, tied, or glued onto slabs of bark, branches, or driftwood, and then hung on a wall or suspended in mid-air. The exception is pink quill (*T. cyanea*), which is commonly available in pots. Some other species do have a few roots, but their primary purpose is to latch tightly onto their support, not to absorb water and nutrients. Like all bromeliads, tillandsias absorb moisture from the air through specialized scales on their leaves—one reason many members of this family are called air plants. They also absorb nutrients through their leaves, like other bromeliads, but unlike other bromeliads, they do not form a cup or tank in which they can store water.

The slender foliage is the definition of understated, running a small gamut from narrow to thread-like. So, when a tillandsia flowers at three to four years old, it's comes as a shock that such a tiny bit of gray-green fluff can produce such astonishingly large and bright flowers. In many tillandsias the inflorescence is flattened like a feather, taller than the plant and standing above it, with bright red or pink bracts. The common name pink quill is appropriate because its inflorescence does resemble a bright pink quill feather used for writing. Purple, violet, or blue flowers peek out from between the very closely spaced bracts, and the plant can be in bloom for months. Of course, like all bromeliads, after the plant flowers, it dies a deliciously slow death, cloning itself all the while by producing several pups around its base. Most pink quill tillandsias are sold potted, since that's the easiest way for growers to produce them. However, you could grow this epiphyte, like all its brethren, on a slab of bark, an untreated board, or some other wooden perch if you want to.

OPTIMUM HOUSEHOLD ENVIRONMENT

Read the Introduction for the specifics of each recommendation.

MEDIUM LIGHT. Bright filtered light from an east or west window is best in the summer. In winter they can handle a couple hours of direct sun from an east window.

MODERATE TEMPERATURE. Daytime 70 to 80°F, nighttime 60 to 70°F.

Tillandsia (aka air plant, sky plant).

MODERATE WATER. Spray the entire plant with filtered, rain-, or distilled water twice a week. Make sure the base of the plant does not sit and soak in a puddle of water. Also be sure the plant dries out within four hours. Your plant rots if it's too wet for too long. Don't use tap water for these plants; they are sensitive to the chemicals it contains.

HUMIDITY. Tillandsias are very well adapted to dry air and need no supplemental misting beyond their regular water spray.

POTTING MEDIUM. For pink quill, use any good organic potting medium designed for

Tillandsia.

semi-terrestrial orchids, one that incorporates organic fertilizer, mycorrhizal fungi, and other beneficial microbes. For all other tillandsias, no potting medium is needed.

FERTILIZER. Use any balanced liquid organic fertilizer mixed at half-strength and spray it on the leaves once a month through the growing season. In winter, apply fertilizer every other month.

POTTING. Once your plant is fastened to its wooden perch you won't have to reposition it. After the mother plant dies you'll probably want to reposition the pups. Handle the pup gently and position it on its side on the slab of bark. Cover the roots, if there are any, with a little bit of moist sphagnum moss. Tack three or four small nails into the slab all around the base of your plant. Wrap plastic-coated wire around the head of one of the nails, then wrap the wire across the base of your plant over to another nail and wrap the wire around that nail's head. Continue wrapping from nail to nail until your plant is securely bound to the slab with a crisscrossed network of wire. Tuck moistened sphagnum moss all around the base of the tillandsia and the wire to hide the wire. Hang the plant in a warm, humid, shaded location until it's established on its new perch.

PROPAGATION. Tillandsias are easy to propagate by separating the pups after the mother plant has died and fastening them to a wooden support.

COMMON PROBLEMS

Watch for brown leaf tips (page 246), mealybugs (page 262), and root rot (page 272).

Urn plant

Urn plant (*Aechmea fasciata*) is a big (2 to 3 feet tall and 2 feet wide), bold, extremely attractive bromeliad with an astonishingly bright, shocking pink inflorescence. Its numerous 18- to 36-inch-long, 2-inch-wide, stiff and leathery leaves are silver with gray-green bands. Some cultivars have creamy stripes on the edges of the leaves, and some are brushed with purple. The waxy leaves are edged with black spines and are spiny at the tips. Like all bromeliads, urn plant's leaves absorb moisture from the air through specialized scales. Most bromeliads have leaves that form a "vase" that holds water, and in urn plant the overlapping bases of the leaves form this watertight cup in its heart. In nature, the leaves absorb nutrients from anything that falls into the water tank, a feature that makes bromeliads very easy to fertilize by just spraying the foliage. Some nutrients are absorbed immediately by the leaves and some accumulate in the tank to be taken up later. Any fertilizer that reaches the potting medium is taken up by the roots.

Urn plant blooms in the spring when it's three to four years old. The spectacular inflorescence, which grows up out of the central tank, is taller than the leaves. It is a bright, frosty pink with a large number of bright pink bracts at the tip of the stalk that form a rounded ball. Violet flowers peek out from between the pink bracts, and the plant blooms for months. The violet flowers turn red as they age. Once your plant has flowered, it slowly dies over the course of a year. As it dies, however, it clones itself by producing two or three pups around its base. If your plant is in flower when you purchase it, don't fret when it begins its decline. It will produce pups, and in another three to four years the pups flower. Most urn plants are sold potted, since that's the easiest way for growers to produce them. However, you could grow this epiphyte on

Urn plant (aka silver vase plant).

a slab of bark, an untreated board, or some other wooden perch if you want to.

OPTIMUM HOUSEHOLD ENVIRONMENT

Read the Introduction for the specifics of each recommendation.

MEDIUM LIGHT. Bright filtered light from an east or west window is best for urn plant.

MODERATE TEMPERATURE. Daytime 70 to 80°F, nighttime 60 to 70°F.

MODERATE WATER. Urn plant obtains most of its water from its tank. Keep about 1 inch of water in the tank. Empty the tank and refill it with fresh distilled water or rainwater every two to three weeks or so. Moisten the potting medium at the same time but not so much that it becomes saturated and soggy. A little water frequently is the ticket, and too much water can easily lead to root rot. Don't use tap water for these plants; they are sensitive to the chemicals it contains.

HUMIDITY. Urn plant prefers moderate humidity. Mist your plant occasionally with a spray bottle of water on a mist setting, or use a handheld mister. Put the pot in a saucer or tray of water, making sure the bottom of the pot never sits directly in the water by raising the pot up on pot feet or pebbles. Consider putting a humidifier in the room if the air in your home is very dry.

POTTING MEDIUM. Use any good organic potting medium designed for semi-terrestrial orchids, one that incorporates organic fertilizer, mycorrhizal fungi, and other beneficial microbes.

FERTILIZER. Use any balanced liquid organic fertilizer mixed at half-strength and spray it on the leaves once a month through the growing season. In winter, apply fertilizer every other month.

POTTING. If you grow urn plant in a pot, young plants need up-potting to a container with a diameter 2 inches larger than the current pot. Up-pot them in the spring. Use a shallow pot, wider than deep, and be gentle; this plant has only a few shallow roots. An 8-inch pot is plenty big enough for a mature urn plant. Once it matures it does not need up-potting; and, of course, once it flowers it's going to die.

To grow it on a slab of bark or piece of driftwood, gently knock the plant out of its pot and shake off most but not all of the potting medium. Handle the roots gently and position your plant on its side on the slab of bark. Cover the roots with a little bit of moist sphagnum moss. Tack three or four small nails into the slab all around the base of your plant. Wrap plastic-coated wire around the head of one of the nails, then wrap the wire across the base of your plant over to another nail and wrap the wire around that nail's head. Continue wrapping from nail to nail until your plant is securely bound to the slab with a crisscrossed network of wire. Tuck moistened sphagnum moss all around the roots and the wire to hide the wire. Hang the plant in a warm, humid, shaded location until it's established on its new perch.

PROPAGATION. Urn plant is easy to propagate by separating the pups after the mother plant has died. When the pups are 6 inches tall pot them up in the same kind of medium as the parent plant but keep them in a loose clear plastic bag in warm temperatures for a month until they're established. Alternatively, attach the pups to a wooden perch as just described.

COMMON PROBLEMS

Watch for brown leaf tips (page 246), scale insects (page 262), and root rot (page 272).

Cacti and Succulents

Agave

Three of the approximately 450 species of agaves, many of them very attractive specimens, are often grown as houseplants. Parry's agave (*Agave parryi*), like all its cousins, is an evergreen succulent perennial. It has stiff, thick, 12-inch-long steel-blue leaves shaped like broadswords and tipped with long, ebony-black spines. The edge of each leaf is saw-toothed with small black spines. The overlapping leaves grow into a perfect ball, like a giant artichoke 2.5 feet tall and wide. On the back side of each leaf, lace-like whitish patterns left by the older leaves add interest. Queen Victoria agave (*A. victoriae-reginae*) makes a lovely, very long-lived houseplant, growing slowly to only 10 inches high and wide. The white marks on the backs of its leaves stand out in contrast to the dark green color. *Agave americana* matures at an impressive 4 feet tall and wide, way too big for the average home, but fortunately this slow-growing species can be enjoyed as a houseplant for years while it is young.

It is unlikely any agave grown indoors as a houseplant could ever have enough energy to produce a flower stalk. Be sure to locate spiny specimens where admirers and passersby will not get stabbed in the ankles or knees. Also, the sap of agaves irritates some people, causing contact dermatitis.

Agave (aka American aloe, century plant, maguey, mescal).

OPTIMUM HOUSEHOLD ENVIRONMENT

Read the Introduction for the specifics of each recommendation.

HIGH LIGHT. Agaves need full direct sun to prosper in the home environment. In winter give them a south window that cools off at night.

HIGH TEMPERATURE. Daytime 75 to 85°F, nighttime 65 to 75°F. In winter grow them ten degrees cooler, day and night.

LOW WATER. During the growing season, water whenever the top of the potting medium becomes dry to a depth of 2 inches. Water less frequently in winter.

HUMIDITY. Agaves are adapted to very dry, desert conditions and do not need supplemental humidity.

POTTING MEDIUM. Use any good organic, fast-draining, cactus and succulent potting soil that incorporates organic fertilizer, mycorrhizal fungi, and other beneficial microbes.

FERTILIZER. Use any balanced organic fertilizer. Apply once a month through the growing season. Do not feed these plants in winter.

POTTING. Agaves grow extremely slowly and need to be up-potted only every three years or so. When your plant needs up-potting, shift it to a container with a diameter 2 inches larger than the current pot. Choose a heavy, shallow pot to help keep your agave from falling over. Re-pot every few years or so. Agave species and hybrids vary enormously in mature size, so your final pot size varies according to the mature size of your plant.

PROPAGATION. Agaves are propagated by seed or by potting up pups.

COMMON PROBLEMS

Watch for shrunken, wrinkled leaves (page 255), mealybugs (page 262), and root rot (page 272).

Aloe

All the approximately 400 species and hybrids in *Aloe* are excellent container specimens, with showy, tubular flowers in brilliant reds, oranges, and yellows. But only a few of these desert-dwelling succulents make good houseplants. Of these, *A. vera* is the most popular. Others to consider as houseplants are *A. aristata* (lace aloe) and *A. humilis* (spider aloe) at 8 to 10 inches tall, and *A. variegata* (tiger aloe), with zebra-striped leaves, to 12 inches tall.

Aloe vera grows 1 to 2 feet tall and 6 to 12 inches wide with rosettes of stiff, thick, fleshy leaves. The leaves are 18 inches long, gray-green,

Aloe (aka Barbados aloe, burn plant, Chinese aloe, first aid plant, Indian aloe, medicinal aloe, true aloe).

Spider aloe.

spotted with whitish flecks, and armed with whitish teeth all along the edges. It is a tropical, evergreen perennial that produces pups, new little clones of itself, all around its base. When three to four years old, *A. vera* blooms in the summer with clusters of small, tubular yellow flowers on 3-foot-tall stalks. It needs good light to flower. If aloe does not flower for you, try giving it more light. If you put it outdoors for the summer, hummingbirds will be sure to find the flowers and delight you with their antics. *Aloe vera* has been used medicinally for millennia and is a common ingredient in commercial cosmetics, skin creams, and sunburn lotions. Cutting or breaking a leaf in half releases the healing, mucilaginous sap, which can then be rubbed directly onto the skin.

OPTIMUM HOUSEHOLD ENVIRONMENT

Read the Introduction for the specifics of each recommendation.

HIGH LIGHT. This succulent likes very bright, filtered light and grows well in a south, east, or west window. It tolerates direct sun very well as long as you acclimate it to the intense light and heat slowly over a period of a couple of weeks. The leaves turn orange at the tips in full sun.

MODERATE TEMPERATURE. Daytime 70 to 80°F, nighttime 60 to 70°F.

MODERATE WATER. Water whenever the top of the potting medium becomes dry to a depth of 1 inch and try to keep the leaves dry. Water very sparingly in winter.

HUMIDITY. Like most cacti and succulents, aloe

tolerates the dry air of our homes very well.

POTTING MEDIUM. Use any good organic, fast-draining, cactus and succulent potting soil that incorporates organic fertilizer, mycorrhizal fungi, and other beneficial microbes.

FERTILIZER. Use any balanced organic fertilizer. Apply once a month through the growing season. When your plant goes dormant in winter, stop feeding it.

POTTING. When aloe needs up-potting, shift it to a container with a diameter 2 inches larger than the current pot. Aloe grows slowly and needs re-potting only occasionally.

PROPAGATION. Aloes are easy to propagate by carefully separating the pups from their mother.

COMMON PROBLEMS

Watch for sunburn (page 256), scale insects (page 262), and root rot (page 272).

Ball cactus

Most of the time when you find a cactus labeled "ball cactus," it will be one of the 25 or more *Parodia* species. As youngsters, all ball cacti are indeed round as a ball, but as they age they become columnar. They have deep furrows between raised longitudinal ribs and variously colored hairs and spines on the tops of the ribs. In addition to their pretty flowers, the patterns and shadows formed by the ribs and spines add visual interest to these little guys. Place them where they invite close inspection all year long. All produce pups around their base.

When young, balloon cactus (*Parodia magnifica*) is less than 10 inches tall and wide. As it ages it elongates, growing 18 inches tall and 3 to 6 inches thick, with deep furrows between raised longitudinal ribs or ridges. The tops of the ribs are covered with long, flexible, golden spines that are thin and hair-like. Flowers are 2

Ball cactus.

inches wide, borne on the top of the plant, and are pale, almost translucent, sulfur-yellow.

Lemon or golden ball cactus (*Parodia leninghausii*) starts out as a small ball well armed with soft, long, yellow spines. It earns another common name, yellow tower cactus, with age, reaching 3 feet tall and 5 inches thick. Its stems are heavily ribbed, hairy on the top of the ribs, and spiny. It flowers reliably every summer, even while it is still very small, bearing numerous 2-inch-wide, funnel-shaped yellow flowers with whitish stigmas on its crown.

Silver ball cactus (*Parodia scopa*) has showy white hairs in tufts at the base of clusters of long yellow spines. The white hairs give the whole top of the plant a silvery look. This one also

Balloon cactus.

has yellow flowers clustered on its crown, each with a bright red central stigma. Like the previous two species, it is a small ball when young, growing to a 20-inch-tall, 4-inch-thick column with age.

OPTIMUM HOUSEHOLD ENVIRONMENT

Read the Introduction for the specifics of each recommendation.

HIGH LIGHT. Give your ball cactus bright filtered light, not full sun, from a south or west window all winter long. In summer move it outdoors where it will be in partial shade during the heat of the afternoon.

MODERATE TEMPERATURE. Daytime 70 to 80°F, nighttime 60 to 70°F. In winter grow it five degrees cooler, day and night.

MODERATE WATER. Through the growing season, water whenever the top of the potting medium becomes dry to a depth of 1 inch. In winter, water much less and wait till the top of the potting medium becomes dry to a depth of 2 inches.

HUMIDITY. Ball cactus tolerates the dry air of our homes very well, like most cacti and succulents.

POTTING MEDIUM. Use any good organic, fast-draining, cactus and succulent potting soil that incorporates organic fertilizer, mycorrhizal fungi, and other beneficial microbes.

FERTILIZER. Use any balanced organic fertilizer. Apply once a month through the growing season. When it goes dormant in winter, stop feeding it.

POTTING. When ball cactus needs up-potting, in two to three years, shift it to a container with a diameter 2 inches larger than the current pot.

PROPAGATION. Ball cactus is easy to propagate from seed or by potting up pups.

COMMON PROBLEMS

Watch for sunburn (page 256), scale insects (page 262), and root rot (page 272).

Barrel cactus

Golden barrel cactus (*Echinocactus grusonii*) is the most widely grown houseplant cactus. It is a sculptural plant of great character and beauty, deeply furrowed and strongly ribbed. Dense golden spines on the tops of the ribs are long and straight, sometimes slightly curved, and occasionally white instead of the usual yellow. The plant forms a perfect ball when young, becoming more oval in age. Really old plants can get 5 feet tall and 3 feet wide. When they are about 20

Barrel cactus.

years old, plants bear small, 1- to 2-inch-wide, yellow flowers in a ring around the top of the plant. This cactus readily produces pups around its base.

Young plants of compass barrel cactus (*Ferocactus cylindraceus*) occasionally make good houseplants. This species is a ball when young and grows very slowly into a cylindrical shape. In nature, specimens lean to the south, facing the sun, with the lower half of the plant lying flat on the ground (hence the common name). Flowers are 3 inches wide, bell-shaped, yellow-orange, and borne in a ring on the top of the barrel. The barrel itself is deeply ribbed and densely clothed in red spines that turn gray as they age. The compass barrel is formidably spiny even when young, so careful placement in your home is paramount to avoid lacerating ankles

Golden barrel cactus (aka mother-in-law's cushion).

and knees of human residents. Fishhook barrel cactus (*F. wislizeni*) is very similar, except that the flowers are red, red with yellow edges, orange, or just plain yellow. It has viciously hooked stout spines (ouch!) and also needs careful placement in the home.

OPTIMUM HOUSEHOLD ENVIRONMENT

Read the Introduction for the specifics of each recommendation.

HIGH LIGHT. All three barrel cacti need full sun. If you have just acquired one, however, it may not have been grown in full sun; you'll have to acclimate it carefully so that it doesn't get sunburn.

LOW TEMPERATURE. Daytime 65 to 75°F, nighttime 55 to 65°F.

LOW WATER. Water whenever the top of the potting medium becomes dry to a depth of 2 inches. In winter water even less but don't let the plant dry out completely.

HUMIDITY. These cacti tolerate dry air extremely well so no additional humidity is necessary.

POTTING MEDIUM. Use any good organic, cactus and succulent potting soil that incorporates organic fertilizer, mycorrhizal fungi, and other beneficial microbes.

FERTILIZER. Use any balanced organic fertilizer. Apply once a month through the growing season. Do not feed these plants in winter.

POTTING. Every year in spring, when your young barrel cactus needs up-potting, shift it to a container with a diameter 2 inches larger than the current pot. Older plants need re-potting every two to three years. Be sure to wear gloves and handle it carefully.

PROPAGATION. Barrel cacti are easy to propagate from seed or by potting up pups.

COMMON PROBLEMS

Watch for leggy growth (page 251), mealybugs (page 262), and root rot (page 272).

Cereus cactus

Cereus cactus (*Cereus repandus*) is generally 2 to 4 feet tall when grown as a houseplant. Its short but sharp spines are borne on columnar blue-green stems. Only large, older specimens will flower, but when they do, it is a show. The flowers are huge, 6 to 8 inches long, and spectacular. They're white, they open only at night, and each lasts only a single night, but the plant continues to flower over several months in summer. The 2.5-inch-round, purplish red and yellow fruits, known as Peruvian apples, have tasty white flesh and tiny crunchy seeds. The stems of 'Monstrosus' twist and swirl into exotic sculptural shapes. Another common cultivar, 'Ming Thing Blue', also with fantastically shaped stems, is especially appealing because of its blue-green jade color. You'll want to place any cereus cactus carefully, to avoid painful jabs by its spines.

OPTIMUM HOUSEHOLD ENVIRONMENT

Read the Introduction for the specifics of each recommendation.

HIGH LIGHT. Cereus cactus grows best in full, direct sunlight but will also do well in very bright, filtered light. When you acquire yours, find out if it has been grown in full sun or in filtered light. If the latter and if you want yours in full sun you'll need to acclimate it so that it doesn't sunburn.

MODERATE TEMPERATURE. Daytime 70 to 80°F, nighttime 60 to 70°F. In winter grow it ten degrees cooler, day and night.

LOW WATER. Water whenever the top of the potting medium becomes dry to a depth of 2 inches. Water even less often in winter but don't let the plant dry out completely. When its stems get slightly spongy, water it.

HUMIDITY. This cactus is adapted to dry air and no misting is required.

Cereus cactus (aka column cactus, giant club cactus, hedge cactus, Peruvian apple cactus, Peruvian torch).

POTTING MEDIUM. Use any good organic, cactus and succulent potting soil that incorporates organic fertilizer, mycorrhizal fungi, and other beneficial microbes.

FERTILIZER. Use any balanced organic fertilizer. Apply once a month until the plants go dormant in winter.

POTTING. When your cereus needs up-potting, shift it to a container with a diameter 2 inches larger than the current pot. Up-pot young plants in spring, older plants only when necessary. Large cereus cacti are quite top-heavy, so choose a heavy pot to keep them from toppling over. And wear gloves to protect yourself from the spines.

PROPAGATION. Cereus cactus is easy to propagate from seed and stem tip cuttings, or by potting up pups.

COMMON PROBLEMS
Watch for sunburn (page 256), mealybugs (page 262), and root rot (page 272).

Chin cactus

Most popular varieties of chin cactus (*Gymnocalycium mihanovichii*) have an odd appearance. They look like a spiny, bright red baseball stuck on top of a green stick. The red balls are natural mutants that have no green chlorophyll in their tissues. The whole plant is bright red, pink, orange, or yellow, and, since it is not green at all, it is impossible for it to manufacture food for itself through photosynthesis. It has to be grafted to a different plant or it will die. The green "stick" it's grafted to is almost always a queen of the night (*Hylocereus triangularis*) cactus, but it could be any number of different green cacti. The "stick" must make enough food to keep the mutant red cactus ball alive and healthy. These colorful mutants are quite

Chin cactus (aka blondie, hibotan, hibotan nishiki, moon cactus, red cap cactus, red-top cactus, ruby ball).

common and readily available as grafted plants in garden centers and even in big box stores. In 'Hibotan Nishiki', a newer mutation, bright red sectors alternate with green on the same plant. Because these plants are partially green they can make their own food and grow on their own roots, so they don't have to be grafted. Both 'Hibotan Nishiki' and the non-mutant green species of chin cactus are available from specialist suppliers.

Chin cactus.

The wild form of chin cactus is a small, green flattened ball about 4 inches tall and 5 inches wide that produces abundant pups all around its base. The colorful mutants retain this ability, and you'll often see grafted plants with multiple, brightly colored pups. Flowers of the wild species are yellow with orangey brown tints at the base and tips of the petals. The flowers of the colorful mutants are pink. Chin cactus flowers don't open wide and flat as so many cacti do. The flowers remain narrowly tubular even when fully mature. If successfully pollinated (unlikely for a houseplant), small purplish red berries result.

OPTIMUM HOUSEHOLD ENVIRONMENT

Read the Introduction for the specifics of each recommendation.

HIGH LIGHT. The colorful mutant cactus on top of the green "stick" burns if it gets too much light. And yet the green cactus understock must have sufficient light to make enough food to supply itself and the mutant. Finding the right balance can be tricky, so bright filtered light with no direct sun is best for this plant.

MODERATE TEMPERATURE. Daytime 70 to 80°F, nighttime 60 to 70°F. In winter give them 55 to 65°F, day and night.

LOW WATER. Water whenever the top of the potting medium becomes dry to a depth of 2 inches. If your cactus starts to feel soft and spongy give it a little more water. In winter water less but don't let the plant go totally dry.

HUMIDITY. Chin cactus does not need supplemental humidity.

POTTING MEDIUM. Use any good organic, cactus and succulent potting soil that incorporates organic fertilizer, mycorrhizal fungi, and other beneficial microbes.

FERTILIZER. Use any balanced liquid organic fertilizer. Apply at half-strength once a month. Do not feed this plant in winter.

POTTING. When your plant needs up-potting, shift it to a container with a diameter 2 inches larger than the current pot. Re-pot every couple of years.

PROPAGATION. Chin cactus is tricky to propagate. Its pups are easily separated from the mother plant but, since they are not green, they must be grafted to an appropriate understock.

COMMON PROBLEMS

Watch for sunburn (page 256), spider mites (page 263), and root rot (page 272).

Christmas cactus

Christmas cacti (*Schlumbergera russelliana*, *S. ×buckleyi*, and *S. truncata*) are true cacti, like their desert-dwelling cousins, but unlike them they are tropical evergreens. These leafless, spineless, shrubby epiphytes have jointed, flattened, leaf-like stems. Each joint of the stem is a flat, 1.5-inch-long pad with soft, pointed teeth or scallops on the edges. With age plants get 2 feet high and 3 feet across. Forty years of faithful bloom is not uncommon. The stems are easily separated at the joints and will readily root to make new plants. Gorgeous, tubular flowers appear in fall and winter, making these cacti holiday favorites. Flowers are about 3 inches long and can be white, scarlet, pink, orange, yellow, or purple. Hundreds of cultivars have been developed by breeders, and these usually appear in abundance in garden centers and supermarkets between Thanksgiving and Christmas.

These cacti are stimulated into flowering by the cool temperatures and short days (or more precisely, long nights) of fall and winter. Commercial growers force them into flower for the holidays by controlling daylength and temperature. At home, you can force your plant to flower at any time by putting it in a dark closet where it

Christmas cactus (aka Thanksgiving cactus, crab cactus, holiday cactus).

will get no light at all for eight days or so. Bring it back into the light, and it will bloom in about six weeks. You can also stimulate blooming by lowering the thermostat at night to 55°F.

OPTIMUM HOUSEHOLD ENVIRONMENT

Read the Introduction for the specifics of each recommendation.

MEDIUM LIGHT. Christmas cactus does best in bright filtered light. It does not tolerate full sun and is easily burned by it. Keep your plant in an east window but protect it with gauzy sheers if the joints start to turn red—a symptom of too much light. If it isn't getting enough light then it will not be able to flower very well, so finding the correct balance is important.

MODERATE TEMPERATURE. Daytime 70 to 80°F from spring to the end of summer, 55 to 60°F in autumn and winter. To stimulate flowering keep nighttime temperature at 55°F.

LOW WATER. Christmas cactus is more drought tolerant than many houseplants—after all, it's a cactus. During the growing season, spring through summer, keep the potting medium lightly moist by watering sparingly but frequently. Water once a week, just enough so that the water begins to come out the drainage hole in the bottom of the pot. Stop and give it no more till next week. In fall and winter, water about once a month. Never keep your plants in soggy soil because overwatering will kill them.

HUMIDITY. Christmas cactus likes high humidity and will appreciate some additional humidity if your home is dry. You can help it out by misting it a couple times a week with a spray bottle of water on a mist setting, or use a handheld mister. You can also set the pot on top of a tray filled with gravel and water. Just be sure the pot is raised up above the surface level of the water.

POTTING MEDIUM. Christmas cactus will grow well in ordinary organic potting soil mixed

Christmas cactus, flower.

50/50 with sand to improve drainage. The growing medium needs to be free-draining but humus-rich. Some garden centers sell a mix of soil specifically designed for cacti. It's mostly sand and works well for regular cacti, but not for your Christmas cactus. However, it works well if mixed 50/50 with ordinary organic potting soil, to increase its water-holding capacity.

FERTILIZER. Use any balanced liquid organic fertilizer. Apply at half-strength every other week in spring and summer, once a month in fall and winter.

POTTING. Christmas cactus do not need large pots to grow and bloom well. They seem to be happiest, flowering every year, when their roots are a bit crowded. Early summer is the best time for re-potting. As your plant ages you will need to up-pot it every two to three years. However, you'll probably never need a pot larger than 12 inches in diameter.

PROPAGATION. You can easily create as many Christmas cactus plants as you want by breaking or twisting off pieces of stems with at least three or four joints or pads to use as stem cuttings.

COMMON PROBLEMS
Watch for sunburn (page 256), aphids (page 260), and root rot (page 272).

Crown-of-thorns

This sprawling, succulent, woody shrub hails from Madagascar. So, although its common name is picturesque and accurately describes its densely spiny stems, crown-of-thorns (*Euphorbia milii*) was not the plant used in the crucifixion of Christ. Crown-of-thorns gets 2 feet tall, at most, indoors in a pot. Its actual flowers are so tiny you can barely see them, but they're borne in a small cluster that is flanked by two, much larger and brighter petal-like bracts. These bracts are typically brilliant red but can also be pink, white, or pale yellow. They contrast beautifully with the bright green leaves, which are 2.5 inches long and 0.5 inch wide. Even though the clusters and colorful bracts are small, they're borne in great numbers and make this easy plant very showy in bloom. Stems, armed with thick, black, 0.5-inch-long spines, are hard and woody near the base of the plant and softer and more succulent toward the tips. Stems have lots of small leaves in their upper reaches, especially on new growth. Plants shed older leaves from the lower stems and branches and get leggy with age.

❶ Site this plant in an out-of-the-way place, and use gloves when working on it. Sensitive people develop skin rashes from contact with its milky sap, and the sap is toxic to people and pets when ingested, causing severe irritation of the mouth and gastrointestinal tract, swelling about the eyes and mouth, excessive salivation, and vomiting. Should these occur, call your local emergency hotline, poison control center, or vet.

Crown-of-thorns (aka Christ plant, Christ thorn, Siamese lucky plant, silverthorn).

OPTIMUM HOUSEHOLD ENVIRONMENT

Read the Introduction for the specifics of each recommendation.

MEDIUM LIGHT. Very bright, filtered light, or direct sun for three or four hours daily, serves this plant well.

MODERATE TEMPERATURE. Daytime 70 to 80°F, nighttime 60 to 70°F.

MODERATE WATER. Through the growing season, water whenever the top of the potting medium becomes dry to a depth of 1 inch. In winter, water whenever the top of the potting medium becomes dry to a depth of 2 inches.

HUMIDITY. Crown-of-thorns tolerates dry air very well and does not need to be misted.

POTTING MEDIUM. Use any good organic, cactus

and succulent potting soil that incorporates organic fertilizer, mycorrhizal fungi, and other beneficial microbes.

FERTILIZER. Use any balanced organic fertilizer. Apply every two weeks until the plants go dormant. In winter, apply at half-strength once a month.

POTTING. When crown-of-thorns needs up-potting, in late winter or early spring, shift it to a container with a diameter 4 inches larger than the current pot.

PROPAGATION. Crown-of-thorns is easy to propagate from stem tip cuttings.

COMMON PROBLEMS

Watch for leaf drop (page 249), scale insects (page 262), and gray mold (page 268).

Crown-of-thorns, yellow form.

Donkey tail

Super easy and low maintenance, donkey tail (*Sedum morganianum*) makes a delightfully odd companion because its long, dangling stems really do look like the thick tails of some animals—except that they're gorgeous, waxy, and blue-green. The stems are clothed in hundreds of small, 0.75-inch-long, fleshy, blue-green, teardrop-shaped leaves. Because of the way the leaves overlap, stems also resemble braided tresses or thick ropes. The lax, trailing stems, 3 feet long and 1 inch thick, are often seen in hanging basket combinations. The one drawback of this houseplant is that the pretty leaves fall off with every bump or touch, leaving bare, ratty-looking stems behind. It is very fragile and needs extra careful handling. In summer, well-grown specimens produce clusters of small pink to red flowers at the tips of their cascading stems. 'Burrito' has shorter stems and smaller leaves that are packed more tightly together. It is also distinctly bluer than the typical species.

OPTIMUM HOUSEHOLD ENVIRONMENT

Read the Introduction for the specifics of each recommendation.

HIGH LIGHT. Donkey tail prefers really bright light, even full sun, but it will suffer in extreme heat. A half-day of sun from an east window works well. South windows work if protection from afternoon heat is possible. It's probably best to avoid west windows. If you take it outdoors for the summer, give it morning sun with partial shade in the afternoons; it will sunburn badly unless gradually acclimated to the intense light and heat of a summer afternoon.

LOW TEMPERATURE. Daytime 65 to 75°F, nighttime 55 to 65°F. In winter give them 55 to 65°F, day and night.

MODERATE WATER. In the summer, water

Donkey tail (aka burro's tail, lamb's tail, horse's tail).

whenever the top of the potting medium becomes dry to a depth of 1 inch, and keep the potting medium lightly moist but never soggy. In winter, water whenever the top of the potting medium becomes dry to a depth of 2 inches.

HUMIDITY. This succulent tolerates dry air very well; however, it does not like drafts and will throw its leaves on the ground in protest.

POTTING MEDIUM. Use any good organic, cactus

Donkey tail.

and succulent potting soil that incorporates organic fertilizer, mycorrhizal fungi, and other beneficial microbes.

FERTILIZER. Use any balanced organic fertilizer. Apply once a month until the plant goes dormant in winter. Stop feeding in winter.

POTTING. When your plant needs up-potting, carefully shift it in spring to a container with a diameter 2 inches larger than the current pot. Mature plants that fill their pots are very fragile; they tend to lose their leaves and fall apart when handled. Propagate new plants from stem tip cuttings when re-potting becomes difficult.

PROPAGATION. Donkey tail is easy to propagate from stem tip cuttings and leaf cuttings.

COMMON PROBLEMS
Watch for leaf drop (page 249), aphids (page 260), and root rot (page 272).

Easter cactus (aka Whitsun cactus).

Easter cactus

Easter cacti (*Hatiora gaertneri*, *H. rosea*, and their cross, *H. ×graeseri*) are true cacti, but they do not live in the desert. Like orchids and bromeliads, these tropical evergreens are shrubby epiphytes, and in nature they live on tree branches, high in the cool, moist rainforest canopy. The funnel-shaped flowers of *H. gaertneri* are brilliant scarlet, 1.5 to 2 inches long and 1.5 to 3 inches wide. The flowers of *H. rosea* (pink) and *H. ×graeseri* (brilliant pink to red) are similar. In all kinds, the flowers are borne at the tips of dangling stems and open flat, as they do in most cacti. Plants have a sprawling habit, with jointed, flattened, leaf-like green branches hanging around all sides, which makes them wonderful candidates for hanging baskets. Each stem segment is 1.5 to 3 inches long and 1 inch wide, with little notches on the margins. Like Christmas cactus, Easter cactus's stems can be broken off at the joints and easily rooted to make new plants.

To form flower buds, Easter cacti need a cold treatment in November, December, and January. Flowers open in late spring, as their common name suggests. Oval, red fruits form after the flowers fade, if they have been pollinated. If you spot these fruits developing, pinch them off so your plant wastes no energy making fruits filled with seeds. It will bloom better next year if you remove the fruits.

OPTIMUM HOUSEHOLD ENVIRONMENT

Read the Introduction for the specifics of each recommendation.

HIGH LIGHT. Bright filtered light with no direct sun is best.

MODERATE TEMPERATURE. Daytime 70 to 80°F, nighttime 60 to 70°F. In November, December, and January give them 45 to 55°F nights to initiate flower buds.

MODERATE WATER. Water whenever the top of the potting medium becomes dry to a depth of 1 inch. Strive for consistently moist (but not soggy) soil. This plant starts to shed stem segments if it gets too much or too little water. Taper off on the watering when the plant has finished blooming and resume normal watering when it starts into active growth again.

HUMIDITY. Easter cactus likes high humidity and will appreciate some additional humidity if your home is dry. Mist it a couple times a week with a spray bottle of water on a mist setting, or use a handheld mister. You can also set the pot on top of a tray filled with gravel and water. Just be sure the pot is raised up above the surface level of the water.

POTTING MEDIUM. Easter cactus grows well in ordinary potting soil mixed 50/50 with sand to improve drainage. The growing medium needs to be free-draining but humus-rich. Some garden centers sell a mix of soil specifically designed for cacti. It's mostly sand and works well for regular cacti, but not for your Easter cactus. However, it works well if mixed 50/50 with ordinary organic potting soil, to increase its water-holding capacity.

FERTILIZER. Use any balanced liquid organic fertilizer. Apply at half-strength every other week in spring and summer, once a month in fall and winter.

POTTING. Easter cacti do not need large pots to grow and bloom well. They seem to be happiest when their roots are a bit crowded. Up-pot every two to three years to a container with a diameter 2 inches larger than the current pot. You'll probably never need a pot larger than 12 inches in diameter.

PROPAGATION. You can easily create as many Easter cacti as you want if you make stem cuttings by breaking or twisting off pieces of the jointed stems with at least three or four joints or pads.

COMMON PROBLEMS

Watch for flower bud drop (page 248), mealybugs (page 262), and soft rot (page 274).

Gold lace cactus

Gold lace cactus (*Mammillaria elongata*) is deceptively small. It begins life in your home with individual stems that look like fingers, each about 6 inches long and 1 inch thick. Soon it begins to produce pups around the base of the stem. These produce more pups until this diminutive cactus becomes a densely packed cluster of hundreds of cylindrical stems, filling up and dangling over a 12-inch pot. Each stem is covered in harmless 0.5-inch-long, golden yellow, coppery brown, or white radial spines. Clusters of spines grow from tiny nipples that cover the body of this cactus in an attractive double spiral pattern. The spines radiate sideways, making them a flat starburst that can't stab you. A few cultivars of this very popular and easy-to-grow species have a couple of straight central spines poking out of the middle of the clusters that can, and do, stab you.

Starry, 0.5-inch-long and -wide flowers in very pale yellow, sometimes tinged with pink, bloom in spring. They are borne in a ring at the tips of the stems, but they open sequentially, one or two, sometimes three at a time. Small pink, berry-like fruits that turn red when mature

Gold lace cactus (aka golden star cactus, golden lace, ladyfinger cactus, ladyfinger).

follow the flowers. Brown seeds fill these fruits. Unusual variants of or hybrids involving this species include 'Cristata' (brain cactus) and others like it. In these cristate (crested) forms, the stems grow flat and wide, losing their cylindrical shape and becoming fan-like. A well-grown cluster of a cristate variety becomes a round, undulating mass of interlocking fans that really does look like a brain.

OPTIMUM HOUSEHOLD ENVIRONMENT

Read the Introduction for the specifics of each recommendation.

MEDIUM LIGHT. Give gold lace a half-day of direct sun from an east or west window.

HIGH TEMPERATURE. Daytime 75 to 85°F, nighttime 65 to 75°F. In winter grow it ten degrees cooler, day and night.

LOW WATER. Water whenever the top of the potting medium becomes dry to a depth of 2 inches. Give it less water in winter but don't let it dry out completely.

HUMIDITY. This desert-adapted cactus tolerates dry air quite well and needs no supplemental humidity.

POTTING MEDIUM. Use any good organic, cactus and succulent potting soil that incorporates organic fertilizer, mycorrhizal fungi, and other beneficial microbes.

FERTILIZER. Use any organic fertilizer, in either a powder or liquid formulation. Apply at half-strength once a month through spring and summer. Do not feed your cactus in winter.

POTTING. When gold lace cactus needs up-potting, every two to three years or so, shift it to a container with a diameter 2 inches larger than the current pot. Use a shallow pot, wider than deep.

PROPAGATION. Gold lace cactus is easy to propagate from seed or by potting up the pups.

COMMON PROBLEMS

Watch for sunburn (page 256), mealybugs (page 262), and root rot (page 272).

Haworthia

These striking little plants are choice succulents that are easy to grow, low maintenance, and almost indestructible. Haworthias look like miniature aloes with zebra stripes; the most desirable species for growing indoors are *Haworthia attenuata*, *H. bolusii*, *H. fasciata*, and *H. maxima*. These stemless, evergreen perennials have thick, very tough, pointed leaves in a basal rosette. The dark green leaves are variously marked with pure white bands, stripes, and dots that are raised up above the surface of the leaf. Some haworthias have white markings only on the underside of the leaf and some have them on

Haworthia (aka pearl plant, zebra plant).

both sides. Cultivars are available with variously colored leaves from purplish bronze to bronzy orange, even yellow and chartreuse. Individual plants grow about 3 inches tall and wide, but they get wider by producing a few pups around the base of the mother plant, forming clusters. Plants flower in the winter. A 16-inch-long, wiry stalk emerges from the center of the plant and bears tiny white flowers. You can cut the flower stalk off when the flowers fade.

OPTIMUM HOUSEHOLD ENVIRONMENT

Read the Introduction for the specifics of each recommendation.

HIGH LIGHT. Give your haworthias very bright indirect light all year long. They are very tolerant of full sun, but you'll have to acclimatize them to it gradually or they will sunburn.

MODERATE TEMPERATURE. Daytime 70 to 80°F, nighttime 60 to 70°F. In winter give them 60°F days if possible.

LOW WATER. Water whenever the top of the potting medium becomes dry to a depth of 2 inches.

HUMIDITY. No supplemental humidity is necessary.

POTTING MEDIUM. Use any good organic, cactus and succulent potting soil that incorporates organic fertilizer, mycorrhizal fungi, and other beneficial microbes.

FERTILIZER. Use any balanced organic fertilizer. Apply at half-strength once a month through spring and summer. Do not feed your plants in fall and winter.

POTTING. This plant sheds some of its older roots in the spring so, every year or two, re-pot them in spring. When your plant needs up-potting, shift it to a container with a diameter 2 inches larger than the current pot. Choose a wide, shallow pot for these shallow-rooted beauties.

PROPAGATION. Haworthia is easy to propagate by potting up the pups.

COMMON PROBLEMS

Watch for sunburn (page 256), mealybugs (page 262), and root rot (page 272).

....

Hedgehog cactus

Grapefruit- to peanut-sized, these ball-shaped cacti with sharp spines have comparatively huge, outstandingly beautiful flowers. Peanut cactus (*Echinopsis chamaecereus*) has cylindrical stems about 0.5 inch thick and 2 to 3 inches long that resemble peanuts in the shell. The tiny plants produce improbably large, bright scarlet flowers, to 3 inches long and half as wide, in late spring and early summer. A large number of pups grow around the base of the mother plant, eventually making a large cluster of crowded stems to 12 inches wide. The little stems fall off the plant easily, especially when you're up-potting the cluster, but these can be rooted and grown into another plant. Easter lily cactus or sea urchin cactus (*E. oxygona*) has curved, 1-inch-long spines. It grows as a round ball, like a green softball or grapefruit, and eventually gets as large as 12 inches tall. It too produces lots of pups around its base, forming large clusters to 2 feet wide over time. Its gorgeous, imposingly large pink or white flowers are produced sporadically all summer. The flowers, borne from the sides of the plant's body, are 6- to 8-inch-long tubes with a flattened starburst of radial petals at the top of the tube. Each flower opens just before sunrise and lasts a single day, but a large, well-grown plant in full bloom can open as many as 50 or more flowers at once—a spectacular sight. Many hybrids have been created between these and other species of *Echinopsis*. These hybrids, with flowers ranging from white, pink, red, and scarlet to magenta, orange, and yellow, are very popular houseplants and are widely available in garden centers everywhere.

OPTIMUM HOUSEHOLD ENVIRONMENT

Read the Introduction for the specifics of each recommendation.

MEDIUM LIGHT. Give these cacti a summer vacation outdoors in filtered light. Bring them indoors fall through spring—they're not frost tolerant—and give them bright light. Indoors or outdoors, they can take a half-day of full sun but be careful to acclimate them if they've not been exposed to the intense light and heat of direct sunlight before.

MODERATE TEMPERATURE. Daytime 70 to 80°F, nighttime 60 to 70°F. In winter give them 55 to 65°F, day and night, to set flower buds.

Hedgehog cactus.

MODERATE WATER. Through the growing season, water whenever the top of the potting medium becomes dry to a depth of 1 inch. In winter, water whenever the top of the potting medium becomes dry to a depth of 2 inches.

HUMIDITY. These plants are adapted to dry air and do not need supplemental humidity.

POTTING MEDIUM. Use any good organic, cactus and succulent potting soil that incorporates organic fertilizer, mycorrhizal fungi, and other beneficial microbes.

FERTILIZER. Use any balanced organic fertilizer. Apply once a month through the growing season. Do not feed these plants in late fall and winter.

POTTING. When your plant needs up-potting, shift it to a container with a diameter 4 inches larger than the current pot.

PROPAGATION. Hedgehog cacti are easy to propagate by potting up the pups.

COMMON PROBLEMS

Watch for sunburn (page 256), mealybugs (page 262), and root rot (page 272).

Hen and chicks

Numerous species and hybrids in the genus *Echeveria* are called hen and chicks, including *E. elegans* and *E. secunda*. These little evergreen beauties are easy to grow and very low maintenance. They make splendid potted plants, with a basal rosette of leaves that looks more like a bright green lotus flower than a stem with leaves. The thick, waxy leaves also come in lavender, rose-red, very dark reddish purple, silvery blue, powder blue, and mauve. Some varieties have markings or blushings of pink, red, bronze, or purple that can intensify when plants get sufficient sunlight. Leaves can also be variously frilled, crimped, or waved. They are imbricate:

Hen and chicks (aka echeveria).

the longest leaves are on the bottom of the rosette and the shortest leaves are on the top, so that no leaf completely shades out another. The rosettes, from 4 to 6 inches across, are borne on short stems that generate lots of pups. These "chicks" can easily be separated from the mother "hen" and potted up to make new plants. Small, nodding, bell-shaped flowers are borne on tall, branched stalks that arise from the center of the rosette; flowers are pink, lined with either yellow, orange and yellow, or red and yellow. Many growers just nip off the flower stalks as soon as they start to form so that the perfect symmetry of the foliage is not disturbed.

OPTIMUM HOUSEHOLD ENVIRONMENT

Read the Introduction for the specifics of each recommendation.

HIGH LIGHT. Give these succulents very bright light all year long. Give them a half-day of direct sun in summer but be careful to acclimate them slowly to the full intensity of the light.

MODERATE TEMPERATURE. Daytime 70 to 80°F, nighttime 60 to 70°F.

MODERATE WATER. Through the growing season, water whenever the top of the potting medium becomes dry to a depth of 1 inch. Water less often in winter.

HUMIDITY. These plants do not require supplemental humidity.

POTTING MEDIUM. Use any good organic, cactus and succulent potting soil that incorporates organic fertilizer, mycorrhizal fungi, and other beneficial microbes.

FERTILIZER. Use any organic fertilizer, in either a powder or liquid formulation. Apply at half-strength every two weeks through the growing season, once a month in winter.

POTTING. When your plant needs up-potting, every two years or so, shift it to a container with a diameter 2 inches larger than the current pot.

PROPAGATION. Hen and chicks is easy to propagate by potting up the chicks and from leaf cuttings.

COMMON PROBLEMS

Watch for sunburn (page 256), mealybugs (page 262), and root rot (page 272).

Jade plant

A handsome small tree with multiple trunks, sturdy limbs, and succulent leaves, the jade plant (*Crassula ovata*) is a beloved and common sight in homes everywhere, as well as in offices, public buildings, and shopping malls. Sometimes sculpted and almost bonsai-like, these plants develop great character with age. They are also easy to grow, quite low maintenance, and so easy to propagate, you can give new plants away to your friends. Jade plant rarely gets more than 2 feet tall as a houseplant. It's a winter-flowerer, bearing clusters of small, inconspicuous pink or white flowers at its branch tips, but it doesn't bloom until it's ten or more years old. That's okay, because thick trunks and branches with their shiny green leaves are the real beauty of this plant. The 2-inch-long, thick, oval leaves of jade plant are a rich jade green that often develops red tints in high light situations.

When you receive or purchase a jade plant you may find that there are as many as five plants crowded into the pot. Growers pot up that many cuttings in order to give the pot a fuller look. In the spring, take the plants out of their pot and separate them. Pot each one in its own pot. Not only will each grow better and be healthier, but the tree-like character of the plant will be better displayed.

OPTIMUM HOUSEHOLD ENVIRONMENT

Read the Introduction for the specifics of each recommendation.

MEDIUM LIGHT. A half-day of filtered light from an east or west window is a perfect site for jade plant.

MODERATE TEMPERATURE. Daytime 70 to 80°F, nighttime 60 to 70°F. If you have a large, older plant and you'd like it to bloom, give it 55 to 60°F, day and night, for six weeks in winter.

LOW WATER. Through the growing season, water whenever the top of the potting medium becomes dry to a depth of 2 inches and water even less in winter. If the plant starts dropping leaves, then it's not getting enough water so up the ante a bit. Try watering it when the medium is dry to 1.5 inches. Be careful though; jade plant quickly succumbs to root rot if it's overwatered. Monitor the potting medium closely to make sure it is never soggy. Do not let the pot stand in water in its saucer.

HUMIDITY. Jade plant is well adapted to dry air and needs no supplemental humidity.

Jade plant (aka friendship plant, friendship tree, lucky plant, money tree).

POTTING MEDIUM. Use any good organic, cactus and succulent potting soil that incorporates organic fertilizer, mycorrhizal fungi, and other beneficial microbes.

FERTILIZER. Use any balanced organic fertilizer. Apply at half-strength every two weeks from spring through fall. Do not feed your jade plant in winter.

POTTING. Up-pot young plants in the spring. Choose pots with a diameter 2 inches larger than the current pot. Re-pot older, mature plants every two to three years.

PROPAGATION. Jade plant is easy to propagate from 3-inch-long stem tip cuttings and leaf cuttings.

COMMON PROBLEMS
Watch for leaf drop (page 249), mealybugs (page 262), and root rot (page 272).

Kalanchoe

Kalanchoes (*Kalanchoe blossfeldiana*) are attractive little plants that appear in full bloom by the thousands every winter holiday season. They have very large clusters of very small flowers in brilliant shades of red, pink, orange, white, and yellow. Some people choose to treat kalanchoe as a temporary holiday decoration and discard it as soon as it's finished blooming. But this herbaceous evergreen perennial is easy to grow, will bloom again fairly easily, and lives for at least three years, if you care for it. And since it's a pretty plant even when not in flower, it is well worth keeping around for an encore. Well-grown, mature specimens grow slowly into bushy, rounded mounds, 18 inches tall and 20 inches wide. The thickish succulent leaves, 2 to 4 inches long, are bright green with red, slightly scalloped edges. The plant covers itself with flamboyant flowers in winter, and the flowers last a long time, putting on a good show for weeks.

Kalanchoe (aka flaming Katy, Christmas kalanchoe, florist kalanchoe, Madagascar widow's-thrill).

To set flower buds, kalanchoe needs to have a light treatment, then a cold treatment, and finally, a dark treatment of 14-hour nights for 30 consecutive days. Making this happen is easier than it sounds. Put your plant outdoors for the summer so it's exposed to long summer days. In autumn it will naturally be exposed to cool temperatures sufficient to meet its need for the cold treatment. Just be sure to bring it back inside before the temperature drops below 40°F. Then put it where it won't be able to "see" any artificial light at night. If you handle it this way, it'll be back in bloom in January and February. If you'd like your kalanchoe back in full glorious bloom in time for the winter holiday season, cover it with a lightproof cover every night for the month of September.

❶ All parts of this plant are toxic to people and pets, including the water in a vase of the flowers. The plant contains cardiac glycosides, which directly interfere with the electrolyte balance within the heart muscle, causing nausea, drooling, vomiting, dilated pupils, tremors, seizures, abnormal heart rhythm and rate, and life-threateningly high potassium levels. If anyone ingests this plant, call your local emergency hotline, poison control center, or vet.

OPTIMUM HOUSEHOLD ENVIRONMENT

Read the Introduction for the specifics of each recommendation.

HIGH LIGHT. Indoors, kalanchoe does very well with full, direct sun from a south, east, or west window. Outdoors, in summer, provide filtered or dappled shade.

HIGH TEMPERATURE. Daytime 75 to 85°F, nighttime 65 to 75°F. In winter give it 60 to 70°F, day and night. In autumn give it cool temperatures outdoors, 55 to 65°F, to initiate flower buds.

MODERATE WATER. Water whenever the top of the potting medium becomes dry to a depth of 1 inch.

HUMIDITY. Kalanchoe does not need supplemental humidity.

POTTING MEDIUM. Use any good organic, general-purpose potting soil that incorporates organic fertilizer, mycorrhizal fungi, and other beneficial microbes.

FERTILIZER. Use any balanced organic fertilizer. Apply once a month through the growing season. Do not feed the plants in winter.

POTTING. When your plant needs up-potting, in early summer, shift it to a container with a diameter 2 inches larger than the current pot.

PROPAGATION. Kalanchoe is easy to propagate from stem tip cuttings.

COMMON PROBLEMS

Watch for failure to flower (page 247), spider mites (page 263), and stem rot (page 275).

Living stone

"Bizarre," "unbelievable," and "amazing" are some of the things people say when they first see a living stone (*Lithops* spp.). It looks nothing like a plant but does look exactly like a stone, or pair of stones, actually. Two rounded leaves, separated by a slit, nestle close together at ground level, disguised as pebbles. That's all you see until, surprise, the thing produces a flower. And it's a big flower too, considering the tiny size of the plant. Some 300 different types of living stones are in cultivation— some are species but many more are cultivars, whether selections or hybrids. Colors are various, from cream, gray, brown, and red-brown to green, and the size, though always small, varies as well. In general, the whole plant is about 1.5 inches wide. All forms store water in their leaves, which allows these succulents to

Living stone (aka pebble plant, flowering stone).

persist under extremely inhospitable environmental conditions.

These crazy little plants have virtually no stems. Any tiny bit of stem that the plant has is underground. The top of each thick leaf is flat and either smooth or pebbled in texture. Each spring, the plant grows a single pair of new leaves, which slowly emerge through the fissure between the two older leaves. As the two new leaves grow larger, the old leaves shrink, eventually disappearing altogether. Occasionally, the plant produces two new sets of leaves instead of just one, and becomes double-headed. As time goes by, the double-heading process continues, and each plant eventually forms a colony. Flowers are often larger than the plant itself, with many thin, strap-like petals, in yellow or white. The flowers, one for each pair of leaves, emerge from the slit between the two leaves each fall, opening wide in the afternoon and closing up tight at night; some are sweetly fragrant.

OPTIMUM HOUSEHOLD ENVIRONMENT

Read the Introduction for the specifics of each recommendation.

MEDIUM LIGHT. Living stones prefer a half-day of full sun, preferably from an east window during the cool of the day. The intense heat and light of full afternoon sun from a west window should be filtered a bit to moderate the heat load because the plants suffer from sunburn when exposed to full sun and high heat.

HIGH TEMPERATURE. Daytime 75 to 85°F, nighttime 65 to 75°F. In fall, winter, and spring, grow them ten degrees cooler, day and night.

LOW WATER. Proper watering is the key to success with these plants. In summer, and again in winter, give them almost no water at all. Give them a tiny drink only if they become badly wrinkled. There are two times a year when living stones actually need a little water. The first time is in the spring after the new leaves have developed and the old leaves have shriveled. The second time is in the fall when the flowers appear. During these times, water whenever the medium is dry to a depth of 2 inches.

HUMIDITY. Living stones do not need supplemental humidity and will, in fact, suffer if humidity is too high. They do not do well in terrariums, for example.

POTTING MEDIUM. Use any good organic, cactus and succulent potting soil that incorporates organic fertilizer, mycorrhizal fungi, and other beneficial microbes and mix it 50/50 with sand.

FERTILIZER. Use any balanced organic fertilizer. Apply once in spring when the new leaves are growing, and once in fall when flowering begins.

POTTING. When this very slow growing plant needs up-potting, every five years or so, shift it to a container with a diameter 2 inches larger than the current pot. Choose a pot deep enough to accommodate its taproot.

PROPAGATION. Sometimes a plant develops multiple heads and can then be divided. Living stones are easy to propagate from seed, but your plant makes seeds only if you hand-pollinate its flowers with pollen from a second, genetically different plant.

COMMON PROBLEMS

Watch for sunburn (page 256), spider mites (page 263), and root rot (page 272).

Mother of thousands

Mother of thousands (*Bryophyllum daigremontianum*) has thick, evergreen, succulent "leaves"—actually leaf-like structures called cladodes—6 to 8 inches long and 3 inches wide. They are blue-green on the upper surface, blotched with purple on the undersurface, and have saw-toothed, sometimes purple edges. The teeth are not sharp and won't cut you. What's interesting is that in the notches between the teeth, teensy little plantlets form. These clones develop roots while still attached to their mother. Then they fall off, land on the ground, take root, and grow. By the thousands, in every single pot of all the nearby houseplants. Hence the common name. In many countries, this plant is ranked as a noxious, invasive weed. You can probably guess why. The main stems of this plant get 2.5 to 3 feet tall and often need to be staked to remain upright. They produce lateral roots as high as 6 inches from ground level. Tall, old plants tend to lean sideways and when the lateral roots touch the ground, they too begin to grow. Eventually they develop stems and become a clone of the original. This playful succulent very rarely flowers indoors, but if it ever does you will see small, smoky lavender-pink, bell-shaped flowers. They're borne in large clusters on 12-inch-tall stalks that develop on the tips of the main stems. After it flowers the plant generally dies, leaving behind countless copies of itself.

Mother of thousands (aka alligator plant, alligator's tongue, devil's backbone, Mexican hat plant, mother of millions).

❗ All parts of this plant are toxic to people and pets, including the water in a vase of the flowers. The plant contains bufadienolides, chemicals that react with blood sugar to form cardiac glycosides, which in turn interfere with the heart muscle's electrolyte balance, causing nausea, drooling, vomiting, dilated pupils, tremors, seizures, abnormal heart rhythm and rate, and life-threateningly high potassium levels. If anyone ingests this plant, call your local emergency hotline, poison control center, or vet.

OPTIMUM HOUSEHOLD ENVIRONMENT

Read the Introduction for the specifics of each recommendation.

HIGH LIGHT. This plant tolerates full, direct sun and the heat load of a south or west window very well. It also does well in bright, filtered or dappled light.

MODERATE TEMPERATURE. Daytime 70 to 80°F, nighttime 60 to 70°F.

LOW WATER. Water whenever the top of the potting medium becomes dry to a depth of 2 inches. Water less in winter.

HUMIDITY. Mother of thousands is well adapted to dry air and needs no supplemental humidity.

POTTING MEDIUM. Use any good organic, cactus and succulent potting soil that incorporates organic fertilizer, mycorrhizal fungi, and other beneficial microbes.

FERTILIZER. Use any balanced organic fertilizer. Apply at half-strength once every three months.

POTTING. In the spring, when your plant needs up-potting, shift it to a container with a diameter 2 inches larger than the current pot.

PROPAGATION. Mother of thousands is easy to propagate by planting the little plantlets.

COMMON PROBLEMS

Watch for plant sprawl (page 253), spider mites (page 263), and root rot (page 272).

Orchid cactus

There are more than 7,000 named hybrids and species in this cactus group, all with huge, stunningly gorgeous flowers in every shade of purple-red, red, pink, orange, apricot, yellow, white, and multicolor blends. Orchid cacti are mainly *Epiphyllum* species and their selections but also intergeneric hybrids involving *Disocactus*, *Pseudorhipsalis*, or *Selenicereus*. Those derived from artificial crosses are sometimes called ×*Disophyllum* (even though not all are hybrids between *Disocactus* and *Epiphyllum*). Orchid cactus is not a desert-dweller; in nature, it is an epiphyte that lives on branches high in the canopy of tropical rainforests. Its stems are 2 to 4 inches wide, flattened, green, spineless, and leaf-like with irregularly saw-toothed

Orchid cactus (aka epiphyllum hybrid, epicactus, epi, leaf cactus).

edges. The stems arch up, out, and down, in 2- to 3-foot-long cascades on all sides of the pot, making these plants superb candidates for hanging baskets. The flowers are borne in spring at the tips or sides of the stems. The funnel-shaped flowers open flat and wide, at the tops of long tubes. They are usually 4 to 6 inches in diameter but can be 9 to 12 inches across. Many of the old-fashioned types bloom only at night, with flowers that last a single night. Modern hybrids tend to be day-blooming with flowers that last two to three days.

For orchid cactus to set flower buds and bloom in the spring, make sure that it is not exposed to any source of light at night in the winter. No desk lamps, night-lights, streetlights, etc. It needs long nights of complete darkness to set buds. It also needs cooler temperatures during this dark treatment. Keep nighttime temperature around 50°F, no warmer than 57°F, through the winter. Give it those long nights and cool temperatures, and this houseplant will reward you generously with its spectacular flowers in spring.

OPTIMUM HOUSEHOLD ENVIRONMENT

Read the Introduction for the specifics of each recommendation.

MEDIUM LIGHT. Give your orchid cactus bright filtered morning light from an east window. Protect it from afternoon heat and light. Give it long nights of total darkness in winter.

MODERATE TEMPERATURE. Daytime 70 to 80°F, nighttime 60 to 70°F. In winter give them 50 to 57°F nights.

MODERATE WATER. Through the growing season, water whenever the top of the potting medium becomes dry to a depth of 1 inch. In winter, water just enough to keep the soil slightly moist.

HUMIDITY. Mist your plant several times a week with a spray bottle of water on a mist setting, or use a handheld mister. Put the pot in a saucer or tray of water, making sure the bottom of the pot never sits directly in the water by raising the pot up on pot feet or pebbles. Consider putting a humidifier in the room.

POTTING MEDIUM. Use any good organic potting medium designed for semi-terrestrial orchids, one that incorporates organic fertilizer, mycorrhizal fungi, and other beneficial microbes.

FERTILIZER. Use any liquid organic fertilizer where the second number (phosphorus) is a lot higher than the other two to promote flowering. Apply every two weeks through the growing season. Do not fertilize in winter.

POTTING. When your plant needs up-potting, every three to four years, shift it to a container with a diameter 2 inches larger than the current pot. Up-pot or re-pot this plant right after it finishes blooming.

PROPAGATION. Orchid cactus is very easy to propagate from stem tip cuttings.

COMMON PROBLEMS

Watch for flower bud drop (page 248), scale insects (page 262), and root rot (page 272).

....

Panda plant

Super easy to grow and tolerant of benign neglect, panda plant (*Kalanchoe tomentosa*) is among the most forgiving of all houseplants. It is a succulent, with thick, water-storing leaves, so it doesn't need much water, and it's very well adapted to the dry air of most homes. Panda plant gets 1 to 2 feet tall and has a stout stem with numerous side branches that give it a tree-like, almost bonsai character. Side branches tend to grow erect at their tips with dense clusters of vertical leaves, whereas leaves near the base of stems are perpendicular to the stems. The densely hairy leaves are oval to egg-shaped

and 1 to 3 inches long. These furry, silvery-velvet leaves are as soft as kitten's ears. With their dark rust-red edges, they are panda plant's most distinguishing feature and the primary reason to grow it in your home. The small, fuzzy, yellowish green, bell-shaped flowers are rarely produced indoors.

❶ Because it is closely related to kalanchoe and mother of thousands, panda plant is presumed toxic to people and pets in all its parts, including the water in a vase of its flowers. Those plants contain bufadienolides, chemicals that react with blood sugar to form cardiac glycosides, which in turn interfere with the heart muscle's electrolyte balance, causing nausea, drooling, vomiting, dilated pupils, tremors, seizures, abnormal heart rhythm and rate, and life-threateningly high potassium levels. If anyone ingests this plant, call your local emergency hotline, poison control center, or vet.

OPTIMUM HOUSEHOLD ENVIRONMENT

Read the Introduction for the specifics of each recommendation.

HIGH LIGHT. Give this plant full sun from a south window, or really bright filtered light. A half-day of sun from an east or west window will also work well. Be careful to acclimatize the plant to full sun slowly.

MODERATE TEMPERATURE. Daytime 70 to 80°F, nighttime 60 to 70°F.

MODERATE WATER. Water whenever the top of the potting medium becomes dry to a depth of 1 inch.

HUMIDITY. Panda plant does not need supplemental humidity.

POTTING MEDIUM. Use any good organic, cactus and succulent potting soil that incorporates organic fertilizer, mycorrhizal fungi, and other beneficial microbes.

FERTILIZER. Use any balanced liquid organic

Panda plant (aka chocolate soldier, cocoon plant, panda bear plant, plush plant, pussy ears).

fertilizer. Apply at half-strength once a month through the growing season. Don't feed the plant in the winter.

POTTING. When this slow-growing plant needs up-potting, shift it to a container with a diameter 2 inches larger than the current pot.

PROPAGATION. Panda plant is easy to propagate from stem tip cuttings and leaf cuttings.

COMMON PROBLEMS

Watch for sunburn (page 256), mealybugs (page 262), and root rot (page 272).

Prickly pear

Prickly pear (*Opuntia* spp.) is the familiar cactus with flat pads that look like the ears on a Mickey Mouse hat. You've probably seen it in dozens of cowboy movies and western landscape paintings. The origin of the common name is obvious: both the plant and its vaguely pear-shaped fruits are covered with vicious spines and/or extremely fine, needle-like hairs (glochids), which penetrate human skin before you even know they're there. The prickly pears you're

Prickly pear.

likely to find as container plants include beaver-tail prickly pear (*O. basilaris*), Indian fig prickly pear (*O. ficus-indica*), and purple prickly pear (*O. macrocentra*). They'll range in size from 20 to 36 inches tall as potted houseplants, and all have flat, ping-pong-paddle-like, jointed stems. The stems are dotted with round spots (areoles), and the spines and glochids grow in tufts on these. The flat pads (*nopales* in Mexican cuisine) are edible, but you have to remove the spines and glochids before you can eat them, and you should wear heavy gloves to do so. They have a slightly mucilaginous texture and taste a little like green beans. Spineless cultivars have been developed specifically for eating. Showy flowers of yellow, purple, red, orange, or white are borne on the top edge of the pads. They open wide, 2 to 3 inches in diameter, with lots of petals, and if successfully pollinated, they'll develop fruit. But again, before you can eat these delicious, tropically flavored fruits, you must first remove all the spines and glochids. Wear heavy gloves and use pliers to pull the big spines off.

OPTIMUM HOUSEHOLD ENVIRONMENT

Read the Introduction for the specifics of each recommendation.

HIGH LIGHT. Prickly pears demand all the light you can provide. Full sun all day from a south window is best, especially if you'd like your plant to flower. Place outdoors in full sun every spring and summer to ensure regular flowering.

HIGH TEMPERATURE. Daytime 75 to 85°F, night-time 65 to 75°F. Prickly pears enjoy high heat loads but will also tolerate more moderate temperatures.

LOW WATER. Water whenever the top of the potting medium becomes dry to a depth of 2 inches.

HUMIDITY. Prickly pears do not need supplemental humidity.

POTTING MEDIUM. Use any good organic, cactus and succulent potting soil that incorporates organic fertilizer, mycorrhizal fungi, and other beneficial microbes.

FERTILIZER. Use any balanced organic fertilizer. Apply at half-strength once a month through the growing season. Do not fertilize in winter.

POTTING. When your plant needs up-potting, shift it to a container with a diameter 4 inches larger than the current pot.

PROPAGATION. Prickly pear is easy to propagate from seed or by rooting whole pads.

COMMON PROBLEMS

Watch for failure to flower (page 247), scale insects (page 262), and root rot (page 272).

Rat tail cactus

This is another epiphytic cactus, but unlike Christmas cactus, Easter cactus, and orchid cactus, rat tail cactus (*Disocactus flagelliformis*) is spiny, and vehemently so. The shallowly ridged, cylindrical stems are so densely clothed in whitish, orange-brown, or golden yellow spines that sometimes you can barely see any green on them. The spines, though small (0.1 inch long), are sharp and abundant, so err on the side of caution and wear heavy gloves when potting or working with this plant. This fast-growing cactus produces multiple stems, 0.5 to 1 inch thick and as much as 4 to 5 feet long, forming large clumps that look like ropes cascading from their pot or hanging basket. The tubular flowers are 2 to 4 inches long and wide, bright pinkish violet-red, and borne in abundance from the tips and sides of the dangling stems in spring. Each flower lasts two to three days and flowers are produced for about two months. Hybrids with other species are available, and many are less demanding of high sunlight. They also have larger flowers, and a broader range

Rat tail cactus.

of flower colors including bright orange, pink, and purple. The stems of these hybrids are dark green with much deeper ridges and furrows than the species.

OPTIMUM HOUSEHOLD ENVIRONMENT

Read the Introduction for the specifics of each recommendation.

HIGH LIGHT. Rat tail cactus really wants full, direct sun all day from a south window in order to do its best and flower well. It will tolerate a half-day of sun from an east or west window, or really bright filtered light, but it may not flower well. Given low light it won't flower at all.

MODERATE TEMPERATURE. Daytime 70 to 80°F, nighttime 60 to 70°F. In winter, when the plant is resting, give it 55 to 65°F days, and don't let the temperature drop below 45°F.

MODERATE WATER. During the growing season, water whenever the top of the potting medium becomes dry to a depth of 1 inch. In winter, water much less frequently, just enough to keep the potting medium from drying out completely.

HUMIDITY. Rat tail cactus does not need supplemental humidity.

POTTING MEDIUM. Rat tail cactus will grow well in ordinary potting soil mixed 50/50 with sand to improve drainage. The growing medium needs to be free-draining but humus-rich. Some garden centers sell a mix of soil specifically designed for cacti. It's mostly sand and works well for regular cacti, but not for your rat tail cactus. However, it works well if mixed 50/50 with ordinary organic potting soil, to increase its water-holding capacity.

FERTILIZER. Use any balanced liquid organic fertilizer. Apply at half-strength every two weeks through the growing season. Do not fertilize in winter.

POTTING. Re-pot annually when the plant has finished flowering. When your plant needs up-potting, shift it to a container with a diameter 2 inches larger than the current pot.

PROPAGATION. Rat tail cactus is easy to propagate from stem tip cuttings.

COMMON PROBLEMS

Watch for failure to flower (page 247), mealybugs (page 262), and root rot (page 272).

Snake plant

We've grown this plant, our mothers grew it, and so did our grandmothers. It's been very popular for a long time. And deservedly so, because it is a handsome plant with a pronounced vertical presence; and it is both easy to grow and low maintenance. In fact, snake plant (*Sansevieria trifasciata*) seems almost indestructible,

Snake plant (aka bowstring hemp, golden bird's nest, good luck plant, Saint George's sword).

tolerating a very wide range of light, temperature, and water conditions.

Snake plant has no aboveground stems. Its leaves arise directly in a basal rosette from a thick, underground, creeping rhizome, and since the plant doesn't flower indoors, foliage is the primary reason to grow this plant. The stiffly erect, stout leaves feel almost artificial, they're so hard. Each sword-shaped leaf is sharply pointed. Leaves are dark green, with transverse bands of silvery gray-green, much like a snake's skin, and they are sometimes edged with a narrow ribbon of yellow or white, depending on the cultivar. Indoors the leaves rarely exceed 36 inches tall and they are usually 2 to 2.5 inches wide. Some cultivars are much shorter and more compact, with wider leaves. In all the many cultivars, leaves are glossy, with a waxy sheen, and strongly vertical.

❶ This plant is toxic to people and pets and should be kept in an out-of-the-way place. All parts of this plant contain saponins, chemical compounds with soap-like properties which have historically been used as fish poisons and in shampoos. Clinical symptoms are nausea, vomiting, and diarrhea. If you suspect a person or pet has ingested parts of this plant, call your local emergency hotline, poison control center, or vet.

OPTIMUM HOUSEHOLD ENVIRONMENT

Read the Introduction for the specifics of each recommendation.

MEDIUM LIGHT. Give snake plant bright filtered light. No direct sun.

MODERATE TEMPERATURE. Daytime 70 to 80°F, nighttime 60 to 70°F. Don't let the temperature drop below 60°F.

MODERATE WATER. Through the growing season, water whenever the top of the potting medium becomes dry to a depth of 1 inch. In winter, water whenever the top of the potting medium becomes dry to a depth of 2 inches.

HUMIDITY. Snake plant does not need supplemental humidity.

POTTING MEDIUM. Use any good organic, cactus and succulent potting soil that incorporates organic fertilizer, mycorrhizal fungi, and other beneficial microbes.

FERTILIZER. Use any balanced organic fertilizer. Apply at half-strength once a month through the growing season. Do not feed your plant in winter.

POTTING. When your plant needs up-potting, shift it to a container with a diameter 2 inches larger than the current pot. Use a heavy pot to help prevent these tall plants from falling over, or add pebbles to the bottom of the pot to increase its weight.

PROPAGATION. Snake plant is easy to propagate by division of the rhizome and from leaf cuttings.

COMMON PROBLEMS

Watch for sunburn (page 256), mealybugs (page 262), and root rot (page 272).

Tiger jaws

The most widespread and commonly available tiger jaws is *Faucaria tigrina*, with *F. felina* a close second. The name of the genus comes from the Latin *fauces* ("animal mouth"), and the leaves, borne in opposite pairs, do indeed look like the gaping maw of an animal's mouth, or even tiger jaws. What's more, both species have up to ten large, soft, whitish teeth, standing erect along the edges of their succulent, triangular leaves. In *F. tigrina* the teeth are long and recurved, and the 2-inch-long leaves are thinner. In *F. felina* the teeth are shorter, and the 3-inch-long leaves are thicker. Both species have daisy-like yellow flowers, to 1 inch wide in *F. tigrina* and 2 inches wide in *F. felina*. They bloom in the autumn, and the flowers have numerous, very thin petals that have a glossy, satiny sheen. Tiger jaws get about 6 inches tall and spread to form clumps 6 to 8 inches wide.

OPTIMUM HOUSEHOLD ENVIRONMENT

Read the Introduction for the specifics of each recommendation.

HIGH LIGHT. During the growing season give these plants a full day of sun. This much light helps them bloom well in the fall. The plants do best in a south window. A half-day of light from an east or west window also works well.

Tiger jaws (aka cat chap, cat jaws, shark jaws, wolf mouth).

HIGH TEMPERATURE. Daytime 75 to 85°F, night-time 65 to 75°F. Give them cooler temperatures in winter but don't let it get below 60°F.

LOW WATER. Water whenever the top of the potting medium becomes dry to a depth of 2 inches. Water even less in winter.

HUMIDITY. Mist your plant several times a week in winter with a spray bottle of water on a mist setting, or use a handheld mister. During the growing season the plant needs no supplemental humidity.

POTTING MEDIUM. Use any good organic, cactus and succulent potting soil that incorporates organic fertilizer, mycorrhizal fungi, and other beneficial microbes.

FERTILIZER. Use any organic fertilizer, in either a powder or liquid formulation. Apply once a month through the growing season. Do not feed the plants in winter.

POTTING. When your plant needs up-potting, shift it to a container with a diameter 2 inches larger than the current pot. Use broad, shallow pots for these shallow-rooted plants.

PROPAGATION. Tiger jaws is easy to propagate by division and from stem tip cuttings.

COMMON PROBLEMS

Watch for failure to flower (page 247), mealybugs (page 262), and root rot (page 272).

Culinary herbs

What a delight it is to harvest fresh herbs from pots lining your kitchen windowsills. No wonder then that so many people grow certain herbs as houseplants, even if only as temporary ones. All, including many scented-leaf geraniums (page 96), have scented, aromatic foliage that is used in a variety of ways to create dishes and drinks that delight the palate. Some culinary herbs are also used medicinally or are simply valued for their fragrance, but for seasoning your food there's really nothing better than your own, homegrown organic herbs, freshly gathered. Indoors, the best way to keep culinary herbs healthy is to make sure they have plenty of air and space. Place a small fan nearby that blows gently across their leaves. They'll thank you for it.

Basil (*Ocimum basilicum*) is an annual with dozens of available varieties—lemon basil, purple basil, Thai basil—but the typical variety you find at the grocer's is Genovese basil. Buy bags of fresh Genovese basil from the supermarket, trim the ends off the stems, put them in water, and set the jar on a windowsill. Harvest fresh leaves whenever you need them. As time goes by, many of the stems grow roots. Pot these up in 4-inch pots.

Bay laurel (*Laurus nobilis*) is a very pretty, slow-growing, evergreen tree that is quite happy potted and can be grown in a container for many years. To use the leaves, harvest a few and dry them in the sun. The flavor is better from dried leaves, and once dried they'll keep for a year. But discard them after a year because they start to lose flavor. Dry some more fresh leaves to replace them.

Chervil (*Anthriscus cerefolium*) is an annual that quickly flowers and goes to seed in the heat of summer. And of course, it dies after it goes to seed. It does best and lasts longest in the cooler temperatures of winter, and in the light of an east window. Because it's an annual you need to start it from seed or buy young plants at the nursery in order to keep it around.

Chives (*Allium schoenoprasum*) is a very pretty, almost grass-like perennial that gets 6 to 12 inches tall. The tasty leaves are round and hollow and have a mild onion flavor. Harvest by cutting leaves off 2 to 3 inches above the soil line. Chop the leaves for use as a garnish. The pink flowers are also edible.

Cilantro (*Coriandrum sativum*) is an annual that, like chervil, quickly flowers, goes to seed, and dies in summer's heat. Because it's an annual you must either grow cilantro from seed every year, or buy young plants from the nursery to have it available year-round. Cilantro does double duty as a culinary herb because its leaves have one flavor profile and its ripe seeds are ground into coriander, a spice with an altogether different flavor. Cilantro often features in Mexican and Chinese cuisines, but note: when the plant begins to develop a flower stalk, the leaves change flavor. Some people love their flavor in every stage of growth; others relish only the fresh young leaves.

Marjoram (*Origanum majorana*) is a somewhat shrubby perennial closely related to oregano that grows in a clump with upright, branched stems and small, oval, gray-green leaves. Outdoors, marjoram spreads aggressively to 18 to 24 inches tall and wide. It will be much smaller when confined to a pot in the house (and it can't get away from you either).

Mint is a perennial in the mint family. Spearmint (*Mentha spicata*) is a favorite for a lovely,

Rosemary.

ice cold mojito at the end of the day. Pepper-mint (*M. ×piperita*) is more strongly flavored, sharper, almost peppery, thus its epithets. Both these mints spread aggressively out in the garden so keep them under control in pots. Indoors, of course, they can't escape and that's a good thing. Mints root very easily and quickly in a glass of water.

Oregano (*Origanum vulgare*) is a perennial that spreads by underground rhizomes. Its small, gray-green to bright green leaves are strongly aromatic and familiar to most people as a principal flavoring of pizza sauce. Oregano flowers in summer with clusters of small pink flowers. There are numerous cultivars and named varieties with different leaf colors and flavors. Taste before you buy to be sure you like the one you bring home.

Parsley (*Petroselinum crispum*) is a biennial, which means that it will grow leaves in its first year and, in its second year it will flower, set seed, and die. To enjoy it indoors, then, you have to start it from seed or purchase starts from the nursery. Flat-leaf and curly-leaf parsley have very different flavors. Try one of each to see which you'd like to grow.

Rosemary (*Rosmarinus officinalis*), a long-lived evergreen shrub with numerous cultivars, will thrive for years as a potted houseplant. Keep it small (under 2 feet) and bushy by snipping off the twigs to use its abundantly produced, unmistakably flavored leaves in cooking.

Sage (*Salvia officinalis*), another long-lived evergreen shrub, gets 1 to 2 feet tall depending on the cultivar. Some cultivars have purple leaves; others are tricolor with creamy white, purple, and green foliage; and some are variegated with golden blotches. The large, gray-green leaves of 'Berggarten', a favorite cultivar, often find their way into chicken soups and stews.

Tarragon (*Artemisia dracunculus*) is an herbaceous perennial that grows from an underground rhizome to 2 feet tall. Indoors it performs best in an east window and will remain green all winter. Harvest fresh leaves for their delicate anise-like flavor. If you find an offer of

Thyme.

tarragon seeds don't bother with them. They are of Russian tarragon (*A. dracunculoides*), which does not have the distinctive flavor and aroma of true tarragon. True tarragon rarely produces viable seeds and is almost exclusively propagated by division and cuttings.

Thymes are diminutive evergreen shrublets only 8 to 12 inches tall with tiny but strongly aromatic leaves. The numerous cultivars of common garden thyme (*Thymus vulgaris*) include English thyme and French thyme. Cultivars of *T. ×citriodorus* include lemon thyme, orange thyme, and lime thyme. All forms grow happily in 4- to 6-inch pots. Many other species of thyme (woolly thyme, creeping thyme, mother of thyme) widely used as outdoor groundcovers are not culinary herbs.

OPTIMUM HOUSEHOLD ENVIRONMENT

Read the Introduction for the specifics of each recommendation.

HIGH LIGHT. Herbs need full sun. Except as noted (at chervil and tarragon), the all-day-long light or very bright indirect light of a south window is best. A half-day of light from an east or west window also works well, but if your plant starts to get leggy give it more light. Many herbs, especially low-growing ones, do well under artificial lights for 14 hours a day. Keep the lights 6 inches above the leaves.

MODERATE TEMPERATURE. Daytime 70 to 80°F, nighttime 60 to 70°F.

MODERATE WATER. Most herbs should be watered whenever the top of the potting medium becomes dry to a depth of 1 inch. Exceptions are bay laurel, rosemary, sage, and thyme, which should be watered whenever the top of the potting medium becomes dry to a depth of 2 inches.

HUMIDITY. Herbs generally adapt quite well to the dry air of most homes and don't normally require misting. If the air in your home is excessively dry, mist herbs occasionally with a spray bottle of water on a mist setting, or use a handheld mister.

POTTING MEDIUM. For most culinary herbs, use any good organic, general-purpose potting soil that incorporates organic fertilizer, mycorrhizal fungi, and other beneficial microbes. For bay laurel, rosemary, sage, and thyme use a well-drained, organic, cactus and succulent potting soil. If you can't find an organic cactus potting soil that incorporates organic fertilizer, mycorrhizal fungi, and other beneficial microbes, you can make one by mixing sand 50/50 with a general-purpose medium that has all these healthy ingredients.

FERTILIZER. Use any liquid organic fertilizer where the first number (nitrogen) is higher than the other two. Apply at half-strength once a month. Stop feeding herbs in winter.

POTTING. When herbs need up-potting, shift them to a container with a diameter 2 inches larger than the current pot. You'll generally move them from a 4-inch pot to a 6-inch pot. Most of the time you don't need pots larger than 6 inches. If you choose to, and you have the space for it, you could grow bay laurel, rosemary, and sage in pots up to 12 inches in diameter.

PROPAGATION. With the exceptions of chervil, chives, cilantro, and parsley, which are grown from seed, all other herbs are easy to propagate from stem tip cuttings. Most people find rooting herbs in water is simple and easy. When the cuttings have plenty of roots, pot them up into 4-inch pots. You can also root cuttings in potting mix by using rooting hormones.

COMMON PROBLEMS

Watch for leggy growth (page 251), aphids (page 259), and powdery mildew (page 272).

Organic Solutions to Common Problems

COMMON GROWING CONDITION PROBLEMS

Every plant portrait lists the most common problems that occur for each plant. However, you may encounter less common problems as well. If something is not quite right with your plants and you've ruled out a pest or disease, look at the photos and read the descriptions in this section to find a diagnosis and safe, organic solutions.

Accordion-folded leaves. New, young leaves of certain orchids (alicearas, beallaras, dancing ladies, pansy orchids, spider orchids) tend to stick together as they grow when the humidity is too low or the plant doesn't have enough water. Leaves that are stuck together cannot free themselves, but they keep trying to grow. As a result, the leaf becomes pleated and folded. Accordion-folded leaves will not outgrow this condition. Although unsightly, it is not life-threatening to your plant. Correct the growing conditions, and subsequent leaves will grow normally.

If low humidity is the trouble, raise it by misting your orchids with a spray bottle of water on a mist setting, or use a handheld mister. To determine how often to mist, look at the humidity needs of your plant in its plant portrait. Set your orchid in a saucer or tray of water with the pot sitting on pot feet or pebbles to raise it up above the water. Group your houseplants together to raise the humidity. Put a humidifier in the room. Avoid blasts of hot air from heat registers.

If you believe the humidity is adequate, then insufficient water may be the trouble. Water your orchids more frequently, especially if the air in your home is unusually warm and dry. If humidity is adequate and your frequency of watering is appropriate, check to see if your

Accordion-folded leaves.

orchid needs to be up-potted and the potting medium refreshed.

Brown leaf tips. The tips of the leaves die and turn brown. The cause is low humidity and/or insufficient water. As this condition progresses, leaf edges may also turn brown and die. If tiny black dots develop in the dead brown areas, your plant has a leaf spot fungus infection (page 269).

If low humidity is the trouble, raise it by misting your houseplants with a spray bottle of water on a mist setting, or use a handheld mister. To determine how often to mist, look at the humidity needs of your plant in its plant portrait. Set your plant in a saucer or tray of water

(top left and right) Brown leaf tips.

(above) Accordion-folded leaves.

with the pot sitting on pot feet or pebbles to raise it up above the water. Group your houseplants together to raise the humidity. Put a humidifier in the room. Avoid blasts of hot air from heat registers.

For insufficient water, check to see if your plant's pot is too small for it. If so, your plant needs to be up-potted. Make sure that you provide your plant with all the water it needs.

Edema. Plants develop tiny brown bumps on the leaves. These bumps are firmly attached and cannot be rubbed off with your thumbnail. The bumps are rough to the touch, because they're composed of cork tissue that the leaves produce in response to overwatering. Edema is not

a disease or a pest, and is not life-threatening, but leaves that have already developed edema are going to stay that way. To prevent edema from occurring on new leaves, reduce the frequency and quantity of watering. Increase light and temperature to allow more rapid transpiration. Make sure the potting medium drains adequately and that your plant is not suffering from soggy soil.

Failure to flower. Sometimes houseplants that should produce flowers don't. There are several reasons why a plant fails to flower but the most common are lack of chilling, insufficient light, and lack of long nights. Each of these factors applies to specific houseplants, as follows.

Edema.

Leaf drop.

Lack of chilling: amaryllis, Easter cactus, florist azalea, jasmine, kalanchoe, orchid cactus, and spring bulbs all require a cold treatment in order to set flower buds. The details for each plant's required cold treatment (when, for how long, at what temperature) are given in the plant portraits.

Insufficient light: dendrobium, hibiscus, prickly pear, rat tail cactus, tiger jaws, and wax plant all require sufficient levels of light (whether high or, in the case of wax plant, medium) to have enough energy to produce flowers. Plants that fail to flower because they don't receive enough sun need to be moved to a higher light situation. Alternatively, when curtains are responsible for low light intensity, they can be left open or removed. Increase sunlight carefully and acclimate your plants slowly to avoid sunburn.

Lack of long nights: Christmas cactus, jasmine, orchid cactus, and poinsettia all require a period of darkness in order to set flower buds.

See their plant portraits for details of when and how to provide these long nights, and the duration of this blackout treatment. When you bring your plant out into daylight make sure it cannot "see" light sources at night such as streetlamps, headlights, or electric lighting in your home.

Flower bud drop. Many houseplants drop their flower buds. Gardenia is notoriously finicky and tosses its flower buds on the ground for a variety of reasons. Usually it's because of its requirement for acid soil. Make sure the organic fertilizer you use is designed for acid-loving plants. Gardenias also love coffee grounds, as their portrait notes. If you are certain the soil pH is correct, yet your gardenia (or any other houseplant) still drops its buds, then check to make sure it isn't too cold and that it's getting enough light. For all houseplants, be sure you're not overwatering, as this is a frequent cause of bud drop. Many orchids also drop their flower buds, but the cause is unknown.

Leaf drop.

Leaf drop. Leaves of all plants have a finite lifespan. As a rule plants shed their oldest leaves a few at a time. This is totally normal and not cause for concern. However, when plants drop a lot of leaves all at once, this is not normal. Many plants drop their leaves if overwatered. Have another look at the plant portrait to check the plant's water needs.

False aralia, weeping fig, and others drop their leaves if you move them to a new location. Put them in a permanent location and leave them there. Do not put them outdoors for the summer.

Boston fern, hare's foot fern, and jade plant, among others, tend to be drought deciduous and drop their leaves if they get too dry. Recheck the plant portraits for their water needs.

Donkey tail and lipstick plant are just two plants that drop their leaves if they get too cold. Consult the plant portraits to determine the correct temperature range.

Leaves changing color. Plants with colorful or variegated foliage sometimes begin to lose their bright yellows, whites, reds, or pinks. Leaves can revert to plain green, or just fade and turn pale. Too much or too little sunlight causes the foliage of certain plants to change color.

Arrowhead plant, coleus, and Swedish ivy are all examples of plants with colorful foliage that fades and loses vibrancy with too much sunlight. Move these plants to a lower light situation. Or, instead of moving your plant, add more curtains to reduce light intensity.

Chinese evergreen, croton, polka dot plant, pothos, and variegated cultivars of cast-iron plant and ivy are all examples of plants with colorful, variegated leaves that tend to turn plain green with too little sunlight. Move these plants to a higher light situation. Or, instead of moving your plant, remove some of the curtains on your windows. Acclimate your plants slowly to avoid sunburn.

(top) Leaves on croton begin to lose their bright colors.

(above) Leaves on pothos turn plain green.

Leaves turning brown. Leaves turn brown for a variety of reasons, some of which are perfectly normal and not cause for concern. For example, old leaves in the process of being discarded by your plant often turn brown before they drop. Caladium, Cupid's bow, and Rieger begonias, among others, have a pronounced dormant period in which all the plant's leaves turn brown as the plant prepares to go to sleep. This is also normal, and new leaves will grow when the dormant period is over. But leaves of some plants turn brown because they are sensitive to chemicals or water quality, others to low humidity. These conditions are not normal and are correctible.

Bird's nest and davallia ferns are just two examples of plants that are sensitive to chemicals. Do not spray such plants with insecticides, fungicides, or leaf polishes. Insecticidal soap is safe to use if you need to, but avoid all others.

Many plants (peacock plant, spider plant, orchids, bromeliads) are sensitive to water quality and should be irrigated with filtered, rain-, or distilled water, rather than tap water.

Raise the humidity for maidenhair fern or any plant that has begun to brown by misting it, setting the pot on a tray of water filled with pebbles, or putting a humidifier in the room.

Leggy growth. All plants eventually shed their oldest leaves. As the plant grows taller and as the leaves near its base are shed, the stems or trunk of the plant is revealed. When your plant starts to look like a collection of sticks, each topped by a dust mop of foliage, it has become leggy. Keep in mind that for some plants this look is perfectly normal. Legginess can also occur when plants are grown in too much shade and become tall and spindly as they reach for light.

Plants that have become leggy because they have dropped older leaves need a bit of corrective pruning. Prune them back by about a third

Leaves turning brown.

Leaves turning brown.

to force side branches to grow out and make the plants bushier. Alternatively, pinch out the growing tips of the stems while the plants are still small to avoid legginess from the outset.

Plants that are tall and spindly and have not dropped their older leaves are not getting enough light. Either move these plants to a higher light location or remove curtains that filter the light. As always, slowly and carefully acclimate your plants to higher light intensity to avoid sunburn.

Leggy growth.

Loss of vigor. The flowers of spring bulbs and the smaller, more colorful calla lilies are smaller, and the plants less vigorous than they were in their first year.

Make certain your plant has the proper light regime. Remember, light is food. Also, be sure to provide fertilizer regularly through the growing season and none at all during dormancy. You want the plant to store as much food and nutrients as possible in its underground rhizomes so that it has abundant resources to mobilize the next time it flowers. The more energy it has available from its stores the more vigorous it will be. When the plant is completely dormant put it in a cool place out of the hot sun. Cool temperatures help it conserve stored energy. Treat these plants right and they should reward you with ample flowers every year for years to come.

Needle drop. Norfolk Island pine tends to drop needles on the floor. As with any plant, dropping the oldest leaves (or needles) is normal and to be expected. However, when Norfolk Island pine drops large quantities of its needles, it is experiencing some sort of environmental stress. Although it can grow new needles, it cannot replace ones that have been lost. Norfolk Island pine needs cool temperatures, high humidity, and moderate water to do its best. If the temperature goes too high, the humidity too low, or the plant gets too dry it becomes stressed and starts dropping needles. Avoid putting this plant near sources of hot air like furnace registers, space heaters, or fireplaces. Check the plant portrait for specific requirements.

Plant collapse. All plants wilt, of course, but plant collapse is very dramatic. Nerve plant, in particular, needs ample water, high humidity, and filtered light to stay healthy. It is notorious for having hissy fits and fainting if its potting medium gets too dry, the humidity gets

Smaller, more colorful calla lilies are less vigorous in their second year.

Plant sprawl.

Plant sprawl. Certain plants tend to lean dramatically to one side as they grow larger because their stems don't have the strength to hold them upright. This tendency to lean is exaggerated if the light source always comes from one side, forcing the plant to lean into the light. Pinching off the growing tips of the stems while these plants are young forces them to become bushier and therefore stronger and able to stand straighter. Tying the plant to a bamboo pole or stake also helps it keep its shape. Give the plant a quarter turn every week to keep it growing symmetrically and prevent it from leaning into the light.

Post-repotting collapse. Up-potting and re-potting is a fairly traumatic experience for any plant. Even using the most careful technique, roots get broken or trimmed, stems and leaves are jostled and pruned, and water supply is interrupted. Most plants recover quickly,

too low, or the light too bright. The plant wilts very quickly if it runs out of water. It will rehydrate if watered, but if it's been too dry too long (more than a couple of hours) it won't recover. Just make sure it also has good drainage because soggy soil can be lethal.

but tree ivy is notorious for collapsing completely after re-potting. Give all plants some TLC in a post-repotting recovery room, with a bit of shade and cooler temperatures to minimize water loss while they recover. Gently reintroduce them to their proper light and temperature regimes once they have perked up again.

Premature dormancy. Many houseplants have a definite dormant period at some point in the year. Drought often acts as a trigger for a plant to enter dormancy. Thus, allowing your plant to go dry can cause it to go dormant sooner than it should. False shamrock is especially susceptible to this phenomenon. The leaves of plants other than cacti and succulents turn yellow, then brown, and then drop. In many cases the aboveground plant parts disappear completely. It is not dead, just sleeping, and will resume growth at the appropriate time. When cacti and succulents go dormant in winter they're far more subtle about it—they just stop growing.

Maintain the proper moisture levels to keep a plant active and healthy until the right time for

Post-repotting collapse.

Post-repotting collapse.

Salt burn.

it to go dormant. Check the plant portraits for guidance on frequency and quantity of water for the plant in question.

Salt burn. Leaves that turn brown around the edges, stunted plants, wilted plants, and roots that die at their tips are symptoms of salt burn. The salts show up as a white crust around the edge of the pot or on the surface of the potting medium, especially in dry weather. Any plant can suffer from salt burn due to accumulated fertilizer salts in the potting medium, or salts in the water supply. Common table salt, sodium chloride, is only one kind of salt. Other kinds of salt include mineral nutrients like potassium, phosphorus, and calcium from fertilizer.

Do not use your tap water for your plants if you have hard water with a high mineral content or if you have a water softening system that uses table salt. Instead, use rainwater, bottled water, or distilled water. Whether you have hard water or not, the best practice is to flush fertilizer salts out of the pots once a month by pouring rainwater, bottled water, or distilled water onto the potting medium. Give it a thorough soaking. Then let the pot drain.

Shrunken, wrinkled leaves. All succulents (e.g., agave and aloe) and some orchids (e.g., moth orchids) store water in their thick fleshy leaves. Leaves of these plants become shrunken and wrinkled when plants dry out too much. As soon as you notice this problem, mist and water the plant lightly, but do not soak it. The next day water it lightly again. Wait a couple of days and then water lightly a third time. Shortly thereafter the leaves should have fattened up nicely. Always avoid making the potting medium soggy because the roots of these kinds of plants do not tolerate much water and will quickly succumb to root rot fungus.

Salt burn.

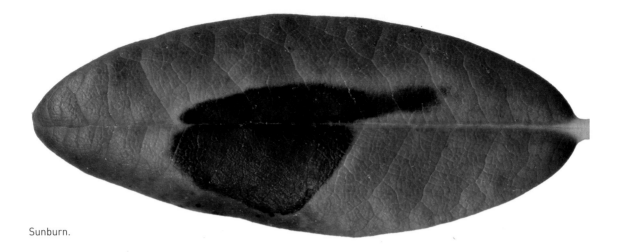
Sunburn.

Sunburn. Leaves develop large black and brown dead patches wherever they have been exposed to too much sunlight. Intense, direct, hot sunlight literally cooks the cells of the leaf and kills them. Your plant will grow healthy new leaves but the dead patches on the old leaves are permanent. Sunburn frequently occurs when a houseplant is moved outdoors for a summer vacation and is inadequately acclimated to its new environment. Solve this common problem by moving the plant to a shadier location. Filter and soften the light by installing sheer curtains or Venetian blinds. Acclimate your plant whenever you move it to a higher light situation.

Whitish spots on leaves. These spots typically show up as lines or rings of pale tissue on the upper surface of the leaves of African violets, gloxinias, and other furry-leaved gesneriads. The spots develop when cold water is dripped onto the leaves. Use a watering can with a narrow spout so you can apply tepid water directly to the potting medium while keeping the leaves dry. You might also try setting the pot in a saucer full of water for 30 minutes. This is called watering from the bottom. Be careful if you try this because it is very easy to forget the plant and

allow it to sit in water too long, which drastically increases the risk of root rot and gray mold.

Wilting. Any plant that cannot move water up to its leaves will wilt. The leaves dangle and become flaccid. The growing tips of the stems droop and point to the ground. The whole plant suffers and, if the situation is not reversed, your plant will die. Wilting is a serious, life-threatening condition that results from four causes.

The most frequent cause of wilting is that you forgot to water your plant. If you find to your horror that your plant has wilted because you forgot to water it, give it water immediately. Most plants will rehydrate quickly and suffer no consequences. If the potting medium is completely dry it may be reluctant to absorb water so immerse the entire pot in a bucket of water until it is completely saturated, then let it drain. Your plant should recover within a few hours. If it does not recover, it's dead.

If your plant has wilted even though you've watered it regularly and the potting medium has ample moisture, suspect root rot, the second most frequent cause of wilting. Gently extract the plant from its pot without breaking stems

Whitish spots on leaves.

Wilting.

or roots. Inspect the root system. If roots are mushy, and gray, black, or dark brown, then the root system has been invaded by a pathogenic fungus that has killed and eaten the roots. See root rot page 272.

A third cause for wilting is that your plant is in a pot that is too small for it. If your plant has wilted, and you're certain you've watered it properly, and you've checked the root system and found it to be alive and healthy, your plant is most likely in too small a pot (rootbound). Plants that are rootbound have essentially filled their container with roots and there is not enough moisture-holding medium left in the pot. The roots run out of water shortly after watering and the plant wilts again. You need to do one of two things. Either up-pot your plant to a larger container with fresh potting medium, or re-pot your plant after trimming away excess roots.

A less frequent but nevertheless important cause of wilting is hot moving air, as from a heat vent or space heater, sucking the water out of the leaves faster than the plant can handle. If your plant wilts and you know it has sufficient water, does not have root rot, and it is not

rootbound, then check for sources of hot moving air. Usually a heat vent from a forced air furnace or an electric space heater will be the culprit. But any plant is likely to wilt when it sits in an open window, in full sun, on a hot afternoon, with the wind blowing.

Yellowing leaf edges. Usually this is perfectly normal and is not actually a problem, though it can be worrisome to the grower. It occurs on the oldest leaves. As your plant grows and makes new leaves the oldest leaves begin to turn yellow, then brown, and then they die. This is a normal part of the aging process for any leaf. Just prune the dead leaves away.

Yellowing leaves. Yellowing occurs for many reasons. It's a bit like having a fever: it tells you *something* is wrong, but it doesn't tell you what. If yellowing leaves have tiny black dots or spots, then you have a fungal or bacterial infection. Have a look at Common Disease Problems on page 266. There may also be colonies of insect pests on the undersides of the leaves. If so, turn to Common Pest Problems on page 259. Yellow

Yellowing leaf edges.

Yellowing leaves.

leaves can also indicate nutritional deficiencies. Check the Introduction and plant portraits, and fertilize your plants in need.

If dots, spots, or insects are absent, and you're certain the nutrient status is adequate, then yellow leaves are diagnostic for too much hot afternoon sun, need for acidic soil, or overwatering. Recheck plant portraits to verify that you are not overwatering any plant. Also make sure the drainage is good. Pay special attention to angel wing begonia, asparagus fern, and gardenia. Use an acid fertilizer for gardenias to acidify the potting medium. Keep asparagus fern out of hot, afternoon sun.

Yellow patches on leaves. Yellow blotches or patches in the middle of the leaf blade, in the absence of tiny brown or black spots or insect infestations, are due to nutritional deficiency. Besides the usual nitrogen, phosphorus, and potassium, your plant needs the secondary mineral nutrients of calcium, magnesium, and sulfur, and the micronutrient iron. Feed your plant

Yellowing leaves.

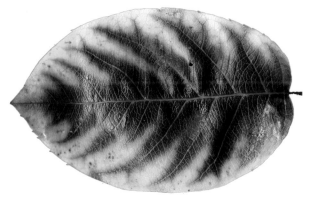

Yellow patches on leaves.

Yellow patches on leaves.

with liquid organic kelp fertilizer to correct the nutritional deficiency. Spray a liquid preparation directly on the leaves. The leaves should turn green again within a couple of weeks.

If the leaves do not turn green again after applying liquid kelp, and small brown spots appear in the yellow patches, you are dealing with leaf spot fungus infection (page 269); if no small brown spots develop in the yellow patches, you are dealing either with an insect infestation of some sort (see next section) or with a virus infection (pages 267, 270, and 271).

COMMON PEST PROBLEMS

Every plant portrait lists the most common problems that occur for each plant. However, you may encounter less common problems as well. If something is not quite right with your plants and you've ruled out improper culture or disease, look at the photos and read the descriptions in this section to identify the culprit (and the symptoms it causes) and solve the problem, safely and organically. Some pests are quite common, while others are not. If you

give your houseplants a summer vacation outdoors, you may find that ants, earwigs, leafhoppers, slugs, snails, and thrips accompany the plants back inside.

The first thing you should do if you have heavy insect infestations is to prune, pick, or break off any part of the plant that is badly affected. Then use other remedies as needed, remembering that even organic solutions can be toxic to people and pets. Take a moment to read and follow all product labels carefully. Clean tools and wash your hands thoroughly with hot soapy water before handling any healthy plants. Be sure to use soap, not detergent, because detergent can burn foliage.

Ants. You are likely well aware of what an ant looks like, and they actually do little damage to your houseplant. But they can be unwelcome in the house; and some bite. Some species bring aphids, mealybugs, and scale insects to plants so that the ants can "milk" them for their honeydew while the pests feed on your plant (honeydew is actually sweet, sticky insect excrement); sounds yucky, but it's actually kind of fascinating to watch. If ants infest your plants, put the pots

Ants and aphids on citrus.

Aphids.

on pebbles in a tray of water, because ants cannot swim. Alternatively, use sticky bands (which work like old-fashioned fly-paper) or spray with insecticidal soap.

Aphids. These tiny, green, woolly-gray, black, or brown, soft-bodied, pear-shaped insects cluster on the undersides of leaves. Look for two tubes on their rear ends to be sure you've spotted aphids. They're hard to see, but if you look closely or with a hand lens, you'll see the tubes. Other symptoms you might see: the tips of stems or branches curl, cup, or deform; or you find a sticky, clear, varnish-like residue on leaves or stems. These pests are very common. Wash aphids off the plant using plain water, soapy water, or rubbing alcohol. Alternatively, spray with insecticidal soap or horticultural oil.

Earwigs. These small brown and black pests have two pincers on their rear ends. They hide during the day and come out at night to eat holes

Earwig.

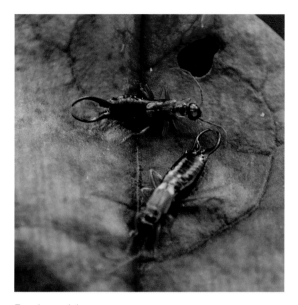

Earwigs and damage.

Leafhopper.

in tender, young leaves. They are uncommon on houseplants but may have hitched a ride into your home on a plant you had outdoors for the summer. You can pick these pests off by hand, but the simplest earwig trap is a moist, rolled-up newspaper. Roll it fairly loosely and secure it with a rubber band. Moisten it slightly and lay it on the potting media in the evening. The earwigs hide in there overnight. Retrieve the paper in the morning, close up the ends, and roll the paper tightly so that earwigs cannot escape. Seal it, along with its hidden earwigs, in a plastic bag and put that in the garbage. Alternatively, spray with spinosad.

Leafhoppers. Another uncommon pest on houseplants, leafhoppers are fast fliers and may disappear before you get a good look. The first sign you'll see are tiny white specks stippling the leaves. Leaf edges might turn yellow, and then brown. If you do get a glimpse of the bug, it is wedge-shaped, greenish blue or brownish gray, and up to 0.5 inch long. These insects may

Leafhopper damage.

enter your home if you've put a plant outside for awhile. They transmit serious bacterial and viral diseases to plants. Solve this pest problem by spraying with insecticidal soap, neem oil, or horticultural oil.

Mealybugs. These pests are very common on houseplants. Your first hint is fluffy grayish white lumps suddenly appearing on the undersides of leaves and where leaves attach to stems. These insects cannot fly. They coat the surface of leaves and stems with clear, sticky, varnish-like honeydew. A gray-black coating (sooty mold) that easily rubs off may grow on the honeydew. Wash mealybugs off the plant using plain water, soapy water, or rubbing alcohol. Alternatively, spray with insecticidal soap or horticultural oil.

Scale insects. Small, gray-white, reddish brown, yellow, or black lumps stick to the surfaces of leaves, or to stems. You can easily remove them with your thumbnail. Like mealybugs and aphids, these buggers coat the upper surfaces of leaves with clear, sticky, varnish-like honeydew. Sooty mold—a gray-black coating that easily rubs off—forms on the honeydew. Scale is very common on houseplants. Pick pests off by hand, or spray with insecticidal soap or horticultural oil.

Slugs and snails. You'll rarely see these two mollusk pests inside, but they do hitchhike on summer vacationing houseplants. Since both of these critters hide during the day, the first

Mealybugs.

Scale on citrus leaf.

Scale on citrus stem.

Slug.

Slug or snail damage.

hint you may have is large irregular holes in the leaves. If you spot slime trails, then you know slugs or snails are the culprits. Pick them off by hand, or trap them by creating hiding places, like a small overturned pot, so that the critters seek refuge at night beneath them. Then you can easily find and destroy the slugs or snails, or move them back outside where they belong. Alternatively, sprinkle iron phosphate on top of the potting medium.

Spider mites. Although a very common pest on houseplants, you'll probably never see a spider mite (unless you have bionic eyes). You will see that leaves are stippled with tiny pale dots that sometimes turn the whole leaf bronze-colored.

Fine webbing, like spider silk, covers leaves and stems over time. Badly infested leaves turn yellow or red and drop off the plant. Wash mites off the plant using plain water, soapy water, or rubbing alcohol. Alternatively, spray with insecticidal soap or horticultural oil.

Spider mite webbing.

Spider mite damage.

Thrips. You will probably have problems with thrips only if you've given your plants a trip to the patio. Thrips are very tiny yellowy orange insects, and you'll likely never see them. They congregate on flower petals and leaves. The symptoms you might see include silvery leaves, slivery streaks on leaves, or damaged leaves that roll up and drop off. Wash thrips off the plant using plain water, soapy water, or rubbing alcohol. Alternatively, spray with insecticidal soap or spinosad.

Whiteflies. You see small, bright white insects fly away when you disturb your plant. Large colonies on the undersides of leaves deposit patches of white residue. These insects, which are very common on houseplants, coat the upper surfaces of leaves with clear, sticky, varnish-like honeydew. Sooty mold—a gray-black coating that easily rubs off—forms on the honeydew. Wash these pests off the plant using plain water, soapy water, or rubbing alcohol. Alternatively, spray with insecticidal soap or horticultural oil.

Thrips damage on citrus fruitlets.

Whiteflies.

COMMON DISEASE PROBLEMS

Every plant portrait lists the most common problems that occur for each plant. However, you may encounter less common problems as well. If something is not quite right with your houseplant and you've ruled out improper culture or pests, look at the photos and read the descriptions in this section to find a diagnosis and safe, organic solutions. Remember, even organic remedies can be toxic to people and pets, so be sure to read and follow all product labels carefully. Diseases on plants are harder to deal with than either adverse cultural conditions or pests. The good news is—diseases are much rarer. If it *is* a disease, 80% of the time it is caused by a fungus.

There is no cure for bacterial or virus infections on plants, so prevention is, as always, the most effective thing you can do. Buy plants from a reliable source and always inspect plants before you buy them. Keep new plants in another room away from all your other houseplants for 14 days; use the same strategy to isolate sick plants. Do not overwater and make sure your plant is in the right-sized pot. Sanitize by removing any infected plant parts swiftly; throw infected plant tissue in the garbage, not your compost pile. Sadly, with all virus infections and rot diseases, you may have no other option but to get rid of the infected plant.

Anthurium blight. This disease is caused by a lethal bacterial pathogen, *Xanthomonas campestris* pv. *dieffenbachiae*. The earliest symptom is the appearance of water-soaked spots on the leaves. Then the spots dry out, turn reddish brown, and develop yellow haloes. When the spots enlarge and invade leaf veins, the disease becomes systemic and life-threatening to your plant. It may be found on any aroid (see sidebar) but commonly infects Chinese evergreen, dumb

Anthurium blight.

Bacterial leaf spot.

cane, and flamingo flower. Sanitize by removing infected plant parts, sterilize your tools, and keep the foliage dry.

Bacterial leaf spot. Spots that have discrete, rounded edges appear on leaves. At first they are translucent, like grease spots on paper. As they increase in size they become angular because the infection is confined by leaf veins. This disease can infect any houseplant but is most common on staghorn ferns and lady's slipper orchids. Sanitize by removing infected plant parts, sterilize your tools, and keep the foliage dry.

Cymbidium mosaic virus. This virus infection is systemic and can occur on any orchid, not just cymbidiums. It rarely kills plants but can disfigure them. Symptoms are variable and include tiny yellowish, whitish, or brown, irregular-shaped spots that enlarge. These spots are sometimes sunken, sometimes not. Unfortunately, an orchid can be infected and have no symptoms at all. Because it is systemic, all parts of the plant—leaves, stems, roots, flowers—carry the disease. Pruners, knives, and scissors carry the virus from plant to plant. Interestingly, this virus has never been found in the wild. It exists only in cultivated orchids and is found in collections worldwide. An ELISA (Enzyme-linked Immunosorbent Assay) test positively identifies any infected orchid, but kits are expensive and the sample you take must be sent to a lab.

Isolate sick plants or quarantine new plants for 14 days. A symptomless but infected orchid can easily infect all your other orchids if you

Bacterial leaf spot.

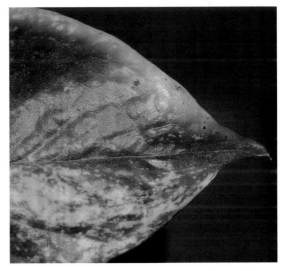

Bacterial leaf spot.

Cymbidium mosaic virus.

Cymbidium mosaic virus.

fail to sterilize your tools. If possible, clone your orchid to grow a new specimen that is free of the virus.

Gray mold. Gray mold is an infection caused by the fungus *Botrytis cinerea*, a pathogen with a very wide range of victims from houseplants to wine grapes. It starts out as wet, brown spots on leaves or flowers. The plant tissue seems to melt and eventually becomes covered with gray-brown fuzz. That fuzz is composed of millions of spores that float in the air to start new infections on healthy plants. Nip this disease in the bud by removing any infected plant parts swiftly. To prevent new infections, use baking soda spray or spray with a bacterial fungicide (*Bacillus subtilis*).

Leaf gall. Leaf gall is a fungus disease caused by the pathogen *Exobasidium vaccinii*. Among houseplants this fungus infects only florist azalea. In the garden it also infects blueberries, huckleberries, and cranberries, which can transmit the disease to your azalea. Infections occur on leaves and sometimes on flowers and stems.

Gray mold on Rieger begonia.

Gray mold on geranium.

Leaf gall.

The infected tissue becomes greatly swollen, inflated, and pale green to white, pink, or pale brown. This disease is airborne and spreads via spores. Remove any infected plant parts swiftly. To prevent new infections, use baking soda spray or spray with a bacterial fungicide (*Bacillus subtilis*).

Leaf spot fungus. Small (pinprick- to matchhead-sized) brown or black spots that look a bit like freckles develop on the leaves. Often, but not always, the leaf begins to turn yellow where the spots are located, and/or the spots may develop yellow haloes. The spots are sometimes surrounded by a narrow purple band. The spots are almost always round, not angular, because these fungi are capable of eating their way through the veins of the leaf. As time goes by, the spots get larger and the leaf becomes more yellow. These symptoms are caused by one of several different fungal pathogens that infect the foliage of houseplants. All produce spores that drift through the air to land on healthy leaves. The spores germinate and the fungus attacks your plant. These leaf spot fungi

Leaf gall.

Leaf spot fungus.

Mosaic virus.

disfigure your plants and they spread to other plants, but they are only lethal when plants are already weak. Remove any infected plant parts swiftly. To prevent new infections, use baking soda spray or spray with a bacterial fungicide (*Bacillus subtilis*).

Mosaic virus. Mosaic viruses are a very large group that includes tobacco mosaic virus, cucumber mosaic virus, common bean mosaic virus, and many others. Most of these viruses were named for the plant they were first discovered on, for example, tobacco mosaic or TMV. It does not mean that TMV infects only tobacco and nothing else. In fact, TMV is worldwide and infects more than 150 different kinds of plants, including some houseplants. The symptoms of a mosaic virus are irregular zig-zag yellow streaks and patches of yellow mottles or specks on otherwise green leaves. Like the orchid viruses, plants can be infected with a mosaic virus and remain symptomless. Mosaic viruses are systemic and are transmitted from plant to plant by pruners and scissors. Be sure to sterilize tools.

Mosaic virus.

Mosaic virus on holly fern.

Isolate sick plants or quarantine new plants for 14 days. If possible, clone your plant to grow a new specimen that is free of the virus.

Ringspot virus. This systemic virus infection can occur on any plant but is most common on orchids. It rarely kills plants but does disfigure them. Symptoms are variable and include spots on leaves and off-color streaks on the flower petals. The leaf spots are often concentric yellow rings with brown centers. Unfortunately, a plant can be infected and have no symptoms at all. Still worse, a symptomless but infected plant can easily infect all your other plants if you fail to sterilize your pruners. Because it is systemic, all parts of the plant—leaves, stems, roots, flowers—carry the disease. Pruners, knives, and scissors carry the virus from plant to plant. An ELISA (Enzyme-linked Immunosorbent Assay) test positively identifies any infected plant, but kits are expensive and the sample you take must be sent to a lab.

Ringspot virus.

Ringspot virus on corsage orchid roots.

Powdery mildew.

Isolate sick plants or quarantine new plants for 14 days. A symptomless but infected orchid can easily infect all your other orchids if you fail to sterilize your tools. If possible, clone your orchid to grow a new specimen that is free of the virus.

Powdery mildew. Symptoms of this fungus include grayish white patches growing on the leaves, stems, and flowers. Your plant looks like it's been dusted with flour that rubs off easily. Leaves eventually develop dead, brown patches and become deformed. Powdery mildew is a disease caused by a number of different pathogenic fungi. All these different fungi have white mycelium that grows on the surface of the leaves and all produce airborne spores. Remove any infected plant parts swiftly. To prevent new infections, use baking soda spray or spray with a bacterial fungicide (*Bacillus subtilis*).

Root rot. If your plant has wilted even though the potting medium is wet, pull the plant out of its pot. If the roots are gray, dark brown, or black rather than whitish, and mushy rather than firm, your plant has root rot. Root rot is an insidious

Powdery mildew.

Root rot.

Mushy, dead roots.

but preventable disease that can kill your plant before you even know that something is wrong. It's a soilborne fungus disease caused by a number of different pathogenic fungi. Some of these fungi are opportunistic pathogens that are able to invade the root system only after the roots have been broken or cut, or drowned by over-watering. Some are aggressive enough to invade a perfectly healthy root system. All thrive in soggy, waterlogged soil and most disperse their spores in water, not air. In most cases prevention is the only cure for root rot. If your plant is very

valuable and long-lived you might try to save it, but the prognosis is poor. Remove diseased root tissue, and then: discard potting medium, steril-ize the pot and all tools, and spray the roots with Actinovate, an organic fungicide. To prevent new infections, do not overwater and make sure plants are in the right-sized pot, i.e., that the pot is not too big.

Rust fungus. If your plant develops spots on the upper surface of its leaves, flip an affected leaf over and look at the underside. If there are

Rust fungus.

Rust fungus.

Rust fungus.

raised bumps on the undersurface right below each of the spots on the upper surface, and if the raised bumps have colorful, powdery spores, then your plant has one of the many rust fungi. The approximately 5,000 species of rust fungus are host-specific—that is, the rust fungus that infects your flowering maple is not the same one that infects your snapdragons. The spores are airborne and usually rusty red in color. Remove any infected plant parts swiftly. To prevent new infections, spray with a bacterial fungicide (*Bacillus subtilis*) or sulfur.

Soft rot. Fleshy stems, including rhizomes, develop mushy, rotted areas that ooze slime and often smell bad. This is caused by the bacterial pathogen *Erwinia carotovora*. This is a life-threatening disease that kills plants, but the prognosis is not as grim as it is for root rot. Remove infected plant parts. Remove the plant and discard infected potting medium. Sterilize the container and all your tools. Repot the plant in fresh medium.

Soft rot on stems.

Soft rot on pseudobulb.

Stem rot.

Stem rot on prickly pear.

Soft rot on spring bulb.

Stem rot. The stem of your plant turns brown or black at the soil line and becomes soft and mushy. It does not smell bad and doesn't ooze slime. The plant's roots may also become infected. This is a serious, life-threatening disease, caused by some of the same fungi that cause root rot. The disease is preventable with proper watering, but a cure is doubtful and the prognosis poor. Remove infected plant parts. Remove the plant and discard infected potting medium. Sterilize the container and all your tools. Repot the plant in fresh medium.

Recommended Resources

Agrios, George N. 2005. *Plant Pathology*. 5th ed. Elsevier Academic Press.

Deardorff, David, and Kathryn Wadsworth. 2009. *What's Wrong With My Plant? (And How Do I Fix It?)*. Timber Press.

Gardening Solutions, University of Florida, Institute of Food and Agricultural Sciences. gardeningsolutions.ifas.ufl.edu/plants/houseplants/.

Missouri Botanical Garden. missouribotanicalgarden.org.

Pleasant, Barbara. 2005. *The Complete Houseplant Survival Manual*. Storey Publishing.

University of Hawaii, CTHAR Cooperative Extension Service. ctahr.hawaii.edu/Site/ExtHG.aspx.

Useful Conversions

Inches	Centimeters
¼	0.6
½	1.25
¾	1.9
1	2.5
1¼	3.1
1½	3.8
1¾	4.4
2	5.0
3	7.5
4	10
5	12.5
6	15
7	18
8	20
9	23
10	25
12	30
15	38
18	45
20	50
24	60
30	75
32	80
36	90

Feet	Meters
1	0.3
1½	0.5
2	0.6
2½	0.8
3	0.9
4	1.2
5	1.5
6	1.8
7	2.1
8	2.4
9	2.7
10	3.0
12	3.6
15	4.5
18	5.4
20	6.0
25	7.5

Temperatures

$°C = 0.55 \times (°F - 32)$

$°F = (1.8 \times °C) + 32$

Acknowledgments

HOW MANY WAYS can we find to thank our wise agent and counselor, Regina Ryan? Let us count the ways. There are so many we lost count. To all the gang at Timber Press, you go above and beyond: Tom Fischer, Andrew Beckman, Besse Lynch, Brian Ridder, and everyone else who works so hard to produce our beautiful books and let people know about them. Thanks to our writer's group who help steer us onto the right track, especially Rebecca Cantrell and Ben Haggard. We are very grateful to all those who led us to photo ops or took photos for this book: Judith Heath, Roger Heath, Barbara Ansley-Vensas, the Meyers sisters, Brian and Jeanne Glaspell, Ruth Murphy, Ned Ryan, and Camy, Patty, and Jose at Henery's Garden Center, among many, many others. And, as always, thank you dear readers, students, friends, and family for your support and inspiration.

Photo Credits

Barbara **Ansley-Vensas**, pages 59 and 119.

Aquiya / Dollar Photo Club, page 144.

Nino **Barbieri** / Wikimedia Commons, page 86.

Elder Salles / Dollar Photo Club, page 191.

Farm Life Tropical Foliage, page 43.

Floradania.dk, page 112.

gsx750 / Dollar Photo Club, page 228.

Ruth **Hartnup**, page 91.

Judith **Heath**, pages 14 (bottom), 22 (left), and 185.

Roger **Heath**, pages 33, 51, 56, 64, 73, 152, 180, 188, 200, 205, 219, and 234.

ksena32 / Dollar Photo Club, page 207.

maljalen / Dollar Photo Club, page 231.

Nada's Images / Dollar Photo Club, page 217.

ots photo / Dollar Photo Club, pages 97 and 118.

scphoto48 / Dollar Photo Club, page 158.

Jeff **Walls**, page 109.

All other photos are by the authors.

Index

About the Authors

David Deardorff and **Kathryn Wadsworth** are authors and photographers who travel across the country holding popular workshops and lectures. Deardorff's PhD in botany and years of experience as a plant pathologist informs their shared expertise; and Wadsworth's skill as a naturalist and author illuminates the connection between plants and people. Together they have nurtured houseplants and gardens in the Desert Southwest, the Pacific Northwest, and Hawaii. They have appeared on numerous U.S. radio shows, including *Martha Stewart Living*, Joe Lamp'l's *Growing a Greener World*, Ken Druse's *Real Dirt*, and Ciscoe Morris's *Gardening with Ciscoe*, and are the authors of *What's Wrong With My Vegetable Garden?*, *What's Wrong With My Fruit Garden?*, and the award-winning *What's Wrong With My Plant? (And How Do I Fix It?)*. They can be found creating bountiful polyculture gardens in Port Townsend, Washington, and online at kathrynanddavid.com.